II

The author

Andrew Rule has
broken or covered some
of the most notorious
Australian stories of the
late 20th century and
lived to tell the tales
– many of them in this
book. He has had an
interest in crime and
punishment throughout
a career in newspapers,
radio and television.
Since his first book, the
crime classic *Cuckoo*
– included in this
volume – he has
co-written and edited a
series of best-selling
true crime books. He
is currently a feature
writer for *Good
Weekend* magazine.

SEX, DEATH AND BETRAYAL

TRUE CRIMES AND OTHER STORIES

by Andrew Rule

IV

Published in Australia by
Floradale Productions Pty Ltd
September 2004

Distributed wholesale by
Gary Allen Pty Ltd,
9 Cooper Street,
Smithfield, NSW
Telephone 02-9725 2933

Sex, death and betrayal
True crimes and other stories

ISBN – 0 9752318 1-2

The moving finger writes; and, having writ,
Moves on: nor all thy piety nor wit
Shall lure it back to cancel half a line,
Nor all thy tears wash out a word of it.

– Omar Khayyam

Reality … Wow! What a concept.

– Robin Williams

ONE

Supreme Court, 1986

O UTSIDE, it is a radiant spring day; the sort that persuades people to forgive Melbourne its winters. Even in the concrete heart of the city, the streets are splashed with fresh green leaves. There is the promise of a perfect Melbourne Cup week and a broad hint of coming summer.

But the sunshine baulks at the doors of the Supreme Court. Inside, nineteenth century solemnity hangs like an inert gas, sealing out the modern world from a building that is a monument to Victorian-era values and architecture. Splendid cathedrals made men fear God; the gloomy majesty of courts like this made them fear the law.

The corridors echo with the footsteps and muttered conversations of the bit-players in half a dozen dreary legal dramas. But in the cavernous lobby outside the twelfth court there is a larger crowd than usual, and those in it have an air of thinly disguised expectancy. Here, onlookers far outnumber those the Law actually requires to be present. The atmosphere is of an

2

audience waiting for a show to start. There is a buzz of conversation, and the crowd eddies and clots into groups, according to profession and acquaintance.

There are detectives, identifiable from their clothes and the way they move through the crowd with the ease of stockmen among cattle. But this day these men share something extra: behind the in-jokes and camaraderie there is the suggestion of quiet satisfaction.

There are journalists, armed with pens, notebooks, tape recorders and the nervy alertness that comes of gathering facts to a deadline. They stand in knots and drift between the police and a third group – one harder to identify. It comprises four women with much in common. All in their late thirties. All attractive. And all, it seems, under a sort of strain, as if each personality has been stretched by some past event and not yet regained its original shape. They chat animatedly, a little too animatedly, to each other and to the detectives, whom they appear to know well and to trust. But the bonhomie is brittle. Suddenly, one starts crying; the others escort her to a cloakroom. She emerges a few minutes later dry-eyed, smiling and apologetic. It is not the last time she is to cry this day.

Another woman sits alone on the edge of one of the hard benches outside the courtroom. She has brown, curled hair above a face as stony as the tiled floor. She, too, is in her late thirties, but it is obvious she has nothing to do with the other women. She is ill at ease, unwilling to chance meeting others' eyes. She speaks briefly, guardedly, to a detective who approaches. When he walks away she returns to the newspaper in her hand and stares hard at it. In half an hour she doesn't turn a page. This woman has been housekeeper, lover and second wife to the man who will shortly appear before the court.

The time set down for the hearing creeps past. Despite the tragedies and the suffering that have led to this scene, the melodrama is tinged with farce when a prison officer lets slip the reason for the delay ... the prisoner has been accidentally left at Pentridge, and the van has returned for him. There is irony here. The original hearing, set down for three months earlier, was abandoned when the judge failed to appear because he hadn't been notified. This time the prisoner makes the judge wait. The doors are opened and the crowd files in. A packed courtroom waits on the judge and the judged.

THE prisoner's entrance is an anti-climax. For one whose crimes have caused this theatre, the man whom two poker-faced detectives lead to the dock is deceptively ordinary looking. Not much more than middle height, not much less than middle age, not as burly as he appeared in photographs. The impression that he has shrunk in jail is well-founded: one of the detectives mentions later that he has lost 'a good three or four stone' since his arrest eighteen months earlier. He is sandy-haired, with a greying beard that makes him look even more nondescript. He is, in fact, 42, but could be five years older or younger. For what could be the last public appearance of his life, he chooses a light-coloured suit neither expensive nor in glaringly bad taste. He could be a labourer on a day off. Or a farmer on his way to town. Or a salesman. Or a small businessman. All of which, in another life, he has been. He is the sort of man who wouldn't draw a second glance in a pub, or in a church. The sort of man who, as one of his former employers confides later, 'just didn't have "MURDERER" written across his forehead.'

The man in the dock stares at a point somewhere above the judge's head. His face is motionless – and emotionless. As part of court procedure he is asked to confirm his name when it is put to him. 'That's correct,' he says quietly and clearly. They are the only words he speaks in two hours. There is no trace of the

4

Scottish or North of England accent regarded as a vital clue to his identity at the height of the investigation before his arrest.

An investigation unparalleled in Victorian history, lasting almost twenty years and costing millions. An investigation which, despite the brilliance and dedication of a group of country detectives who made it a personal crusade, ended when the wanted man was routinely fingerprinted after a minor offence ... in New South Wales, where police have the power to print suspects the way their Victorian counterparts could not.

As the workings of justice grind on, the detectives sitting drowsily in court ponder the irony. Their man ended by trapping himself through stupidity after all the work they did to trap him through guile. And there was that non-existent accent, one of the shoal of red herrings that bedevilled the case from the start. But most of all they think of how many lives have been blighted by the neatly-dressed monster in the dock. And it churns their guts.

T HE sentencing procedure is a postscript to the main event of six months earlier, a judicial ritual with a predictable result. No-one expects the offender's counsel to produce anything riveting. Faced with appearing for an already lost cause, the barrister selects a standard routine from the advocate's repertoire, and recites a potted – and sanitised – version of the prisoner's life.

Given the enormity of the man's known crimes, and the suspicion of his guilt in others, it jars to hear a lawyer explain with professional sincerity that his client left school early 'not because he didn't like school but because his attitude and inclination was to assist his family.' And only a barrister could gently insinuate that the poor, pregnant teenage wife that the prisoner bashed and taunted with unfaithfulness was somehow partly to blame for his 'dissatisfaction' because of her 'immaturity'.

The lawyer speaks on, earning his fee with the subtle bias he puts on words as deftly as a bowler curls a ball.

Of the time the prisoner faked his own drowning, thus shocking his dying mother into an even earlier grave, the barrister explains he did it 'because he couldn't talk about his problems with his second wife ... he felt hemmed in by relationships'.

In his closing flourishes the barrister produces an unconscious gem of understatement. Describing how his client had spent the two years before his arrest living between his car, a rented room and the bed of his estranged second wife, he says: 'It was a strange sort of a life.'

It was. But no-one except the man in the dock knows how strange.

IAN Armstrong Joblin is what policemen irreverently call a 'trick cyclist'. If he knows this, it probably does not please Joblin, who is accustomed to describing himself from the witness stand as a clinical forensic psychologist before he gets down to the business of labelling barbaric acts with words of many syllables.

In this case, he explains, there was no sign of a physical organic abnormality which might have led to the subject's crimes.

There were two possible reasons for the man's behaviour, he says: hypersexuality and psychological disturbance. 'I spent many hours with him,' he tells the court. 'He seemed quite relieved to be in Pentridge. He often seemed to be quite contrite and remorseful ... but it seems that contrition was no deterrent.'

The prosecutor, John Dee QC, bristles when the psychologist describes the prisoner's armed rapes as a form of 'seduction'. The atmosphere is charged as the silk jumps up. 'You don't say

6

that a man who enters a house by stealth wearing a balaclava and armed with a knife is seducing,' he says incredulously.

It is not a question. The psychologist panics, arguing about the definition of 'seduction'. Then he lets himself be drawn into commenting on a subject which makes the defence counsel wince.

The subject is murder. The double murder to which the prisoner has pleaded guilty six months before. A double murder which, according to the strict letter of the law, has no bearing on the present proceedings, but which in fact hangs over it like a pall.

Drawn on by the prosecutor's baited questions, the psychologist says that from his interviews with the prisoner he thinks the murders 'were not sexually motivated'. The prosecutor pauses for effect, then pounces. With the timing honed by years at the bat table, he produces a police forensic photograph and hands it to the clerk to pass to the witness. 'Would you mind,' he says quietly, mindful that every eye is on him, 'looking at this picture … '

Those who have seen the picture know why the psychologist's face changes colour when he looks a the glossy print. For this is a terrible photograph, taken of a teenage girl's body after it has lain in the bush for sixteen summer days.

The pathologist's words are terrible enough, (*'There was an extreme degree of decomposition and heavy maggot infestation, ligaments and muscles and all the internal muscles having been eaten away …'*) but even if Joblin had read the report, no words could prepare him for the shock of seeing that picture.

And nothing could disguise that the girl was killed in a sexual frenzy.

She is naked from the waist down. And, even in *rigor mortis*, her legs are spreadeagled.

MR Justice Alistair Nicholson is known as a man whose exposure to the sordid parade of criminality seems to have left him neither cynical nor callous; perhaps for these reasons he headed the Victorian Parole Board. The defence barrister, in his closing address, gently explores the judge's attitudes, looking for the combination of persuasive phrases which might unlock a sympathetic response. He must sense he's not making ground. Compassion cuts two ways; this day any kind feelings from the bench is not for the criminal, but for his victims.

'In view of the confusions he has had,' the barrister concludes delicately, 'and despite the enormity of the events of the past, he should not be placed in custody with the key thrown away ... he is deserving of a chance.'

A chance! The detectives stare at the barrister's pinstriped back. A chance, they're thinking, is what this bastard never gave anyone.

The judge shuffles his papers, preparing to address the court before passing sentence. His face is taut with repugnance for the man who has pleaded guilty to raping two women and attempting to rape three others. 'These offences were extremely similar and followed a horrifying pattern,' he begins. 'I am satisfied that on each occasion you watched the victims and the movements of others who lived with them.

'You chose women who were alone or who were caring for young children as your prey. You attacked them at night in what must have been horrifying circumstances. In four cases you had a knife. The fact that you raped these women with children in bed with them just didn't matter to you ... you treated women as some sort of inferior species upon which you could inflict you desires.'

The judge pauses, and his words hang in the air. Those in court who had not known the details of this man's crimes are

8

chilled by them. Fascinated, they look furtively at the prisoner, as if straining to see something outwardly sinister in this nondescript man who was so methodically evil that he timetabled his lust, studying his victims for weeks before striking.

So methodically evil that he chose young mothers, easily forced into submission by the fear that he would hurt their children.

T HE judge announces the sentences. They add up to 30 years jail. The police are professionally inscrutable, but satisfied. In their eyes the quality of justice has not been strained with too much mercy.

They know that the sentence is meaningless, in one sense. The prisoner is already serving life for murder. But they also know how important it is for the victims that justice must be seen to be done, as if the ritual of the court somehow compensates a little for being raped once and haunted forever.

The victims. These are the five women whose determined cheerfulness and strained looks had so marked them outside the court. With the slightest of movements the man in the dock could look at them sitting together a few paces to his right. But in two hours his head does not turn, his face does not change expression.

It is too much for one of the group. As the prisoner steps down from the dock her eyes brim with tears again, and the others comfort her fiercely. It is her fortieth birthday … and the fifteenth 'anniversary' of the night he attacked her.

Stricken as she is, the woman is lucky. Like 30 other women attacked by the man being led from the court, she survived.

Garry Heywood and Abina Madill didn't. And 22 years later, their murders still trouble the town where they lived and died.

TWO

Ardmona, 1964-1966

O N the way to the new share farm Lesley's spirits began to lift, as they always did when Ray was 'being nice', as she put it. 'Being nice' meant not belting her. Even after almost three years of Ray's crude and often brutal ways, Lesley still used the euphemisms of her poor-but-respectable shopkeeping parents. She was like that. There was something pleasantly naive about her that was at once her best point and her worst enemy.

Lesley knew that one irrigation farm was much the same as another: a rectangle among larger rectangles bounded by arrow-straight roads and irrigation channels, the paddocks criss-crossed with checkbanks as predictable as the squares on a chessboard, the orchards as uniform as wheat. It was silly to imagine that grinding over the few miles between Tongala and Ardmona promised a fresh start. And yet, where Ray was concerned, Lesley was still forgiving. Too forgiving, probably. She knew her family and her best friend wondered what she saw in the moody lout at her side; sometimes she wondered

10

herself. At a month past his twentieth birthday, Ray was a couple of inches under six feet, a couple of pounds over eleven stone. Hard and fit, with the strong forearms and hands and the suntanned face of the outdoor worker. Hair, too dark to be called blond, too sandy to be truly auburn, brushed back in the rocker style. Nose long and slightly aquiline, eyes hazel, features regular. Thus sketched, he could have been any young farmer or rural worker. Yet there was an intensity about the young man that set him apart from the easygoing country people.

Perhaps it was this that had attracted Lesley. After three years of marriage and shattered illusions, she still thought he looked handsome dressed up ready to play his trumpet at a dance somewhere, even if he never took her with him and usually came home with lipstick on his collar, lies on his lips, and with a backhander ready if she questioned him. Or maybe, at eighteen, with two babies, she had no choice but to make the best of it.

Behind was Tongala, Stanhope, Yarroweyah and a lot of bad memories stretching back to the time when Ray had 'got her into trouble,' as she put it. He had driven from his father's farm to her parents' shop at Lowesdale for her sixteenth birthday. He gave her a green twin-set and an unwanted pregnancy in the space of an afternoon, then broke off with her the following week before she found out the bad news. Happy bloody birthday, she thought wryly. If she hadn't been pregnant then maybe she wouldn't have gone back to him, married him, and ended up like this, being dragged all over Victoria milking other people's cows.

But it was no good complaining, Lesley resolved. At least there was some sort of hope ahead. Ray was keen on the extra money he could make as a share farmer instead of as a hired hand; if he was happy then there was a chance things would be better. Besides, as she recalled later, 'by that stage I was just going along with him.'

Lesley was an attractive girl: blonde and kind-faced, with a wide mouth that fell into a slow smile, an infectious laugh and a country drawl, all combining to such pleasant effect that most people immediately warmed to her. Except for her father-in-law, a 'pigheaded, bullyish' man who had always preferred to believe ill of her rather than face the truth about his adopted son.

Beside Lesley on the seat of the red EK Holden was her ten-month-old son, Raymond Harold, named after his father and grandfather. It went without saying that the boy hadn't been named for her side of the family. With the eldest, Susan, she'd been able to please herself. Ray hadn't even come to the hospital to see his first-born because he had cleared off to his aunt's place in Melbourne. Where, as Lesley found out years later, he had an affair.

The children were wedged between bundles of possessions. Their furniture had already been sent ahead. It was a sparse collection: bedroom suite, Susan's bed, the baby's cot, a table and four chairs, a television set and a refrigerator.

The red Holden reached Ardmona in late afternoon. Ray, who'd been to the farm to be interviewed weeks before, drove straight to the share farmer's house that was to be theirs for as long as they stayed. They pulled up in the yard beside the house. It was a ramshackle white weatherboard building with a veranda and a steeply pitched iron roof concealing a second storey squeezed into the roof-space. Lesley got out of the car. Her heart sank, though not because the existing occupants obviously hadn't finished moving out. 'Gosh, it's a big place,' she said. As they peered in the kitchen window she felt something beyond the 1960s scorn of anything old. Lesley didn't know the local legend that years before a woman who'd lived there had killed herself after being jilted, but she felt a shiver of apprehension. She had always been intuitive rather than logical. She sensed something sinister.

12

Lesley was pleased when the owners offered to put them up for the night in their comfortable new house next door. Mr and Mrs Gawne and their boys were good people, she thought that evening. Maybe things would turn out all right after all.

THE other share farmers, the Elliotts, were packing the last of their possessions ready to move into Shepparton. Wayne, the oldest son, was impatient. He had other interests, the main one being his girlfriend, a farmer's daughter called Abina Madill. It was a schoolyard infatuation conducted mostly on the telephone. In the previous few months the postmistress at the local telephone exchange had sometimes cut off his long conversations with the girl because they tied up one of the three lines connecting Ardmona and Shepparton. Young Elliott had no reason to take any notice of the new share farmer, Ray somebody or other. The next time he heard of him was 21 years later.

FOR the first year, the Gawnes were happy with their new share farmer. For all his youth – he was twenty – he impressed them as a 'real goer', one of the family recalled later. He was quiet, 'a bit of a loner', but that didn't matter as long as he could handle milking, irrigating and feeding the calves and pigs. It would have been a lot of work for one man, but as so often was the case on dairy farms, the load was shared by the wife.

Lesley, a stranger to farming before she met Ray, had quickly learned to milk after getting married. After that, regardless of babies or pregnancy, she had spent more and more time helping in the shed. At Gawnes', she also had the job of feeding the calves. While she was busy outside, she was to remember with considerable guilt, she was forced to shut her two infants in a room of the old timber house. She later trembled to think what would have happened had a fire started in the old place while she was in the dairy, where the din of the milking machine drowned all other sounds. Such fears didn't seem to bother her husband, who was becoming more self-centred, distant and irritable. He would be violent, then contrite.

While the share farmers were doing a good job, the Gawnes had no reason to take much notice of them. Reg Gawne was busy with the full-time demands of a large orchard and was happy to leave the dairy farming to Ray. Gawnes' teenage son, Stewart, in 1965 completing his last year of school, had the most contact with Ray and Lesley because he often helped them with chores around the farm. Being only a few years younger than the pair, he got to know them a little. The boy sensed that the meek and mild Lesley suffered 'some woeful hidings,' but she always hid the fact. Stewart put this down to pride. Not until much later did he suspect the truth, that Lesley was too frightened to tell anyone.

Stewart did not see the violent side of Ray's character. But he did notice, and never forgot, the faintly obsessive edge to his personality, his strange sense of humour and his strength. Ray, often unshaven and roughly dressed around the farm, took a pride in his strength. He had some exercising equipment, which he used regularly, and he told Stewart that when Raymond junior grew up a bit he was going to start him on weight training.

There was an oversize two-wheel trailer used on the Gawne property for hay carting and other heavy work. Designed to take most of the load forward of the axle, the trailer was brutally heavy to lift on to the drawbar of a tractor. As a teenager, Stewart Gawne could not manage it alone, and he always regarded the job as a test of a farmhand's strength. Where most full-grown men would strain, Ray could do it with ease.

It was early in 1965, before Ray's 21st birthday, that Stewart gained an insight into the man's peculiar idea of a joke. For days Ray hinted mysteriously that he was going to get a new car – a gold Falcon – for his birthday. Stewart was puzzled by this because Ray had just invested his share of the cream cheque on a red Falcon. On Ray's birthday, Stewart couldn't help wandering over to the dairy. Ray looked at him with an oddly triumphant air, reached into his pocket and fished out a new matchbox toy car. 'And sure enough, it was a gold Falcon,' Stewart was to recall. 'He reckoned it was a great joke.'

It seemed to him a puerile and slightly weird prank. In fact, it was a fleeting glimpse of the dark side of Ray's mind. Lesley, had she been brave enough, had she had someone to trust, could have revealed much more about this hidden half of her husband's personality.

Ray's womanising, which Lesley had tolerated almost from the first year of their marriage, had grown more blatant. Lesley knew he had enjoyed an affair with a Numurkah woman, and she also suspected he had sex with a woman working on a nearby farm who visited him whenever Lesley was out of the house.

Lesley would come back from the dairy some mornings to find the other woman in the house with Ray, who had developed the habit of knocking off early while Lesley finished the chores. The woman would stay and watch as Lesley cooked breakfast for Ray and the children. One day Lesley drove to Yarrawonga to the funeral of her aunt. When she got home at eleven o'clock that night, Ray had the woman in the house with him. Stung into a rare display of assertiveness, Lesley abused them both. The woman didn't come back again.

What Ray did when he went out at night was a mystery. If Lesley asked questions, she was told to shut up and mind her own business. If she pressed the point she risked a beating. Without access to the money she helped earn, Lesley was often left without cash and hardly any food while Ray went off at night. He would return after midnight, rise late after Lesley started the milking and then sleep during the day. Often Lesley fed the children Weetbix and milk, or bread and jam with cream from the dairy before they went to bed.

Within months of arriving at Ardmona, Lesley's life had taken on a nightmare quality. Her premonition about the house seemed to her to be depressingly accurate. She was caught in a vice of circumstances, held fast by her own fear. She hated the place, was frightened of being alone there, and yet was left alone most nights of the week. But when Ray was home, things weren't much better. And sometimes much worse. So bad, she sometimes thought, that it seemed he was trying to drive her out.

One day late in 1964 Lesley rebelled. That morning she and Ray had argued. Then he had gone into Shepparton, where she knew he would go to the bank because he was going out that night. 'There wasn't even a can of baked beans in the cupboard, but that wouldn't worry him because he would eat while he was out,' she said later. As the day passed, Lesley grew more determined to get some money to spend on herself and the children.

When Ray returned Lesley refused to help milk. While he was busy in the shed she went out to the car. She knew that he kept cash locked in the glove box of the red Falcon. She levered it open, took £40 and hid it under the stairs.

Lesley was prepared 'to cop a belting' over the money. When he came in, she knew he had already missed the cash. He swore at her and demanded it. She was defiant. 'You're not having it,' she hissed. 'I'm going to buy food for the kids. You're not having that money to spend on some slut!'

Susan, two-and-a-half, and Raymond, fourteen months, cowered when they heard the raised voices. When their father started hitting their mother they started crying. As he swung punch after punch the children backed into an open cupboard recess built to house a refrigerator. Lesley, bruised and bleeding, stumbled in with them and crouched to protect her face and breasts from her husband's fists. The children screamed and clutched at her legs.

'Don't hit Mummy, don't hit Mummy,' little Susan sobbed over and over, in a heartbroken voice her mother never forgot. But he kept hitting. So much that Lesley thought he was going to kill her. One punch left her right arm dangling uselessly, paralysed. She cried out: 'You've broken my arm.' Suddenly, he stopped, and without a word he led her to the bathroom. He turned on the cold water tap over the bath.

Lesley's anger drained away, replaced by absolute fear. 'He's going to drown me,' she thought. There was nothing she could do. Her mind was as numb as her arm. Only when he took her arm and bathed it in the cold water did she realise that she was safe and he was sorry. Not so sorry, though, that he was willing to stay home. He dressed ready to go out as if nothing had happened, like a man cut adrift from the emotional ties that bind normal people. Lesley was shaking with rage and shock. She told him to take the money and go.

As the tail lights of the new red Falcon disappeared down the dirt track to the main road, Lesley rang her parents at Yarrawonga. Sobbing into the handpiece, she asked them to come and get her and the children. It wasn't the first time that kind and long-suffering pair had given her refuge. It wasn't to be the last.

IF, as Lesley suspected, Ray had been trying to goad her into leaving, he seemed to have second thoughts when she actually went. Or he was confused, and didn't know what he wanted from one day to the next. Or he wanted to be cruel to her. Lesley guessed that it was a mixture of all three, further complicated by his insatiable sex drive. One woman had never been enough for Ray, she said later, 'but that didn't stop him being sort of possessive about me ... jealous like a kid.'

Whatever the reason the result was the same. When Lesley took the first faltering steps toward independence, Ray did his best to cripple her chances. This time he had gone too far for Lesley's family to encourage her to go back to him; despite the burden of supporting the children alone she was determined to have a go at surviving without him. For a fortnight, she did. But then he bludgeoned her into submission with tactics as brutal as the beating she'd suffered.

When Lesley had left Ardmona that night, she took only a few clothes because she was angry and confused and wanted only to get away quickly. But in the next few days she talked herself into the bold plan of sharing a flat in Yarrawonga with her sister Dot. They found a cheap and roomy place to rent behind an empty shop, and set about cleaning it. The dream soured when Lesley's father drove her to Ardmona to collect the children's cots and extra clothes. They had chosen a time when Ray would be out, but when she went inside the house she gasped ... everything she wanted was in one bedroom, and the door and the window were boarded up. Lesley and her father went to the police, but already her resolve was dying. She was disappointed, but resigned, when the police politely refused to be involved.

Lesley drove back to Yarrawonga, crestfallen. There seemed to be a tacit code of unhelpfulness in domestic troubles. She went to a solicitor in the town; he was lukewarm about taking any action which would make her independent of Ray. He did not advise photographs of her injuries, nor send her to a doctor to bolster any case she might have. In 1964, it was a man's world. Two days later she went back to the farm. When she went into the house Ray was in the bath. 'What did you come back for?' he sneered, hardly turning his head.

'I'm damned if I know, Ray,' she said softly.

18

THAT night Ray went out. The children's bedroom was still barricaded, so they slept with their mother. When he got home, Ray climbed into bed with them. Ignoring the children, he straddled her and forced her to have sex. She didn't resist. She never had. A month later she was pregnant again. Her third. She was nineteen.

IT was a miserable Christmas in the old white house; it foreshadowed the worst year of Lesley's life. It was her third Christmas with Ray, and she had hoped that for the first time she would be able to invite her parents. But Ray fell into one of his black moods and ordered Lesley to tell her parents not to come. Ray's parents visited to see their grandchildren whenever they liked, she thought, but he seemed insanely jealous of anything or anybody she might enjoy. She was dimly conscious that Ray was adopted – he had never told her, but she sensed it from things she'd overheard – and sometimes she wondered if it had affected him. Something was decaying Ray's personality, and it was growing worse. The moody but personable youth she'd met at seventeen had become frighteningly unpredictable at 21. It seemed to Lesley that 'things built up in him and he had to lash out.'

But Ray's murderous temper was rarely displayed in public. Lesley was the only one to see it regularly. Several times in the cowshed she watched, horrified, as he flogged a cow with an iron leg chain. More than once she had to let the herd out of the yard without finishing milking because Ray had sent the rest crazy by beating one in the bail. Lesley never saw him kill a cow in temper, although she thought him capable of it. Years later a casual acquaintance who sometimes helped in the shed claimed to have seen Ray kill a cow in one of his rages. Because he was responsible for the herd, a missing cow would go unnoticed by Gawnes until long after he left.

It all made Lesley more frightened of him. Then two things happened that turned her tattered affection to ashes, her fear to loathing. One night Ray told Lesley that he was going out to the paddocks to check the watering, one of the all-hours chores on an irrigation farm. He had been gone a long time, which was nothing unusual, when she heard a slight noise on the upstairs landing. Heart thudding, she edged to the door and looked into the hall.

What she saw made her feel sick with fear. The shadow thrown by the light globe dangling over the stairs was moving, swinging back and forth. It was like a scene from a Hitchcock film. Lesley knew that someone must have moved the bulb, someone who would at that moment be watching her from the gloom beyond the light.

She was faint, but the instinct to protect her children made her steel herself. If she could run across the passage into the bedroom she could get Ray's gun. She tensed herself to fling her body across the hall …

Then Ray laughed.

He had sneaked into the house, padded silently up the stairs and manipulated the light from the landing. Just to terrify her.

That was the first time Lesley told him he was 'sick in the head,' a phrase which crept into most of her thoughts of her husband from then on. And it was the first and only time she'd shown any interest in what she later described as the 'dull coloured brown rifle' Ray kept on top of the wardrobe in their bedroom. Lesley's growing fear of Ray set hard the day she came home to find him molesting their three-year-old daughter. She had been in Shepparton. As soon as she got out of the car she could hear the little girl screaming inside the house. She rushed in, stepping over the child's nappy at the front door. Ray was on the bed with the terrified toddler. His pants were down, and he had an erection.

20

Lesley screamed and told him to get out. He looked shocked, as if only then he realised what he was doing.

FROM the day Lesley had first brought Ray home at Yarrawonga four years before, her sister Dot had never liked him. Although Lesley was too embarrassed to tell her everything that happened later, Dot heard enough to confirm her first impressions. But it wasn't until she visited them at Ardmona one day in 1965 that Dot realised there was more than personal dislike.

Tired after playing outside with the children, she decided to rest in their bedroom, which could be reached from the bathroom, which in turn opened onto the veranda. She lay down on the bed, but she felt uneasy. She sensed that she was being watched. She opened her eyes, and looked straight into Ray's. The door into the bathroom was ajar; he had come in silently and was staring at her through the gap.

Dot didn't say anything to Lesley, but afterwards she never trusted Ray. She wasn't surprised when, three years later, her younger sister Cath told her Ray had tried to pull off the bottom of her bikini in a swimming pool. But that was inside the family. People outside it did not see even those subtle signs of how strange the quiet young man at Gawnes' was becoming. He was cunning, and he was a loner. In all his life he'd never had a friend close enough to gauge the changes in him.

LIKE many country boys, Stewart Gawne took a passing interest in firearms. At his age the necessity to kill vermin around the farm meshed neatly with the urge to have some prowess as a marksman. He already had a twelve-gauge shotgun of his own, and when Ray produced a rifle Stewart was quick to have a look at it.

Although Ray had shot since his boyhood in north-eastern

Victoria, his interest in guns seemed not to have waned the way it might have in other men of his age and intelligence. He was as keen as the sixteen-year-old Stewart, and sometimes the pair would stand at the garden gate of the old white house and squeeze off practice shots at tins stuck on a fence post. The weapon Lesley described as a 'dull-coloured brown rifle' Stewart recognised as a .22 calibre semi-automatic Mossberg, a model distinguished by a fold-down plastic pistol grip fitted at the front of the wooden stock.

With target shooting and talk of spotlighting, Stewart and Ray got on well enough, which made a small episode late in 1965 strike a jarring note.

Stewart was towing a portable pig-sty to a fresh site with the tractor. As soon as he moved the sty, he saw that he had uncovered a rats' nest. He raced over to the share farmer's house and knocked on the door. When Ray came out he asked eagerly: 'Do you want to shoot some rats?' He had barely put the question when Ray cut him off. 'Nuh,' he said curtly, and shut the door in the boy's face. For all Ray's moodiness, Stewart was surprised. No farmer in his right mind would miss the chance to kill rats, he thought. It didn't strike him then that such rudeness was a good way of discouraging him from asking to borrow the rifle. And that slamming the door might have been more quick thinking than quick temper.

For the Gawne boys, an advantage of living on an orchard was that the barrack-like quarters provided for the seasonal fruit pickers were ideal for holding parties. These were quiet and well-ordered affairs, where most of the guests were too young to drive, or to drink more than a covert sip of alcohol out of sight of sharp-eyed parents. They were not the sort of parties to which Ray and Lesley would be invited. Marriage, children and their status as new employees separated them from the younger set.

22

It was at one of these gatherings in 1965 that an odd thing happened. The party was in progress at one end of the quarters, and Mrs Gawne and some other women were cutting sandwiches for supper in another room. One of the women was standing near a window as she worked. She glanced up, then started in surprise.

At first the others were sceptical, but she was adamant: a man had been looking through the window at her. There was little to be afraid of, but Stewart Gawne realised that the woman – a friend of his family's – was quite upset.

She insisted on fetching Stewart's father and her husband from the main house to look around. The two men satisfied themselves that no-one was hanging around the buildings. Beyond that, it was useless even to try. There was an entire orchard that an intruder could hide in. When they came in for a sandwich and a cup of tea a while later, the woman was still upset.

There was something about the prowler's face she hadn't liked.

A COUPLE of other small disturbances ruffled the peaceful tenor of life in Ardmona that year. So small that only those directly involved were to remember them, and then only vaguely.

One incident was at the old general store, which had served the district as shop, post office and telephone exchange for decades. Many families had scrounged a living at the old store. Three went through it in rapid succession between 1963 and 1966. One of these was a middle-aged couple whose sons had married and who lived alone with their youngest daughter – circumstances that were obvious because of the public nature of their livelihood, though of scant interest to most of those who picked up their bread and mail there.

The storekeeper's daughter, who caught the school bus daily, probably saw little point in pulling the blind when she undressed for bed. Until, that is, one night in 1965.

It happened after she went to bed. She had been asleep, but was woken by a slight noise at the window. She looked up. The shock hit her like iced water. Framed by the architrave was the silhouette of a man in the act of removing the flywire screen. She cried out, and the man ran into the darkness of the nearby orchards. There was no sound when he ran. It was as if he were wearing moccasins. Or barefoot.

Next morning, nerves bolstered by the daylight, the girl was the centre of attention on the school bus. The incident was not reported to the police.

NOT far from the store lived one of the district's oldest fruit-growing families. In 1965 their seventeen-year-old son and one of his sisters were living at home alone. During that year the farm dogs started barking at night, an annoyance which became a pattern over the following months, and which the family put down to someone walking past the house after dark.

At first they thought it might be a neighbour known to wander local roads at all hours, and they were not worried. But the girl, her brother recalled later, got the feeling she was being watched, and started pulling the blinds. The likelihood that whoever was upsetting the dogs was a peeping tom was reinforced by the fact nothing was ever stolen from the farmyard. Convinced that the prowler was coming unpleasantly close to the house, the youth decided to take action. He mentioned the intruder to the neighbours and to his family's farm workers – carefully adding that 'next time' he would reach for a rifle.

This, he calculated, should have solved the problem. But he

24

was wrong. A few nights later the dogs starting barking again. The boy grabbed his .22 rifle, ran outside and fired a volley of shots in the air.

It didn't work. A few weeks later the prowler returned. It was about 2am, and the farmer's son woke up sensing that the intruder was outside. He lay stock still, straining to catch a repetition of the sound that had woken him. Then he heard it: soft footsteps on the garden path under the window at his head.

'He was only three feet away,' he was to recall, reliving that tense moment after 22 years. 'I was an innocent young bloke and I got a hell of a fright. When you're that age you think you're game – but when someone gets that close, it frightens you.'

Another thing happened that night. On his way out the prowler growled at the dogs, ordering them to lie down. What struck the boy was that he didn't know the voice. There was, perhaps, a subtle clue to the prowler's identity which escaped the teenager. Whoever it was had growled at the dogs with the automatic assurance of a lifetime habit.

Farmers aren't afraid of farm dogs.

THE next time the dogs barked late at night, the orchardist's son took his rifle and fired off a twenty-round magazine into the dark. 'I sprayed them around at leg height,' he said later. 'I can still remember one slug glowing red, streaking through the air like a tracer.'

He was to do the same thing half a dozen times, and even hatched an elaborate plan to hide on the roof in a sleeping bag and ambush the brazen intruder. But, as suddenly as they'd started a year before, the visits stopped. The farmer's son remembers 'very vividly' that the last one was at the beginning of the fruit picking season. Early February, 1966.

THREE

Missing persons, 1966

THE times they were a-changing. On the other side of the world teenage pop stars were driving psychedelic Rolls Royces, making millions from tapping the restless energy of their generation. A generation, as one of its pop anthems went, that was dancing to a brand new beat.

In Shepparton, as in any Australian provincial city, the baby boom teenagers whose parents had waltzed and fox-trotted at sedate country dances flocked to see the new groups that radio and television were making into idols. For every Normie Rowe or Billy Thorpe who came to town there was a local band of Beatle-booted, mop-topped kids with heads filled by rock'n'roll dreams and jungle rhythms.

Those who were young then remember a sort of endless summer of rock dances and concerts, every Saturday night another reel in a real-life teen movie. The cast of mods and rockers were the product of a prosperity which they had grown up taking for granted the way their parents and grandparents never could. This was the first generation which could assume that many of its members would be able to afford motor cars by the time they were twenty, and use them as social toys rather than essential transport. A generation that flouted the religious and moral bonds which had influenced its forebears since Queen Victoria's time. The newly-relaxed drinking laws fudged the old division between what one lot had derided as middle-class Protestant wowserism and the other as working class Catholic intemperance. The permissive society had come to Shepparton.

The orchards and canneries, farms and factories brought wealth and workers to the town, strengthening its position as the capital of central Victoria. In the post-war boom years, Shepparton had boomed more than most towns, greedily embracing the trend to turn Australia into an ersatz California: drive-in theatre, bowling alley, supermarkets, big car yards and the hamburger shops, cafes and coffee lounges that were forerunners of the fast food chain stores of the 1970s.

In 1966, Shepparton had 15,000 people and was growing fast, with thousands more in the intensively-farmed districts outside the city limits. The population explosion brought its pressures – polarities barely noticeable in more staid provincial cities. On one side of town were Housing Commission estates, on the other the big houses of those who had made big money. From both sides of the tracks came a 1960s phenomenon: bored teenagers with money and time to spend.

When they went down the street to hear bands sing cover versions of English songs in American accents, to drink Coca-Cola at the Star Bowl or eat hamburgers at Herco's Cafe, they could have been almost anywhere in the Western world. But when they went home to the drowsy streets, the dairy farms and the orchards, the City of Shepparton went back to its real self. Things were changing, but Shep was still just a big country town at heart.

F ROM the night it opened in February 1965, the Shepparton Civic Centre was a huge success. The new cream brick building was a monument to civic pride; it reflected the prosperity of the rich Goulburn Valley irrigation land of which Shepparton was, and is, the commercial heart. The hall boasted a revolving stage, coloured spotlights and space for 2000. An average of 1500 people attended the Saturday night dances, which were advertised as the biggest in provincial Australia. And the steadily more ambitious concerts which were to become a feature that year drew even bigger crowds.

In June 1965, almost 3000 packed the centre to see Billy Thorpe and the Aztecs and local heroes Tony and the Shantells. The Aztecs were billed as 'Australia's top band' and the Shantells as 'Victoria's top band'. Proof of Shepparton's growing status was a long story devoted to the concert in the Melbourne *Sun* under the heading 'Old Shep Goes Hep'. It noted that the Shantells were so popular in their hometown that they had a fan club with more than 1000 members.

The civic centre had been popular all during 1965; its first complete summer season promised to set records. As the weather warmed after Christmas the outriders of the annual invasion of fruit pickers arrived, rolling through town to the orchards in cars covered with the dust of faraway places. By February, with the fruit ripening, the trickle had become a stream which would swell the local population by at least 3000. Most of the pickers were young, unattached, and free with their money and their fists. On Friday nights and Saturdays they flocked into Shepparton like sailors on shore leave; always looking for a good time, often finding trouble. They crowded the pubs, cafes and footpaths, drove slow laps of the main blocks in their cars, wolf-whistled local girls and brawled with local youths. And if they could muster the door money (six shillings and sixpence) and a jacket and tie, they

28

went to the dance in the new hall. That summer the Saturday night dances became bigger than ever, drawing people from a radius of two hundred kilometres the way moths swarm to a lamp on a hot night. Which meant that if an outside promoter wanted to book the civic centre, it had to be a weeknight. Which was why, when promoters trading as Nullabor Tours brought a show they billed as 'The Mod Spectacular' to Shepparton that month, it had to be held on a Thursday ...

THURSDAY, February 10, 1966 As far as Gail knew, Garry Heywood wasn't going out that night. He picked her up after work, as he had most week nights since they'd started going out together the previous November. Then he drove her home, over the river and across the red gum flats to Mooroopna, where she lived with her parents in Toolamba Road. A weeknight ritual that was part of the rhythm of life in a country town.

Gail was a sober and respectable girl. She was also sixteen, dark-haired and pretty. She couldn't help but be pleased to be seen with the tall, fair-haired panel beater she had met at the Saturday night dance just before leaving school. He was popular; he was good-looking; and he cut a dash in his car, an FJ Holden that was the envy of half the teenagers in Shepparton.

The car guaranteed that Garry always had plenty of friends, whether he wanted them or not. And being Garry, he usually did. He liked to bask in the admiration of his peers.

This night, as the deep green Holden idled smoothly away from the kerb outside Midland Housing, where Gail was a receptionist, she neither saw nor sensed anything out of the ordinary. The car, as usual, was spotless. And as far as she could recall later, the blue and grey tartan travelling rug neatly folded in its plastic bag was in its normal place in the back, although she had no reason to check it. Gail knew, as everybody her age did, that there would be a concert that evening at the civic centre. But neither she nor Garry would be paid until the next day, Friday, and so they tacitly agreed to save their once-a-week outing until then. Or that's how it seemed to her. If Garry had other plans at that stage, he certainly didn't tell Gail in the ten minutes or so it took to drive her home to Mooroopna. She assumed he was going home to eat with his family before an early night ready for work next morning.

It was about quarter to six when the green Holden pulled into the drive at Toolamba Road. As Garry backed out, Gail put her hands on the gleaming bonnet as if to help the car by pushing it. Then, still smiling at her little joke, she went inside.

She never saw him again.

A S his girlfriend believed, Garry Heywood did go straight home after he dropped her off, and he did eat with his family. But as his little brother, Allen, soon found out, Garry had decided to go to the concert after all. Allen, who was fourteen, knew this because he washed the cherished FJ Holden for the outing. This pleased him greatly. He hero-worshipped his big brother, and he loved cars.

Garry had brought home the old Holden two years earlier to do up ready for when he got his driver's licence. It had been a cream-coloured jalopy with nothing to recommend it except that he could afford it on apprenticeship wages. The car had become a family project, with Allen working to help strip and restore it in an empty fowlyard behind their parents' modest timber house in Hayes Street. After the mechanical work, which included fitting a high performance head, the Heywood boys spray-painted the body British Racing Green to the best of their considerable ability. The brothers had been born to the trade: their grandfather was one of the first coachwork experts in Melbourne to switch from horse-drawn vehicles to motor cars, and their uncle Dick owned the biggest panel shop in Shepparton. This was where Garry and his father Charlie worked, and where Allen, too, was to do his apprenticeship.

When or why Garry decided to go to the concert was uncertain. He had discussed it with one of his friends, Lindsay Lohse, two days earlier, and might have toyed with the idea then, as he had asked Lindsay to come to the Heywoods' house on that Thursday evening. It transpired that he had definitely made up his mind by the time he finished work at 5pm that day, because it was then that he arranged to pick up one of his workmates, Victor Grosdanis.

While Allen washed the car, Garry sneaked some of his mother's lemons, squeezed them and rinsed his hair with the juice in an attempt to bleach it. When Lindsay Lohse arrived shortly after 7pm Allen pleaded with them to let him come too, but the older pair gently fobbed him off. The kind-hearted Garry, who had been a scout leader, often let Allen come on outings. But this time there might have been plans already laid which would make a kid brother an embarrassment.

Allen mooched inside to watch television. The news was full of the Beaumont case: three children had vanished in South Australia. He talked to his mother about how awful it was, how sorry he felt for the family of the missing children.

ALTHOUGH it was Thursday, with school and jobs to be attended next morning, the concert gave Shepparton a Saturday night atmosphere. The warm weather, the crowds of pickers and the amusement carnival set up near the lake all titillated the mood of pleasurable anticipation. In the car park behind the civic centre that afternoon road crews had been unloading instruments, microphones and other gear to be used that night. It was a good line up, even by Shepparton's high standards: Billy Adams, billed as a star of the 'Go Show'; Yvonne Barrett, just returned from a troop entertainment tour of Vietnam; Roland Storm, billed as a 'Sydney TV idol'; The Changing Times, who had a hit version of the song *Mary Lou*.

All over town, and beyond, young people were getting ready to go out. In a house in Weddell Street, around the corner from Heywoods', a wiry kid called Norm Gillespie was wondering what to wear. Norm was fifteen, and had just started his last year of school and his first year of chasing girls, a pastime he found almost as interesting as playing football. He was the proud owner of a new suit that he had pestered his parents into buying so he could wear it to the Saturday night dances. But this night a jacket and tie were not required, so there were hard decisions to be made about what looked sharp. He settled for narrow-legged trousers, desert boots and an open-necked shirt, then carefully combed his fringe down over his forehead just like the picture of Normie Rowe on his bedroom wall. One reason Norm Gillespie wanted to look good was that he thought he might get a chance to talk to a girl who lived a few blocks away in Maxwell Street. A girl called Roslyn Madill.

Roslyn was fourteen, and the third daughter of Fred Madill, a dairy farmer who had shifted with his wife, Alma, and four daughters from the nearby district of Undera a few years before.

By 1966 their only son, Rodney, was working the farm, and the four girls lived with their parents. The youngest girl was Alison, who was still at primary school. The oldest was Lesley. Between Lesley and Roslyn was Abina, who had just left high school to start work in the office of Heywoods' panel works.

Norm Gillespie knew Abina and Roslyn well. Like him, they were members of the Presbyterian Fellowship Association at St Andrew's Church, where they played badminton and tennis. Roslyn was a quiet schoolgirl, the way Abina had been when a sharefarmer's son called Wayne Elliott had kept company with

32

her two years before. But it seemed that in the few months Abina had been working she had been exposed to a more larrikin brand of male company than she was used to at church tennis parties, and her determination to be popular with her new acquaintants was beginning to show. In little things, such as the packet of Alpine cigarettes she tucked into her handbag before she went out. And in bigger ones, such as agreeing to meet young tradesmen from Heywoods outside the Star Bowl, at a time when her father and the youth who thought of himself as her boyfriend believed she would be at the concert.

At sixteen Abina was attractive, but more because of her vivacious personality than any classic beauty. 'A young girl full of life,' was the way Norm Gillespie was to remember her. For the concert she wore a matching skirt and blouse, stockings, new white sandals and a white shoulder bag.

Although his wife was going to visit friends at Undera that evening, Fred Madill, a cautious father, did not deviate from his usual custom of taking his daughters by car rather than letting them walk after dark. He backed his car out of the drive of their neat, violet-coloured weatherboard house in Maxwell Street about 8.30pm, with Roslyn and Abina aboard. On the way they picked up a girl of Abina's age, Jan Frost, who lived a few doors away in the same street, and a younger girl called Rae Croxford. When they reached the civic centre there was so much traffic that Mr Madill couldn't park and escort the girls to the door. He let them out in the street and went home satisfied that Abina's latest boyfriend, a young mechanic called Ian Urquhart, would bring the two sisters home at midnight after working late at the local Ford dealers.

By the time Fred Madill's car turned the corner his daughters had chosen different ways. Roslyn and Rae Croxford went into the hall, but Abina and Jan Frost walked straight towards the Star Bowl bowling alley. Abina and Jan had met for a malted milk at lunch time that day, and Abina had confided to Jan that she had arranged to meet boys from her work at the bowling alley. Jan had not intended to go to the concert, but later had argued with her boyfriend and decided to keep Abina company rather than moon around alone.

They reached the bowl about 8.45pm.

Waiting for them was the dark green FJ Holden, by this time with four boys in it. Garry Heywood always had plenty of mates.

IN the hour and a half after leaving home Garry and his car had been busy. Lindsay Lohse asked him if he would drop him at the farm where he worked after the concert. Garry said he was broke and low on fuel. He pulled into a service station in Corio Street and Lindsay bought fifteen shillings worth of petrol, which more than half filled the tank. It was generous, although Lohse would have done his mate a bigger favour by crying broke. Running out of petrol might have provided a miracle later that night.

By 7.30pm the wandering green Holden had reached Victor Grosdanis's place in Ford Road on the outskirts of town. When they arrived Victor was still getting ready. After a hurried wash Victor got into the back seat, clutching his tie in his hand. He never did get to put it on that night, and left it on the seat.

At 7.55pm, on the way back into the town centre, the boys picked up Garry's cousin, Paul Heywood, who was waiting in Shepparton's main thoroughfare, Wyndham Street. Paul, sixteen, was still at school, but his parents were away that night and he was free to go out and stay out as long as he liked. Back on the road, the boys decided to have a drink in preparation for the night's events. Heywood turned left out of Wyndham Street, past the police station and over the bridge towards Mooroopna. Soon after 8pm the Holden drew up outside the Cricketers' Arms Hotel, where there was less chance of being

34

caught drinking under age, or being seen by any of their older relatives. Although only sixteen, Grosdanis looked the oldest and he fronted the bar to buy each round of beers. They drank quickly, and by the time they left 25 minutes later the beer was beginning to take effect. Lohse and Grosdanis bought five cans of beer each to add to four cans of vodka and orange Grosdanis had bought earlier.

By 8.30 they were on their way to the Star Bowl. They parked outside just before Abina and Jan walked up.

Jan had reason to feel faintly uneasy. If she hadn't argued with her boyfriend and if Abina's boyfriend hadn't been working until 10 o'clock, then they wouldn't be in what could easily turn into an embarrassing situation.

As soon as she got in the front seat with Garry and the boy Lohse she knew they had been drinking. Nobody said anything about going anywhere, but after a lap of the block Garry drove down behind the lake and parked near the swimming pool. It was just after 9pm. The girls drank vodka and orange, the boys drank more beer and became more boisterous. Jan wanted to go back to the concert, but Abina didn't. It was a long way to walk in new shoes. After about half an hour Garry decided to drive back to the civic centre. He parked in Welsford Street in front of the hall.

Garry and Lindsay went inside the hall; Lindsay shouted Garry the door money. Jan, Abina and the two other boys walked around the block. Joan Dealy, who had known Abina from primary school at Undera, saw Abina and one of the boys walk through the public gardens opposite the civic centre just after 10pm. By 10.15 Abina, Jan and the two boys were back in the Holden.

INSIDE the hall, Garry was intent on having a good time. He tried to kiss Kathy Payne, who was there with a friend of Garry's, Walter Cazervan. She walked away. He also approached a girl called Sandra Wallace, who was with a group of friends. He asked if she or any of the other girls wanted to come for a ride in his car. They declined. Garry was talking loudly, and an attendant asked him to leave. After chatting with the doorman he sneaked back in and sat at the front of the hall with Lindsay. But the attendant saw him and told him to get out again.

It was about 10.30pm when Garry reached his car. Soon after he got there Jan, who had been sitting uncomfortably in the front seat with Paul Heywood, made an excuse and left. Before going she asked Abina several times if she wanted to come with her. Abina didn't. Jan walked towards the hall, then saw her boyfriend, Max Hart, drive past. Relieved, she went over to join him.

Garry asked his cousin and Victor Grosdanis to get out of the car so that he could drive down to the lake with Abina. They objected, and said they wanted some guarantee that he would come back and drive them home by midnight. Garry gave Victor a set of keys and Abina gave him her wristwatch.

Then Garry drove off, with Abina still sitting in the back seat. It was about 10.45pm.

G ARRY Heywood came back to the civic centre that night. But he was there earlier than his friends expected, and somehow they missed him.

About 11.15pm, just before the concert ended, a girl who knew Garry by sight saw him leaning on a rail on the left-hand entrance of the foyer. He was looking into the hall, as if watching for somebody. The observer, Eileen O'Brien, noticed he was wearing a brown jumper and an orange checked shirt similar to that of her brother, Patrick, who was with her. A few minutes later another girl, Patricia Webber, left the hall with some friends and turned into Welsford Street to walk home. She had gone only a short way when she saw Heywood drive past in his green Holden. The car turned left out of Nixon Street and drove south along Welsford Street at a normal speed, then turned right. The girl did not notice if there was anybody else in the vehicle.

She was the last person in Shepparton to see Garry Heywood alive.

THE Urquharts were all hard workers. Their father, David Urquhart, was a Scot who made adjectives like 'dour' and 'canny' seem pale. He was a fiercely independent man whose main achievement in life had been to raise six healthy children while working on an orchard at Lemnos, a few kilometres out of Shepparton. It wasn't easy. As youngsters the older children milked six cows by hand, separated the cream, fed the skim milk to the pigs and then walked the two kilometres to school. In the early days they had been so poor they had one bicycle between them, but Urquhart senior punished any hint of dishonesty. His children loved him, but until the day he died they were a little frightened him, awestruck by the sacrifices he'd made to give them a start in a new country. It was not until the children were in their teens that they discovered they had older sisters in Scotland: two girls who had been left with relatives as infants while their parents migrated to try to escape the deepening depression.

David would spellbind his children during the evening walks around the orchard which he made a family ritual. He showed them how the different breeds of spiders spun their webs, where the birds built their nests, and much else of the natural world around them. It was just after one of these walks, in the late 1940s, that Mrs Urquhart collapsed; it was the first sign of the Parkinson's disease that was to kill her.

Mrs Urquhart was pregnant when the disease was diagnosed. When the baby was born David called the children together, announced that they had a new brother, and asked them to suggest names. From the chorus of suggestions he chose Ian, Duncan and Ross, which was what the baby was christened. For one with so many Scottish names, Ian Duncan Ross Urquhart was later to get a distinctively Australian nickname: 'Chilla'.

Ian was five when his mother died. But from the time he was born she had been so ill that his elder sister, Heather, then twelve, had stayed home from school to look after them both. Heather and her sisters Ivy and Cath, hardly more than children themselves, helped bring Ian up. Even after Heather left home at seventeen to board in Shepparton she saw the boy constantly. She was as anxious about his welfare as her mother would have been. The Urquharts were a clannish lot, and they looked after their little brother well.

Like his brother, David junior, Ian showed a mechanical bent which was encouraged by their father's practical knowledge of farm machinery. A neighbour, a policeman who owned a small block, had reason to recall how useful and willing the Urquhart boys were. He was ploughing his paddock one day when his borrowed tractor broke down. Ian and David Urquhart saw him tinkering with the old machine as they walked past on their way home from school, and they volunteered to have a look. To the man's surprise, the boys found and fixed the fault and had the old machine running again within a few minutes. Neither the policeman nor anyone else who knew the Urquharts was surprised when first David, then Ian, landed apprenticeships at the local Ford dealers, C.T.G. Smith Motors.

Which is where, on the night of February 10, 1966, the Urquhart brothers were working late on an important job. Ian was eighteen, he had a girlfriend, and there was a concert on, but work came first. It was the way they had been brought up. He must have wondered sometimes over the next six years whether being so conscientious was worth it.

W HEN the Urquhart boys finished work at 10pm, according to statements they later made to the police, David dropped Ian at his new lodgings in Orr Street. After a shower and change of clothes – a sequence of events later queried by detectives – Ian walked to the Taverna Espresso coffee lounge in Fryers Street. By the time he reached the cafe, the bands at the concert had started the second bracket; the crudely-amplified music drifted into the warm summer night. The streets were dim because of statewide restrictions imposed by an electricity workers' strike.

When Urquhart got to the coffee bar he found his friend Peter Hazelman sitting with three others, Kevin Stewart, Buck Knight and Bill Van Viess. He sat and chatted with the others. He had plenty of time to kill; he had arranged to pick up Abina at midnight and there wasn't much else to do but talk cars. After about half an hour the other three left, so Peter and Ian decided to go and sit in Peter's car, a fawn Austin A 90. The pair had moved to the Orr Street lodgings only a few days before. For both it was the first flutter of independence after leaving the family cocoon. Orr Street was hardly more convenient than being at home, but what they paid for as well as bed and breakfast was a feeling of controlling their own destiny. It was to be short lived.

Outside, the streets were busy with the spillover from the concert and the carnival. The boys drove around aimlessly for a while. They pulled up outside the Chateau Brion restaurant in Fryers Street and sat in the car listening to the radio. They could see enough of Welsford Street near the civic centre to tell when the show was finished. At 11.20pm they saw the concert-goers spilling onto the street. Peter started the Austin and drove slowly past the civic centre to give Ian a chance to see Abina waiting in the crowd on the footpath.

Ian was getting anxious. He hadn't known Abina long but she

was the first girlfriend he'd had, apart from schoolboy crushes. He asked Peter to drive to the Madills' house in Maxwell Street. When they reached the house they parked for a few minutes, saw there was no activity and turned back towards the civic centre. They arrived just before midnight.

Roslyn Madill and her friend Rae Croxford were standing in the street talking to someone in a car. Peter pulled up, and Ian called the girls over and asked where Abina was. Roslyn hesitated, then told him the truth. Abina was driving around with Garry Heywood, her boss's nephew with the flash car.

Ian's adolescent pride was wounded. 'I'll kill the bastard, I'll belt him,' he said. It was a natural reaction, full of the exaggeration of anger. The girls got into the Austin for the promised ride home. They dropped Rae Croxford off, then went to the Madills.

When they arrived, Ian asked Roslyn to signal by turning on one of the house lights if Abina was home. She nodded, and went inside. No light came on.

It was fifteen minutes after midnight. The first day of the rest of Ian Urquhart's short life had just begun.

IAN Urquhart wasn't the only one to worry about Abina in the first hour of that Friday. Soon after he and Peter Hazelman brought Roslyn home, Abina's friend Jan and her boyfriend Max arrived at Jan's house in Maxwell Street. As soon as they saw Ian and Peter sitting in the Austin outside Madills, Max reversed his Holden so that Jan could speak to them about Abina. After a couple of minutes Ian and Peter got in Max's car and the four drove off to look behind the lake. Jan pointed out where she thought Garry Heywood's car would be, just past the parking bay near the swimming pool. But it wasn't there. They kept driving along the gravel road that wound through the red gums right around the lake to Wyndham Street.

40

Along the way Peter Hazelman noticed a few cars parked among the trees; he took no notice of what makes they were, apart from the fact that none was Garry's Holden. To complete their circuit they drove down Wyndham Street before turning off to return to Madills' to see if Abina had come home while they were away. The carnival had shut down and the streets were almost deserted: there was no way they could have missed Heywood's car if it had been anywhere in Wyndham Street.

By Peter Hazelman's reckoning they arrived back at Madills' house about 12.45am. This made sense, no matter how slowly they drove, it would not take more than half an hour to circle the lake, and he was certain they had started the search not long after dropping Roslyn Madill home at the (easily verifiable) time of 12.15am. Peter's account of what happened that night tallied perfectly with that of Jan and Max, for the very good reason that they were all telling the truth.

But there was, strangely, a difference between the statements detectives took from each of the three a few days later. Whereas Jan and Max were quoted as saying they had arrived in Maxwell Street just before 1am and had then taken until 1.45am to drive around the lake, Peter Hazelman – and, presumably, Ian Urquhart – insisted that it had been some 45 minutes earlier. Hazelman stuck to that time despite some heavy-handed interrogation over the following weeks.

It could have been that somebody's watch was wrong, or that in the confusion either Peter Hazelman or the other two had lost track of time. Or it might have been that somebody was already trying to build a case against Ian Urquhart: somebody who needed a time gap long enough for the boy to have committed a double murder before rushing back to wait innocently outside Madills' house.

But the strange workings of the police inquiry were to come

later. In the early hours of Friday, February 11, everybody was working together to find the two missing teenagers. After arriving back at Maxwell Street, Ian and Peter climbed back in the Austin outside Madills' and waited, while Max dropped Jan off at her parents' house a few doors down. Jan went inside to face a sleepless night; Max drove back up to Madills. Max knew Abina well, and he worked with Ian Urquhart at Smith Motors. He was worried.

IN the Madill household, the alarm was not raised until after 1am. Mr Madill had gone to bed early, was asleep when Roslyn got back, and did not know anything was amiss until his wife came home from visiting at Undera and woke him to say that Abina wasn't home. The couple went outside several times to see if there was any sign of her. About 2am Mr Madill drove to the police station. When he left he noticed that the boys were not parked in front of his house. They had gone off on another drive to look for Heywood's car, something they did several times that night.

Mr Madill could not raise anybody at the police station, because the two night duty officers were on patrol. He drove home, rang the station, and was told that the divisional van would come around as soon as possible. By this time the three boys were back, parked outside the house.

WHEN the police van pulled in behind the cars outside Madills', the glare of its headlights made it impossible for the boys to tell what the new arrival was. But Ian Urquhart thought he knew; he leapt out and ran back, fists cocked as if to punch the driver. He stopped in surprise when he realised that it was a police van, not a dark green FJ Holden. Instead of Garry Heywood, he was faced by two uniformed policemen who wanted to know what was going on.

42

It was a spontaneous action in keeping with the anxiety and anger Urquhart had displayed for the previous two hours. It strains credibility and common sense that a teenage apprentice mechanic would produce such an inspired off-the-cuff perform-ance to bolster an alibi. Like the one-hour discrepancy among the various statements taken a few days later, it didn't add up.

CHARLIE Heywood was wakened by the knocking. He wasn't sure what time it was, but he knew it was late. There was no traffic on the main road at the bottom of the street, and there was the hush that descends in the hours just before dawn.

He opened the door. On the step were a policeman and a man about his own age, Fred Madill. He was surprised at what they told him. He knew that Abina Madill worked in the office at the panel works, but he had never seen Garry in her company. He hadn't even been sure the boy was going out that night until he and his wife arrived home about 8.30pm from an outing early in the evening. By that time Garry had gone.

He went to the bedroom Garry shared with Allen. Fear bit into him when he saw Garry's bed was empty, except for Jenny, the old terrier, who always sneaked in with the boys. Allen stirred, and asked what was up. Charlie tried to hide his alarm from the boy, but he knew something must be wrong to keep Garry out hours after midnight. They started work at 7am.

By this time Mrs Heywood was awake and upset. Her husband tried to reassure her, then he joined Fred Madill and drove around checking cars parked outside motels and any other likely spots. After that they parted, and Charlie woke up Garry's mates at their homes. But no-one knew anything; none of them had seen Garry since before 11 o'clock. He seemed to have vanished …

At the police station Fred Madill was formally filing his daughter as a missing person. It was 3am.

FIRST Constable Frank Eyre had started his shift at 11pm and would finish at 7am. His partner for the night was Constable John Quirk, who started at 9pm and finished at 5am. Having two men on duty overnight in Shepparton was the police force's concession to the fruit-picking season. But despite the concert and the carnival the night of February 10 had been peaceful: no fights, no accidents, hardly a drunk in sight. When Fred Madill reported that his daughter had not arrived home after the concert, it didn't seem like much. Teenagers, being exactly that, were known to be late home occasionally. Sometimes they got back next morning, other times it might take a few days, or weeks, but they usually turned up.

The first time the two policemen went to Madills' house, they didn't know the girl was with Garry Heywood. But they knew Heywood's car well, and Frank Eyre thought later that if they'd seen it earlier that night he would have remembered. It was understandable that the Madills and the Heywoods were upset, but it seemed pretty clear at the time that the kids had 'shot through'. That is, it did until Eyre found the car.

It happened just after 5am. Eyre dropped his partner home in the south end of Shepparton and was driving back to the town centre along Wyndham Street when he saw the green FJ on the west side of the road, facing the lake. The car was parked roughly, as if by someone who didn't care, or who was in a hurry. It was a little askew, with the front wheels on a left lock and a long way from the kerb. The windows were down, a tie was dangling from the offside rear door and the keys were missing. The policeman walked to the front of the car and felt the motor.

It was, he recalled later, 'stone motherless cold'. It must have been there for hours.

Eyre was thoughtful as he drove back to the station. He

decided that before he knocked off he would ring Peter Parkinson, an ex-homicide detective who had been transferred to Shepparton not long before. But first there was the business of telling Charlie Heywood he'd found his boy's car.

AS soon as he saw the Holden, Mr Heywood knew that Garry had not parked it. He climbed into the front seat with a heavy heart. Allen and his sister Lorraine slid into the car beside their father. One of them produced a spare key and slid it into the ignition. Then they drove the only clue to Garry's fate slowly home. The Heywoods were bewildered and scared. They knew what the police didn't: Garry would never run away and leave that car behind.

IN the cowshed at Gawnes', Lesley turned on the old wireless in time to catch the 6am news on 3SR. As if to spite her, the Righteous Brothers hit *Unchained Melody* blared from the big, fabric-covered speaker. Lesley remembered the song for a long time afterwards because the station played it at the same time every morning for weeks.

She was more miserable than usual. Not only had Ray gone out the night before, he wasn't home in time to start the milking with her. The time pips sounded, and the newsreader started his list of items. One of them caught her attention. Two Shepparton teenagers were missing. The details were sketchy … they were last seen in a dark green FJ Holden near the civic centre … police would like to hear from anyone with information about their movements. For no particular reason, Lesley felt a pang of apprehension. The old intuition thing, she thought. It was silly, but she couldn't help worrying about where Ray had been. A few minutes later he stepped quietly into the shed. Lesley gave him a black look and said nothing. They worked in silence. They usually did.

I N Mooroopna a couple of hours later, Garry Heywood's girlfriend, Gail, was having breakfast when she heard a later version of the same news bulletin on the big radiogram in the kitchen. By this time the names of the missing pair were being broadcast.

Gail caught the bus to work, still in a fog of confusion. The fact that Garry had been with Abina didn't worry her; she was young and naive, and assumed that Garry had been giving Abina a ride home from the concert when they'd disappeared. But why had he gone out in the first place? And what on earth could have happened to him? One thing she was sure about, as was every other teenager who knew Garry well: there was no way that the pair had run away. Apart from all the other reasons, she knew he was flat broke and had a week's wages owed to him.

The disappearance caused some talk among the bus passengers, but most buried their heads in the Melbourne *Sun*. It was a big day for news. The notorious murderer William O'Meally had attacked a warder in Pentridge. Sir Robert Menzies had announced his retirement from parliament. And a top Sydney detective was joining the hunt for the Beaumont children.

P ARKINSON, a much younger policeman was to say years later, 'was a real hero when he came to Shep from homicide ... like something out of New York'. This was probably intended as a compliment. But there were those not so admiring of the former homicide detective who might also have used the New York analogy.

For a boy born and bred on a farm in the Riverina, Peter Parkinson had fast picked up a lot of big city habits, although former colleagues remembered there was always a touch of the cowboy about him. In the bush, the strapping young man had shorn sheep and occasionally fought in the boxing tents; in Melbourne he joined the police force and soon became a slick city detective. A handsome man with dark, curly hair and impeccable clothes of the trench coat and snap-brim hat variety, he could have walked straight off the set of television's *Homicide*. But the charming and persuasive manner veiled a tough, streetwise character. While working in the homicide squad under the notorious Jack Matthews in the early 1960s, he earned a reputation remembered, for varying reasons, years after his retirement.

While in the squad, Parkinson was involved in the investigation of 35 murders. His biggest job was the 'mafia murders', the outbreak of violence among Italian fruit and vegetable stallholders at Melbourne's Victoria Market. But, ironically, it wasn't until he left Russell Street to go to the country that the biggest case of his career came within reach. Characteristically, he grabbed it.

He had gone back into uniform to go to Shepparton as a senior constable in February 1965. The move, he said later, was on doctor's orders: one of his children had severe asthma and needed a drier climate than Melbourne.

By chance, going to Shepparton also enabled him to renew acquaintance with Jack Matthews, who had been made superintendent there. And, as it turned out, with Sergeant Jack Ford, who was still in the homicide squad. Both Ford and Matthews were later to serve prison sentences after being convicted of perverting the course of justice following the abortion inquiry.

But that was all well after 1966. That year, early in the morning of Friday, February 11, Parkinson took a telephone call at home from Frank Eyre. His astonishingly detailed memory of events of two decades before, delivered as carefully as court evidence, begins with that call ...

'I was on day shift on Thursday, with a rostered rest day on Friday. I was rung fairly early that Friday morning. He (Frank Eyre) said: "We have got a problem with a couple of young people that have disappeared. It seems to look a bit serious. Do you think you could come in and have a look?"

'My reaction was: "Who is it?' When he mentioned Garry Heywood I was more interested because he lived around the corner from me. I lived in Hare Street, which dead-ended right at his parents' house. Each day I'd see him washing his car. This was an immaculate car. It was a British Racing Green FJ Holden, which was the really in thing for any young feller at that time.

'I went to the station, where the uniformed constables had detained four people: Ian Urquhart, Peter Hazelman, Jan Frost and Lindsay Lohse (sic). I was filled in by the constables on what they knew: when they had gone to the concert, that the car had been found at the lake, and that these four had been looking for Abina Madill.

'But before questioning the four kids I went to Heywood's address and took possession of Garry Heywood's car, took it to the police station and locked it in a garage and put the key in my pocket. I was careful not to touch any printable surfaces.

'Then I questioned the four of them separately and carefully. Then they left the police station … I felt that it was a serious matter. Knowing how Heywood treated his car I couldn't have him running off with the girl and leaving it. I felt it was possibly murder – the whole set-up had the smell of it. So I went to the superintendent, who was Jack Matthews, the ex-homicide chief, and I explained the situation to him and my feelings on the matter. He give me the go-ahead to investigate. He said: "Put the whole weekend in at it. If you can't turn up anything by Monday, let me know how you feel then."

'We worked the whole weekend, trying to reconstruct their movements. On the Saturday an old Italian man, now deceased, called Oliveri found Madill's handbag in the bottom of Castle Creek near the bridge. It had her name in it. He had been riding his bike over the bridge and saw it sitting on the

48

sand. 'By this stage the police station was humming. There were calls coming in from the news media and from the public. On the Monday morning I went back to the superintendent. "What are your feelings now, lad?" asked the old boss. I said: "More convinced than ever we have got a double murder on our hands. And I feel the quicker we move into it the better." He said: "Righto. I will back your judgement, lad."

'I said that I'd had the car locked up since Friday and would like to get the scientific branch up to have a look at it, and he said: "We will get 'em all up and you stick to them. I'll get you seconded over into the plain clothes branch." So I contacted homicide, fingerprints, photographic and forensic … and they all arrived that morning before lunch.

'The fingerprint branch printed the car … on top of the driver's door on the green metal surface were the prints of two fingers pointing down. I had no feeling of elation about the prints because it could have been anybody who'd touched the car since it had been washed. We had to print everybody we interviewed to eliminate them. The forensic fellows went completely over the car.

'One thing I remember was that the knob was off the gear stick, it was on the floor. I had left it on the floor. Later when we tested the car on the road we noticed that because of vibration at around 70 miles per hour the knob would unscrew itself from the gear stick and fall on the floor, so we knew it had been hunted (driven hard) by the killer.

'On that Monday we immediately started a murder file and set up a room, an old room near the disused cells in the backyard of the station. We rang the PMG and they sent a bloke straight around and he ran a line out to the room. Then we grabbed a few typewriters and by sunset that night we were set up. The only thing we were short of were cars, so we used our own. You'd think nothing of jumping in your own car and doing 50 miles, as long as you were getting the job done. Every person that we interviewed or there was any contact with we put on file and indexed. I worked alongside the homicide detectives under Sergeant Henry Morrison. I was more or less his co-ordinator. I didn't know it then but that week was the first of a year in which I never had a day off. After a long day's work, if you walked into a pub people would say: "Have you got that bastard yet?"

'It was an intensive, tiring, painstaking investigation …'

And a useless one. But that, naturally, would be not stressed by a retired man filtering his memories through the lens of 21 years.

Other people were to remember things a little differently.

WHEN the Heywoods got home with Garry's Holden after fetching it from the lake, they parked it on their front lawn. After attempting a breakfast which none of the family had much stomach for, Allen recalls that he started washing the FJ, as if by going through the familiar routine he could end the nightmare; that somehow Garry would come whistling up the footpath, ruffle his hair, throw a few mock punches and take him for a ride. He picked up the hose and started at the back of the car, but before he went any further than the boot his father stopped him. Instinctively, Charlie Heywood was wary of disturbing the car too much. His caution was fortunate for the police. By the time Parkinson picked up the car later that day 'to preserve the crime scene' the way he'd learned in the homicide squad, the pair of finger prints on top of the driver's door could easily have disappeared.

Lorraine, Garry's married sister, was living at home while her husband was building a house. She was almost eight months pregnant with her first child, and by the mid-morning she was pale with worry. Lorraine, like Allen, had helped

Garry restore the car and she knew in her heart that only something terrible would make him leave it, to let a stranger drive it. But at the same time she and her parents and little brother nursed the hope that there was some harmless explanation they hadn't thought of. Some minor accident? A late party somewhere from which the Holden had been stolen?

Anything, however unlikely, was preferable to the awful probability of murder.

Lorraine and her mother went out to the car and looked through it. There was something out of place, something missing. Then she realised what it was: the handsome blue and grey checked rug that her parents had given Garry for his eighteenth birthday. So was the plastic bag that he kept it in. When the police came to get the car they told them about the rug; about how Garry always kept it in the back of the car. It seemed an important piece of information at the time, but it might have been better if they had not been so observant.

The rug was to lay one of the biggest false trails in a case that was littered with them, leading investigators on fruitless interstate junkets when the answer to the riddle was hidden on their doorstep ...

But that was later. On February 11, 1966, the screw tightened another turn for the Heywood family when the big detective stepped into the Holden and drove it away.

It was as if to say that Garry wouldn't be needing it any more.

IAN Urquhart and Peter Hazelman had dozed fitfully in their car outside Madills' place until about 7am. When he woke Ian was still angry. They drove off, looking for breakfast and Garry Heywood.

Two hours later Catherine Hogan, housekeeper for Paul Heywood's parents at their house in Fairway Court, was just starting her morning's work. Mr and Mrs Heywood, Garry's uncle and aunt, were still in Melbourne. When the woman arrived she noticed that Paul was on the telephone, talking to someone about Garry. When he hung up, he told her that his cousin was missing. Then he went to school.

Five minutes later Peter Hazelman's Austin pulled into the drive, although the housekeeper did not recognise either the driver or the boy who got out of the car and walked up the drive.

The boy was about eighteen, had fair hair and was wearing blue combination overalls with AMPOL on the pocket. But the most striking thing about him was his face. It was white with strain. He asked: 'Is Heywood here?' When told that Paul had just left for school, the boy replied: 'I came to clean him up.' Asked why, he allegedly said: 'I was supposed to pick up a girl at the civic centre at eleven o'clock and they took her away.'

At least, that was the way Urquhart's answer was noted when detectives interviewed the housekeeper later. Which begs the question: why should Ian Urquhart say he was to pick up Abina at eleven o'clock when he had, on the evidence of her family, clearly arranged to pick up both her and her sister Roslyn at midnight? For that matter, why should Ian Urquhart, when talking to the housekeeper, mention the time at all? If he did, it was a convenient detail for anyone looking for elusive circumstantial evidence.

FOR the Heywoods and the Madills that first weekend was a foretaste of nightmare. With every hour the parents knew it was more likely that their children had come to harm, but for the first two days it seemed to them that no-one in authority shared their concern. Many tended to dismiss the disappearance as another case of runaway teenagers. But from the beginning the families and friends of Abina and Garry could not convince themselves of the runaway theory, as much

52

as they prayed for a telephone call from Melbourne or interstate proving them wrong. So when faced with a lukewarm response for mounting a full-scale search within 24 hours of Garry's car being found, Charlie Heywood and Fred Madill started looking themselves.

The Heywoods took Jenny, their terrier, who was devoted to Garry and knew his scent. With Mr Madill they started searching the red gum flats beside the Goulburn river. The task was huge, but it relieved the agony of waiting at home for the news they feared.

They found nothing. Ironically, it was a chance find by a stranger on Saturday, February 12, that galvanised the police into action. An old man, Alfonso Oliveri, was riding his bicycle over the Castle Creek bridge on the highway twenty kilometres south of Shepparton when he caught a glimpse of something white in the dry creek bed below. He dismounted and scrambled down the bank. It was a girl's handbag. Inside was the usual unremarkable clutter: a small amount of money, paper tissues, one full and one empty packet of Alpine cigarettes, a powder compact, and a key holder with Shepparton Motor Panels printed on it. There was also a metal disc with the word 'Billy' engraved on it, an object which was to puzzle police for almost two decades.

But it was the name and address written inside the bag that caused the uniformed constable to call for his superiors as soon as the old man handed in the bag later that day. Neatly printed on the inside lining was: Abina Madill, 17 Maxwell St. Shepparton.

It was hard to believe that Garry Heywood might run away without his week's wages and his prized car. It was harder to believe that a girl would throw away her handbag unless she was under duress. Those who had been dismissing the teenagers' disappearance with dirty wisecracks fell silent.

To detectives the handbag almost certainly meant murder. But was it necessarily double murder? That question was to cause the Heywood family more anguish before another week was out.

On Monday, February 14, the day decimal currency was introduced to Australia, the serious hunt began.

The search and rescue squad arrived from Melbourne to join dozens of local volunteers, including every able-bodied worker from Heywood's panel works, which had closed its doors. The searchers started beating through snake-infested forest along the river.

A light aircraft, boats and skindivers were also brought in. Meanwhile, homicide squad and forensic police were setting up what they thought of as temporary quarters at the police station. None could have guessed how long they would be there.

That day *The Herald* became the first Melbourne paper to pick up the story. And the front page lead of the *Shepparton News* stated that police were 'gravely concerned'. Everybody knew what that meant. They were looking for bodies.

IAN Urquhart had a problem. The police were looking for a murderer, and he had what could be construed as a classic motive: jealousy. The fact that there was no material evidence, or anything in his behaviour or his statements which suggested guilt, did not matter. Until somebody better came along, he was the nearest thing to a 'good suspect'; and for years his tragedy was that no better suspect ever turned up.

This didn't just pre-suppose that a country teenager could commit a double murder in a jealous rage and then mask his guilt as coolly as a professional killer. It also pre-supposed, because the suspect had friends whose statements corroborated his and gave him a watertight alibi, that three other teenagers were accessories to a monstrous crime; a crime which involved killing one of their own friends.

It strains belief, but it happened.

The first gruelling interview came on Monday, February 14. Jan, friend of both Abina and Ian Urquhart, was called in during the afternoon. Her boyfriend Max was brought in later that night. Peter Hazelman was seen next day. The three went in to the CIB office as ordinary, country kids who were puzzled and worried about Abina's fate, and determined to help in any way they could.

They came out – hours later – bewildered and angry about a system they'd been grown up learning to respect. They said later that they were unhappy about answering some questions put to them, particularly questions about their own personal lives which they considered offensive and irrelevant to Garry and Abina's disappearance.

It was the beginning of a bitterness that was to alter the course of their lives. But Ian Urquhart suffered worse.

ON Tuesday, February 15, the number of volunteer searchers swelled to more than a hundred, and the police circulated radio descriptions of the missing pair to every State. Already the diplomatic euphemisms about 'grave concerns' had been dropped; the *Sun* bluntly stated in a headline that murder was feared. Still the families clung to the threads of doubt which were left. Mr Madill was quoted as saying that Abina might have gone to Melbourne because her handbag was found near the highway leading that way. It seemed a forlorn hope.

There was huge public interest in the case, but the news-papers were struggling for fresh angles. In the absence of anything genuinely new and important, the trivial was puffed into seeming significance and rumour thrived. All of which hindered the search for truth – and put great pressure on already overworked police to come up with something.

Theories abounded. On Wednesday, February 16, police

appealed for a 'party of Melbourne rock'n'roll fans who had been at the concert to come forward. The same day the *Shepparton News*, in the unmistakably rhetorical style of its police roundsman Laurie Sweet, asked: 'Did a fight at the back of Shepparton's civic centre have anything to do with the mysterious disappearance of a teenage couple who have vanished without trace?'

Meanwhile, there were reports that the couple had been seen at Mildura and other river towns near the South Australian border, and that police were interested in tracing two Queenslanders who had reportedly 'left town in a hurry' the previous Saturday.

Next day, Thursday, it was revealed that police had recovered an 'undergarment' of Abina's hidden under a rock in the town. After re-interviewing one of the boys who had been with Garry and Abina on the night they disappeared, detectives soon established that the find was of no consequence, but the story was made public anyway.

A little tact would have saved a lot of pain for the Madill family. But, as Abina's older brother Rodney was to comment a long time after, some detectives of those days treated his parents rather callously.

On Friday morning, February 18, Garry and Abina had been missing for one week. Superintendent Jack Matthews pledged to keep up the search to the end. To that stage there had been reports of girls matching Abina's description at Mildura, Kerang, Sale, Wodonga and a district near Sydney.

Shepparton was a town in shock. Soon it was to be under siege. Two more homicide detectives left Melbourne to join their two colleagues already in Shepparton. One of them was Senior Detective Noel Murphy, whose reputation as a street-wise operator approached that of Peter Parkinson.

Saturday, February 19, was duck opening day. Police urged

shooters to watch for clues, particularly Garry Heywood's blue rug. The local pony club turned out 32 riders to help with the search. Mr Madill told the newspapers: 'We don't know which way to turn. If they have run away, I implore them to come home or let us know where they are … '

Next day the Melbourne reporters went home.

F OR the Heywoods the cruellest cut of all came early on Sunday morning, February 20. It was inevitable and understandable that the police would act on the growing suspicion that Garry had killed Abina and was being protected by his family. But that didn't make it any easier for the Heywoods when the time came.

At 9.30am that Sunday detectives turned up at Heywoods' house and escorted Charlie Heywood to the police station. They were taking the nest of murderers theory seriously; the missing boy's grieving father was questioned vigorously by a group of detectives which included Matthews, Murphy and Parkinson. While he was being detained one of the forensic police and a member of the search and rescue squad searched Heywoods' house.

Neither the questioning nor the search produced any result. The expert homicide investigators from the city couldn't understand it. With their experience, their training, their intuitive ability to 'smell a crook', they could not have been blamed for thinking they would be able to clean up the mystery in the first week. But by Monday, February 21, it was looking as if they might be in for a long and tiring investigation.

They could hardly have guessed that it would see most of them out of the job.

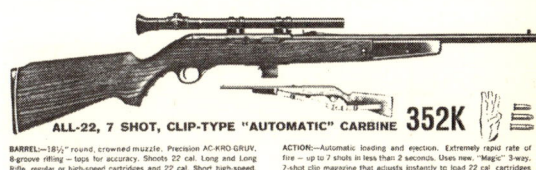

ALL-22, 7 SHOT, CLIP-TYPE "AUTOMATIC" CARBINE **352K**

BARREL:—18½" round, crowned muzzle. Precision AC-KRO-GRUV, 8-groove rifling — tops for accuracy. Shoots 22 cal. Long and Long Rifle, regular or high-speed cartridges and 22 cal. Short high-speed.

STOCK:—Genuine American walnut with Monte Carlo and pistol grip. Hand rubbed to a rich, lasting beauty. Two-position, extension fore-end of black Tenite. Sling swivels and web strap on left of stock. Butt plate with white liner.

SIGHTS:—Open rear with adjustments for windage and elevation, and Sporting Front. Receiver grooved for easy scope mounting.

ACTION:—Automatic loading and ejection. Extremely rapid rate of fire — up to 7 shots in less than 2 seconds. Uses new, "Magic" 3-way, 7-shot clip magazine that adjusts instantly to load 22 cal. cartridges in any one of the 3 popular lengths. Positive safety, at side of receiver, "right under your thumb."

WEIGHT:—About 5 lbs. **LENGTH:**—Over all 38". Easy take down.

SCOPE:—Shown is Mossberg's 4-power Model 4M4 with slide-on mount, a very desirable accessory. See page 7.

FOUR

Homicide, 1966

MURCHISON East is a pair of road signs sandwiching a hotel, a railway station, a store, a set of saleyards and a few scattered houses, all overshadowed by a cluster of silver wheat silos visible across the Goulburn Valley plain long before a traveller reaches them. Its excuse for a separate existence from Murchison proper, which nestles on the Goulburn River's opposite bank several farms away, is that it marks the complicated intersection of the Goulburn Valley Highway, the road from Bendigo, and the Tocumwal to Melbourne railway line.

It would flatter this aimless collection of buildings, imply some sort of non-existent charm, to call it a hamlet. To all but the handful of locals who get their beer, bread and mail there it is merely an irritating slow spot on the way to somewhere else, a butt for 'blink and you'll miss it' jokes.

But despite the humdrum ugliness of the highway frontage, there is something familiarly Australian about the cream-

58

painted, red-roofed, weatherboard railway station shaded by its ragged row of pepper trees. It could be part of any sleepy country town anywhere. So could the dusty gravel road that winds behind it and heads north through the paddocks towards the tree-lined river, then turns sharp right and goes nowhere in particular before rejoining the highway towards Shepparton.

The anonymity of the road is reflected in its variety of names. Locals refer to it variously as the river road, the station road or Cassidy's road; the first two labels for obvious reasons, the third because a local farming family held land on the western side of it for more than a century. Despite the number of choices, or perhaps because of them, in 1966 no signpost marked the road's entrance onto the highway just west of the railway line. Most travellers, concentrating on the railway crossing and converging traffic from the Melbourne road, would never notice it, even in daylight.

And at night, only someone who had been there before could pick the turn-off.

Peter Jacobi was one of few people not living at Murchison who knew the river road by day or night. When he stepped off the train at the little station under the pepper trees about 11am on Saturday, February 26, he headed straight for a nearby house with the assurance of someone on familiar ground. With him was another youth, Phillip Ashton. Both carried shotguns, Peter's a vintage double-barrelled English model his grandfather had given him. They were on a weekend shooting trip. At seventeen they were old enough to go away alone, young enough to enjoy the novelty of independence.

The boys were from Melbourne, Peter Jacobi from Box Hill, his mate from Montrose. But young Jacobi's family originally came from Murchison East; he had been born there and had often visited his grandparents after his family moved to Melbourne. It was to their farmhouse that he was leading the

way when they got off the train, which they'd caught at
Spencer Street at 8.15 that morning.

The boys wasted no time. After Phillip was introduced to the
old people, they bolted down a quick morning tea and headed
off to one of Peter's favourite haunts to get in a shot before
lunch. It was a warm day, but the pair walked quickly, pleased
to stretch their legs after the train journey. They went down the
river road for fifteen minutes, then climbed through a wire
fence on their left and struck out across a paddock owned by
the Cassidy family. By cutting across the paddock on an angle
they hit the boundary fence between Cassidy's and the crown
land about 250 metres from the road. Just before reaching the
fence, which they crossed to get into the forest, they smelt
something dead. This was not unusual in summer, when the
stench of a dead animal can linger for weeks.

The bush on the crown land next to Cassidy's was grazed
under lease, and so was park-like and clear of undergrowth
beneath the trees. It was an excellent place to ramble, and
although it was the wrong time of day to see rabbits or foxes the
young shooters were not disappointed with their walk. They
wandered through the gums for an hour before turning back.

Again they set out to cut across the corner of Cassidy's
paddock to the road, but this time they struck the fence at a
different spot. It was then that they saw the body they'd smelt
an hour earlier.

It wasn't an animal.

It was, unmistakably, a girl.

Peter Jacobi has seen plenty of bodies since that day, having
later joined the police force. But he has never seen one that
affected him the same way. It wasn't just that she was black
from exposure and fearfully decomposed; it was obvious that
she had died violently and in terror. The body was naked from
the waist down. Like everyone else in Victoria the boys knew

60

that two teenagers were missing, but they were too shocked by what was lying on the ground to make the connection. They felt sick. They turned and hurried across the paddock. Beyond the trees the heat was fierce, so they slowed to a brisk walk when they reached the road. The closest house was Cassidy's, a kilometre away. It seemed a long way to carry bad news.

JOHN Barron Cassidy, better known as Jack, still had not eaten lunch when the two lads hammered on his door. They were strangely flushed, and not just from exertion on a hot day. One he recognised as the grandson of one of his neighbours, the other was a stranger.

A body, they said. A dead girl down near the fence at the edge of the bush. As their story tumbled out, Jack Cassidy wondered if it had anything to do with the missing teenagers from Shepparton who had been so much in the news for a fortnight. Better see Bernie Robins straight away, he decided.

Senior Constable Bernard Robins was just about to take the first mouthful of a hot midday meal when Cassidy and the two boys parked outside the Murchison police residence. When he heard their story he knew the mystery of the missing teenagers was probably solved, and in the way that everybody feared. Resignedly, he asked his wife to put his lunch in the oven to keep it warm. There wasn't much chance he'd get back to it.

They drove back over the bridge along the highway to 'Murch East', as the locals called it. Left turn into the little road behind the station, past the railway houses backing onto the line, and down the dusty gravel road to the corner where a big mallee gate led into the bush paddock. The mallee gate was always kept shut, but the Cassidys had been puzzled to find it open about two weeks earlier when checking how their heifers had strayed onto the road from the crown land they leased ...

They climbed out of the car, jerked open the gate and walked along the fence. Precisely 413 feet, as it was later measured. Robins held his breath and approached the body. He picked up the right hand and looked at the ring. 'That's her,' he said.

Abina Madill. Born September 17, 1949. Died on or about midnight, February 10, 1966.

ROBINS went to Cassidy's to make the first in a chain reaction of telephone calls that had Murchison East buzzing with police by mid-afternoon. Peter Parkinson and Joe Ogden drove straight down from Shepparton, 37 kilometres away, and made arrangements to secure the crime scene until the team of specialists needed at a homicide could be gathered to start their painstaking tasks. Before they arrived a traffic patrolman, Brian Barnfield, drove down from the highway and took statements from the two teenagers.

Police don't like murders without bodies. Now, at least, they had a body. But only one, a point which Jack Cassidy was pondering. A few days before, he recalled, he had smelt something dead near a clump of saplings inside his paddock. At the time he assumed it would probably be a dead dog, as it was not unusual to have carcasses dumped in the bush at the bottom of his property. Now, with the girl being found within a few hundred yards of the saplings, he told police about the 'dead dog'. It would be the first place he'd look for Garry Heywood. Or what was left of him.

The farmer was right. The police found the second body among the saplings. About six feet tall, dressed in narrow-legged black trousers, desert boots and an orange checked shirt. There was a box of matches and two shillings and fourpence in the trousers pocket, and a bullet hole in the left temple.

Shot and dumped like the dog Jack Cassidy thought he had smelt.

62

Garry Charles Heywood. Born August 19, 1947. Died on or about midnight, February 10, 1966.

BAD news travels fast. Garry Heywood's sister Lorraine and her husband were out when they heard the first radio bulletin about the bodies at Murchison. By this time Lorraine was only four weeks off giving birth, but she knew she could handle the crisis better than her mother. She and her husband drove straight to her parents' place to try to ease the shock.

Mr and Mrs Heywood were bottling fruit. It was one of the routine mechanical tasks they had been trying to fill their time with. As soon as Lorraine walked in they knew something was wrong.

'Mum and Dad,' she said gently. 'We've got some terrible news. We think they've found Garry's body with the girl's … '

FIRST Class Constable Bob Dowdell, solid country police- man and father of a big family, was playing tennis at Orrvale, just out of Shepparton. When he came off the court at 5pm he got the message left for him by Sergeant Thomas, who'd rung from the police station. He was to report for duty at the state forest at Murchison, to stand guard over the bodies. Dowdell went home, changed into his uniform and drove his own car to Murchison. By the time he got there the shadows were beginning to lengthen; it was a warm, still summer evening.

As soon as he got out of his car, the smell hit him. It seemed to hang over the whole forest. The odour of a putrefying human body was indescribably worse than any other, he was to say later. It permeated his hair and the weave of his clothes. Years later, the memory still made his broad face pucker with revulsion. He saw the girl's body first. Her skull had been broken like an eggshell. The rest of the body was shrunken by the heat so that it looked like a child of twelve or thirteen, he thought. Along the fence and through the gap to the clump of saplings he walked, skirting the forensic experts going about their job of reducing the haphazard details of murder into precise scientific observations.

Dowdell saw that the boy's body had not decomposed as much as the other because the trees had shaded it from the sun. It was bloated with the gases trapped inside the gut. He shuddered, unable to share the black humour and professional detachment of the homicide men around him. This was too close to home. He knew Garry Heywood, 'a happy, fun-loving boy, good-natured and normal,' who for years had come out to his place to ride horses. His wife played croquet with Mrs Madill, who was a respected member of 'a good Christian family'. And he had teenage kids of his own.

It was a long night on guard duty, watching over a ghoulish scene lit by portable generators.

Dowdell arrived home a little before dawn. He took off his clothes outside the house, and walked in almost naked. He burned some of them, scrubbed others. And although he shampooed his hair repeatedly and had shower after shower to get rid of the smell, it was days before his wife would let him in the same bed.

O N the afternoon and evening that the bodies were found the police concentrated on plotting every detail with diagrams, maps and photographs before the corpses could be removed late that night.

While the Senior Government Pathologist, Dr James McNamara, carried out post-mortems next day at the coroner's court in Melbourne, forensic police got down to the tedious and vital part of their job. Starting early that Sunday morning Senior Constables Kevin Murdock and Henry Huggins began a systematic search.

64

The question of what had happened to the girl's missing clothes was quickly answered. They were found about 75 metres north of her body. Strangely, they were not scattered. Someone had neatly folded the skirt, placed the girdle on it, then put one of Abina's new white shoes on top. The other shoe was lying on the ground alongside.

Missing from the tidy little pile were Abina's stockings. One was found a few feet away from the other clothing. It was knotted into a tight loop, and dark fibres found caught in the weave were later identified as coming from Garry Heywood's trousers, indicating that the stocking was used to tie his legs. Traces of blood were found on the stocking, and underneath it was a small patch of blood-soaked earth. Nearby was Garry Heywood's jumper, which had been turned inside out. When examined, it was clear that the jumper had become impregnated with grass seeds, bark and leaves before being taken off, as if the wearer had been rolling on the ground. It also had traces of blood.

Another stocking was found about 25 metres away, roughly a third of the distance between the pile of clothes and where Abina's body was found. It also was tightly knotted in a loop, as if used to bind the arms or legs of one of the victims.

All of which indicated that the killer was cold-blooded and methodical. But it did not give a clue to his identity.

MURDOCK and Huggins soon found two clues they expected to find – and a third which seemed a stroke of rare good fortune. They did not need a post-mortem to Heywood had been shot with a small calibre firearm; the neat hole in his left temple made that clear enough. They found what they were looking for early on Sunday morning, lying in the fallen leaves about two metres from his body.

A spent .22 shell.

Another shell was found near the bloodstained and knotted stocking which was later identified as having tied Heywood's legs some time before he was shot. There was no apparent injury inflicted on either body by this shot, prompting speculation as to whether the killer had missed his aim or fired a shot to frighten his victims into submission.

The shells were important, but it was the discovery of a small piece of black plastic that made Murdock and Huggins satisfied with their efforts. They found it about two metres from the bloodstained earth and knotted stocking, and they guessed it was almost certainly part of the murder weapon. With a little good luck and a lot of painstaking work a clue like that could lead straight to the killer. As it turned out, with a lot of bad luck and a little slipshod work, it led nowhere.

B RIAN Thompson's quiet Sunday morning at home in Chadstone ended with a telephone call he'd been half expecting. When he got in to the forensic science laboratory in Spring Street the head of the homicide squad, Frank Holland, was waiting for him with the bullet the pathologist had taken from Garry Heywood's skull a few hours earlier.

The slug had flattened on impact, and looked an ugly mess. But underneath the mushroomed nose, Thompson knew, the base would be intact. He washed the slug and mounted it under a microscope. Sure enough, on the last bit of the bullet to leave the weapon, were the rifling marks gouged into the soft metal as it had spun down the barrel. To a trained eye the grooves on the slug were a signature. Scribbling on a foolscap pad as he worked, Thompson counted eight grooves, and noted their width compared with the width between them. Then he started checking against the ballistics records of the 160 types of .22 calibre weapons in the firearms library. When he finished he had a list of nine makes of rifle which had the same rifling pattern as the murder weapon. Next day, Frank Eyre arrived from Shepparton with the two spent shells and the piece of black plastic found at the murder scene. As soon as Thompson looked at the ejector marks on the shells, he knew they had both been fired from the same self-loading rifle.

There was only one self-loading model on the list of nine makes he had made the day before: Mossberg.

Thompson hardly had to look at the piece of black plastic. He knew that it was the plug which screwed into the butt-end of the receiver of a Mossberg self-loading rifle.

Habitually cautious, he wrote in his report: 'If all three items (i.e. bullet, cartridge cases and plastic plug) are from the one firearm, then the weapon is a .22 calibre Mossberg self-loading rifle.'

FOR the two stricken families in Shepparton life would from now on be filled with unavoidable reminders of their tragedy. One of the first cruel tasks was for each father to make a formal statement. Even the stilted formal style of the policeman taking down the words did not disguise the anguish of Frederick Lynas Madill, third generation farmer, church-goer and father of five.

After outlining the events of the night that his daughter disappeared, he added: 'I cannot think of any reason why any person would want to harm my daughter. Abina was to my mind a normal girl of her years who followed the modern teenage trend. I could not see any difference between her and the other teenage girls in the town ...

'We had shifted into the City of Shepparton from the farm at Undera in either 1962 or 1963, this being for the benefit of the girls' education, employment and social life.

'My wife and I thought that we would have a better chance of looking after them if we made this move.'

THE relationship between the homicide squad of 1966 and the makers of the evergreen television series *Homicide* was close. From when the program had begun two years earlier, the film makers sorted through the neatly solved cases, dusted off any that were promising dramatic material, then worked them up into a script to fit the series' well-defined format. In return, the police were cast as the good guys who always got their man, and got him honourably. The moral was that crime did not pay.

It was great public relations, even if reality did not always fit the cosy matinee formula. Most murders were too banal or too brutal to be portrayed with unblinking accuracy, their investigation too boringly routine to rate as entertainment. But the television series fostered the notion that the squad was an elite force which deftly outwitted the most devious criminal brains. This was not necessarily true.

Although some of the force's brightest and best served in the squad on their way through the ranks, its high rate of solved murders had more to do with the nature of the crime rather than some special brilliance.

The plain fact was that in that era, before drug trafficking added a sinister dimension to their work, homicide detectives dealt mainly with domestic murders. In general, the exceptions to this were gangland slayings, which created public interest but little public anger. The domestics were usually easily solved, and the public wasn't outraged if the occasional painter and docker got away with eliminating a rival.

But with the motiveless and random killing of two teenagers in a town like Shepparton, there was a huge outcry and no obvious culprit. Suddenly, through no fault of their own, homicide detectives were in the uncomfortable position of trying to live up to unrealistic public expectations. The pressure to make an arrest was intense.

68

On Monday, February 28, the investigation widened. Two extra homicide detectives were sent to Shepparton to help the two who were still there, which meant that the homicide men outnumbered the three local detectives. That is without counting Peter Parkinson, seconded from uniform to work with the homicide squad, and Superintendent Jack Matthews, the former homicide chief, who took charge of the inquiry.

The crew was working out of cramped quarters, and faced with searching for a killer or killers in a district crammed with thousands of itinerant fruit pickers who were all potential suspects. It was inevitable in such circumstances that office politics and professional jealousies would surface; it was likely that they would affect the way the inquiry was handled, possibly even dictate its ultimate success or failure.

There was a complicated cross-current of tensions, but the most obvious potential for problems lay in differences between local police and the homicide squad. It was natural that when the homicide squad was called it, the locals would give any help that was asked for, but in the meantime they would get on with their own work – which, in the fruit season, was considerable.

Some who were there were noted an unspoken attitude that if the homicide men were going to get the glory then they could do their own footslogging and their own paper work.

The locals considered that they knew their 'patch' better than anyone else, and that there was no reason to abandon making inquiries in their usual, often informal, way. In the normal course of provincial crime, they were probably right.

Their methods, such as dispensing instant justice to errant youngsters with 'a kick in the tail' instead of laying charges, were appreciated as common sense by the local community. But relying on instinct, local knowledge and memory instead of tedious formalities like writing names and addresses on files was not the way to assist an exhaustive and exhausting murder inquiry. This fact was to have grave and far-reaching consequences.

G ARRY Heywood's girlfriend Gail was sitting alone at home when she heard that the bodies had been found. For her, it was the third miserable Saturday since Garry had disappeared. Apart from going to work, she had hardly gone outside the house. Shepparton had turned into a town of stares and whispers by day, and its streets were almost deserted at night. The dances had all but shut down, and parents drove their children everywhere.

Going to and from work, Gail saw people huddling on street corners, talking of murder. Cranks and gossips were busy. She knew they were saying dreadful things about Garry and Abina and someone called Ian Urquhart. Suddenly, there seemed to be no respect for people's reputations; even Garry's own family had been under suspicion.

'It was weird', she was to say later. One day a man had approached her gloatingly and said Ian Urquhart had told him that 'she had better watch it, because she'll be next.'

It was crazy. And frightening.

B EFORE the bodies were found, Gail had been interviewed by the police only once. Naturally, she had told what she knew, which wasn't much. The well-brought-up daughter of the engineer at the Mooroopna Hospital wasn't the type to be untruthful. The policeman who interviewed her was a Mr Parkinson. He seemed 'very smooth, a real ladies' man,' she was to recall. It was from him she got the impression that Ian Urquhart could be dangerous. The policeman advised her to ask her parents to pick her up from work, which she did. In fact, the day the bodies were found was one of the few times her parents had left her alone. They had gone to Melbourne for the day. When they returned she asked her father to drive her to the Heywoods' place. She liked the family, had always felt welcome when she had visited; she wanted to try to comfort them in some way, to show respect and concern.

While her father waited in the car, Gail steeled herself and walked in. There were a lot of the Heywoods' relatives there. The tragedy had already taken its toll on Garry's mother, a slightly built, kindly and highly-strung woman. Mrs Heywood had lost weight and the will to live. She was smoking and drinking more than Gail had seen her do before, as if that might dull the pain that could be ended only by her own death.

Garry's little brother, Allen, seemed as deeply disturbed as his mother. He had always been sensitive. He was old enough to understand everything that had happened to Garry, but too young to cope with his emotions the way his elder sister, Lorraine, was able to. Gail said what she could, but felt helpless. Then, from out of the black cloud of grief, she was struck by a bolt of bitterness. An old woman, obviously upset, said: 'Go home, there's plenty more fish in the sea.' It seemed gratuitously cruel. Gail, wounded, walked out. It wasn't the last unpleasant experience for her. A few days later the detectives decided to interview her again. Not once, but many times. And each time they would turn up at the office where she worked and order her to come to the station for more questioning. It was her first job; she was sixteen and easily replaceable, a fact she felt keenly. Had she not worked for 'such an understanding company,' she was to say later, she might easily have lost her position.

'Some of the police were real pigs … they would come in to work, wouldn't even identify themselves and ask me to come with them. There were a couple that came on really strong, to the point that they were yelling at me and saying: "You do know something, but you're not telling us!" '

It grew too much for the shy receptionist. One day she refused to go to the station for another round of questioning. The detectives rang Gail's mother, and she told them that her daughter had 'had enough', that if they wanted to see her they could speak to her at home after office hours. Which they did, but only once. After that they stopped questioning the girl.

The experience shook Gail's previous unquestioning faith in the law. For years afterwards, she wondered: 'if that's how they treated witnesses, then how were they with actual suspects?' It was a question that Ian Urquhart and Peter Hazelman, among others, could have answered in detail.

B Y early March, the investigators were in a quandary. The one thing worse than having the several thousand fruit pickers and cannery workers in the district as potential suspects was the prospect of not having them. As the fruit season ended the wandering workforce went interstate chasing other seasonal jobs. To those police with an open mind on the murders, any one of the drifters could have been the killer. For a handful of detectives working under pressure, many of them seven days a week, the absence of strong leads was frustrating. The only alternative was to follow up hundreds of vague possibilities, and that could not be done as thoroughly as they would have liked.

In the first weeks after the bodies were found, a hundred detectives could have been kept busy systematically checking every male in the district, with anybody who refused to be fingerprinted being brought in for further questioning.

But that was a pipedream. In reality, the few homicide detectives who were available could not be posted at Shepparton for longer than two weeks at a time. Because they lived in Melbourne they had to be relieved regularly by fresh crews. This meant that the only policeman with an uninterrupted overview of the case from the beginning was Senior

Constable Parkinson, the recent arrival to the Shepparton uniformed section, whom Matthews had switched to the case because of his previous homicide experience.

The result of this arrangement was that one officer who was officially neither a member of the homicide squad nor of the Shepparton CIB took a big part in running the inquiry. Because of the implied criticism of local detectives, Parkinson's sudden elevation led to ill-feeling at the police station that affected the handling of the case.

The impossibility of interviewing all seasonal workers meant that the investigators had to hedge their bets. They appealed to the public in general, and to orchardists in particular, to report any suspicious behaviour by pickers, and followed up the hundreds of mostly fatuous tip-offs that flowed in. Meanwhile they concentrated on interviewing and re-interviewing the friends and acquaintances of the dead pair.

Still at the top of the hit list were Ian Urquhart and his friend Peter Hazelman. Then came their friends, workmates and acquaintances. Then Garry Heywood's friends, workmates and acquaintances. And so on, like widening ripples in a pond.

ABINA Madill and Garry Heywood were buried on Friday, March 4, six days after their bodies had been found, three weeks after their deaths. Theirs were the biggest funerals ever held in the town.

Abina's funeral service was held at Scots Church in Shepparton at 3pm that day. Garry's was at St Brendan's Catholic Church two hours earlier. Both churches were packed, with mourners spilling out the doors and waiting outside, many of them weeping. Shepparton came to a standstill as each procession crawled its way through the streets to the cemetery. Shops closed their doors and people lined the streets.

By that day Ian Urquhart had already been under siege from

police and public opinion. Stubbornly, he insisted on going to Abina's funeral. He asked his sister, Heather, to get him a dozen red roses and a plain card. On it, in the awkward, childish writing of someone more used to holding a spanner than a pen, he wrote: 'With All My Love, Ian'. When she saw him sign it, Heather thought: 'That card's going to be torn to shreds.' She knew too well that the police's widely broadcast suspicions of Ian had fed the poisonous talk about him. She was frightened that he would be hurt even more by going to the funeral, but how could she ask him not to? It would be betraying his feelings for Abina ... and somehow conceding defeat.

Heather decided that the best thing she could do was go with her brother. They stood at the back of the church, but it wasn't long before those around them started staring, taking their cue from the stony-faced plainclothes police mingling with the mourners. Then heads began to turn from the pews in front of them. Heather was nervous, and took Ian's hand, but he seemed to be lost in his private grief: impervious to the stares of the curious and the whispers of the malicious.

Outside the church he put his arm around her and said: 'You go home.' Then he went to the cemetery to pay his last respects to the girl that, according to gossip, he had killed.

HEATHER tried to get Ian to tell her about was happening each time he was summoned to the police station, to tell her why he was so morose. But he seemed almost ashamed to admit what was happening to him. It got so that he was scared to come home, and would borrow his father's old Volkswagen or a car from one of his friends and camp in it by the river so that he would be hard to find. In the end, Heather could not stand it. She made him promise to contact her if he was asked to submit to more questioning, so that she could accompany him to the station. And she arranged with Smiths' Motors, where he worked, that if the detectives picked him up from work one of his workmates would ring her immediately.

The first time Heather went with him to the station she was as nervous as he was. 'There were five policemen standing in a line, waiting for us,' she said later. 'One of them said sarcastically, "Hello, Ian Duncan Ross Urquhart, who's that?" Ian said: "My sister." And the policeman said: "How come your sister looks like that when you're so damn ugly?" '

After that day, she thought, 'Ian was treated with a bit more respect.' But there were things he didn't tell his sister.

ERNIE Maw was a friend of Ian Urquhart and Peter Hazelman. He knew from firsthand experience some of what they were going through. From the time detectives started questioning Urquhart and Hazelman, Ernie knew his turn was coming. He had, he was to remember, 'carted Urqy and Abina around a lot of times because Urqy didn't have a car.' Another reason for the police to be interested in Maw was that he was a keen shooter, and kept his guns in the boot of his car. The inevitable interview came early in March. Maw followed the same route after work each day, and one afternoon a well-known local detective was parked in the street, waiting for him to drive past. He pulled him over, and asked him to open the boot, where he went through the motions of 'finding' the firearms which he knew were there. He then ordered Ernie to leave his car and come to the station.

Waiting for him were three plainclothes men and a policewoman. One, well known to Maw, was sitting at a table with his leg cocked casually over the corner. He greeted the lad with a friendly smile and started questioning him pleasantly.

'Suddenly,' Maw said later, 'he kicked me fair in the shin as hard as he could. And he yelled: "All right, you little bastard, which one of you shot them and where did you put the gun?" '.

Maw was an orphan who had learned to look after himself early in life, and made of tougher stuff than most of the frightened teenagers the detective had been bullying. He and swung a punch, but was pinioned by the two detectives behind him.

The detective repeated his question. Maw 'turned straight and looked at the policewoman; she stared back at me hard as nails. I didn't answer. I looked at the wall. Then he slapped me in the face and said, "You look at me when I'm talking to you, you little bastard." ' The interview lasted between three and four hours. When it was finished Ernie was, he said later, bloodied but unbowed. 'One of them told me he'd drive me back to my car. I told them to stick it. I walked.'

Years later, as a respectable family man living in Shepparton, Maw had forgiven the detective who belted him that night. But he had not forgotten. And he knew how much worse it was for his mate, Ian Urquhart, and that still made him angry.

A BASIC tenet of detective work is not to reveal everything that is known about a crime, to keep something in reserve that only the guilty could know. That way, if the offender is questioned, he might trap himself by mentioning some detail which no innocent person could know. Another advantage of suppressing some details is that the offender might be lulled into a false sense of security, and so keep some piece of incriminating property or display some bravado or carelessness which attracts police attention. For all these reasons, the three clues the police had at the beginning of the Heywood-Madill case were kept secret.

The first was that the killer had used a Mossberg rifle, from which a piece had been broken and left at the scene. The second was that two fingerprints found on Garry Heywood's car had not been identified as belonging to anyone with legitimate access to the vehicle. The third was that Heywood's blue checked rug was missing from the car. Early in the case, the Mossberg seemed the most valuable clue. It was not until much later, as hundreds of people were fingerprinted for comparison without result, that the unidentified prints took on some importance, though even then not in the eyes of all police.

Regardless of doubts about their value, the prints remained a secret: a copybook example of correct detection procedure. A demonstration of this foresight was given when Heywood's girlfriend, Gail, was fingerprinted for elimination purposes. When she had finished dabbing her fingertips on the ink pad she was told casually that hers were the 'last set of unidentified prints' on the car. It was a neat bit of camouflage, the sort of touch that might eventually have helped to persuade a murderer he had nothing to fear from being fingerprinted in future.

One reporter trusted with the secret of the unidentified prints was Laurie Sweet, police roundsman for the *Shepparton News*, who had a close working relationship with Senior Constable Parkinson. The country newspaperman was to keep the secret for almost seventeen years, as were the Victoria Police. It was a New South Wales policeman who eventually leaked the story to a Sunday newspaper.

Sweet was also entrusted with knowledge of the Mossberg rifle and the missing rug. But neither of these clues was kept secret for long; the police decided to reveal them in an attempt to win useful information from the public.

Both were to prove a waste of time.

ON Wednesday, March 16, the State Government posted a $10,000 reward for information leading to the conviction of the killer or killers of Abina Madill and Garry Heywood. If Lesley heard news of the reward on the radio on the farm at Ardmona it didn't make more than a fleeting impression. She rarely went to Shepparton and was cut off from the fear and suspicion of the townspeople. Besides, she had problems of her own. Ray was getting harder to live with.

For once, Lesley wasn't the only one who was unhappy with him. The Gawnes, too, were worried. For the first year the young share farmer had been a fast worker who got everything done. But it was a lot of work for one man, even if his wife helped, and the tyranny of milking seven days a week seemed to be weighing on him. Even the best sharefarmers grew stale after two or three years of working one property. They needed a break and a move to a new place to become revitalised. The standard of Ray's work had suddenly fallen away to the point that he would milk the cows but hardly bother with anything else. The pigs were neglected, he was slack with the irrigating, and when Reg Gawne came over occasionally to check how the dairy was going, Ray no longer bothered to discuss things with him. He had always been quiet, but now he was moody, almost sullen.

The Gawnes didn't know it then, but Lesley noticed that since the bulk milk vat had been installed in the dairy, Ray had started putting water in the milk to cheat on the volume sold. To her it was another example of the deviousness nobody else seemed to see in him.

Not that Lesley knew everything Ray was doing. He didn't tell her when, one day that March, Reg Gawne sacked him – telling him he wouldn't be wanted once the season finished at the end of June. All Lesley knew was that Ray started scanning the share farming vacancies advertised in the *Weekly Times*. He picked out a job at a place called Mayrung, near Finley in New South Wales, and drove up for an interview. When he got back he was too anxious to wait for the Mayrung owners to contact him. He pestered Lesley to ring them to see if he had got the job. She did, and he had. Ray told Gawnes that he could start at a new farm on April 1 if they would let him go before June.

They obliged. When he had finished the arrangements to shift to Mayrung, Ray seemed more at ease than he had for weeks. Lesley knew they were going to a bigger place with more cows, and would make more money. But when she spoke to him about the new farm he said something which sounded a little out of place. Mayrung was a good place to go, he said, 'because it's at the back of nowhere … '

ON March 29, the police went public on the missing rug. They searched 97 caravans and questioned 300 seasonal workers camping at the Victoria Lake caravan park. The *Shepparton News*, published next day, reported the search and carried a detailed description of the rug and a police appeal for the public's help in finding it.

On April 7, eight weeks after the murders, a special circular was sent to all police stations, although not put on public display. It carried photographs and information about the still-secret Mossberg rifle as well as details of the missing rug.

The city papers had missed the caravan park search a week earlier, and treated the rug as an important 'secret lead' when fed the story about the it the day before the circular was issued. The following week Shepparton police put an identical rug and a photograph of Garry Heywood's car on display in the window of a big Shepparton store, Lunn & Fordyce. Several rugs were brought to the police, but none resembled Heywood's.

ON Sunday, April 17, a telephone call came through to the police station which sounded more promising than any lead to that date. It was from a man known as 'Coogan' Phillips, who owned a panelbeating shop in Mooroopna. He said a youth called Peter McGee, who had been working for him, had suddenly left a few nights before, taking with him $30 from the panel shop, where he had been sleeping in a back room. Phillips said that to find out where McGee had gone he visited McGee's sister, a Mrs Valerie Loffel, at the nearby township of Girgarre. While at Loffel's house, Phillips said, he saw a blue rug with khaki and grey stripes which matched the one on display in the shop window in Shepparton. As soon as he got home he had rung the police.

Within two hours Detective 'Joe' Ogden picked up the rug from Loffels' house. Mrs Loffel told the detective that her brother, McGee, had given her the rug in exchange for two blankets, and that he had told her that a mate of his had given him the rug in lieu of money owed to him. Ogden saw that the rug was identical to Garry Heywood's, except that it no longer had the maker's brand label on it. When the Heywood family confirmed that it was either Garry's rug or an exact replica of it, the detectives started to feel cautiously optimistic. Five days later they found McGee – in Pentridge Prison, on the losing end of a larceny charge. His story was that one night in late February his brother-in-law, Ian 'Snowy' Loffel, had produced the rug outside the Cricketers' Arms Hotel in Mooroopna after leaving the hotel with McGee.

The account was detailed and plausible. McGee said he had waited at Loffel's car at the front of the hotel while Loffel had gone to the hotel lavatory. When Loffel turned up several minutes later he was carrying the rug and a rear vision mirror, both of which McGee assumed he had just stolen. When they had gone home to Loffel's house, McGee said, he had lied to his sister, Mrs Loffel, saying that a friend had given him the rug instead of 'a couple of quid' owed to him. It all tallied with Mrs Loffel's story.

The detectives grew more confident. They had interviewed more than 1000 people, all for nothing. This smelt like the break.

80

IN some ways Ian Stanley Loffel was an ideal suspect. Leaving aside the question of motive, he was all the things that Ian Urquhart wasn't. In his late 30s, Loffel was a drifting labourer and truck driver well-known to police as a thief, pub brawler and heavy drinker with a propensity for violence that made his wife and other relatives fear him.

It seemed clear that if Loffel was not the killer, then whoever had given him the rug was. It meant that Loffel was going to have to come up with some quick answers if he wanted to avoid being charged.

In the event, he did.

Loffel, in the first of what became a series of interrogations over the following year, assured police that he had taken the rug from a dark blue Holden parked outside the Cricketers' Arms Hotel. Obligingly, he provided details. The car, he said, had a 'funny shaped' registration sticker which might have been South Australian. And it had a silver barred rack stuck to the dash which was to hold letters or a packet of cigarettes.

On its own Loffel's statement meant little. In view of his record, there was reason to mistrust anything he said. But there had been a development, which made his story fascinating.

Soon after Loffel was first interviewed police carried out routine inquiries at local garages, asking staff about any suspicious vehicles. On April 23 a mechanic called Des Reid said that about six weeks before he had fitted a set of fog lights to a 'dark blue' FE Holden driven by three young Italians who said they were heading for Mildura. He remembered that they seemed reluctant to leave the car, and that one of them stayed seated in it while he worked. The remarkably observant mechanic remembered two other things about the car. It had South Australian registration ... and he thought there was a silver letter rack stuck on the dash.

Dozens of other people had made similar reports of rough-looking young men, and none had meant anything. But in the light of what Loffel told the police it suddenly took on new importance. The coincidence was striking. The dashboard letter holder referred to by the mechanic Reid had not been mentioned in any press reports.

It seemed to the police that they were close to cracking it.

They were wrong. Five weeks later – after an intensive and much-publicised investigation – the Holden Des Reid had seen was traced to a car yard in Adelaide. But the three youths who had driven it to Shepparton to pick tomatoes had unshakable alibis, and the detectives were left with nothing but a file full of reports of blue Holdens seen all over Australia.

The search for a car matching varying descriptions given by Loffel was to drag on for months. None was ever found. Each time Loffel was interviewed he changed his story. Until, a year later, in a bizarre postscript to the affair, Loffel was to agree to be treated with a 'truth drug' by the police surgeon. This didn't produce any useful answers. Ultimately, after months of speculation that he would be charged with the murders, Loffel was convicted of petty larceny at Shepparton magistrates court. From the dock he parroted off an apology for the trouble he'd caused, and quietly faded from view.

No one was ever to know how Loffel really came by the rug. In fact, investigators raking over the evidence seventeen years later were not sure – despite tests supposedly indicating that it was Heywood's – that it was even the right rug.

WHILE the search for blue Holdens waxed and waned, the rifle inquiry was gathering momentum. Despite the ballistic expert's caution in identifying the weapon, the detectives handling the case decided that it was a million to one against the empty shells and black plastic plug coming from anything but the murder weapon. Therefore they were looking for the owner of a self-loading Mossberg. Police around Australia had been alerted to check any semi-automatic Mossberg rifles heard of in their districts. In the Shepparton area the search was more intense. A list of people who had bought Mossbergs from the local gun dealers was drawn up and the long process of tracing the owners and checking the weapons began.

EACH rifle was test-fired and the spent cases were sent to the forensic science section in Melbourne for comparison with the pair of shells found at the murder scene. Test-firing posed a problem when rifles were brought to the police station. Detectives solved it by putting a drum of water underneath a set of external stairs on the old courthouse and firing into it from above. The water absorbed the impact safely.

It wasn't until May 14, five weeks after the missing rug was made public, that the Mossberg search was thrown open to the media. The story released that day by the homicide chief, Frank Holland, implied that the make of the rifle had just been discovered, disguising the fact that police had been covertly investigating the Mossberg angle for more than two months.

When Holland was quoted as saying that 'an Australia-wide search for the gun began this week,' it was somewhat nearer the truth; the burst of publicity was to help police come close to their ambitious aim of test-firing every semi-automatic Mossberg in Australia.

The shells could have come from any one of four semi-automatic models: the 350 K, 351 K, 352 K, or 352 C. Each of these had the black plastic fitting which had been found broken off at the murder scene. By chance, the only model held in the forensic weapon collection happened to be a 352 K, and it was a photograph of this weapon which got into the newspapers and television. In *The Herald* the picture was run with the caption: 'A rifle of this type – a 352 K Mossberg American automatic – is believed to have been used to kill the Shepparton teenagers.'

The 352 K was unlike the other three models in that it had a fold-down plastic hand grip at the front of the stock, a gimmick which made the weapon stand out from the uniform looks of most .22 rifles, and one which would have appealed to a teenager choosing a 'pea rifle'.

The Mossberg inquiry grew into a separate file, meticulously kept by a promising young homicide detective called Reg Baker, later to become an assistant commissioner. Going public on the rifle seemed a shrewd move; it was becoming less likely every day that the police were going to discover the killer still in possession of the murder weapon. Better, it was thought, to appeal to the public sense of outrage at the murders, and encourage the possibility of people providing information secretly. That way, anyone who did not volunteer a Mossberg for testing would be likely to be pointed out to police by someone who knew they owned such a rifle. And even if the killer had got rid of the murder weapon, police hoped that an acquaintance would remember the rifle and tip them off.

In the event, there was great public cooperation, with information about Mossbergs coming from all over Australia. But apart from the records Baker kept of every rifle test-fired, the Mossberg inquiry was bedevilled by bad luck and sloppy detective work. One of the first steps was to ask the Mossberg manufacturers in the USA to supply details of semi-automatic rifles supplied to Australia. Eventually, the company did this, sending a list of 149 serial numbers. If this sounded like too few, no-one realised it until rifles with the wrong serial numbers started turning up for test-firing. After 150 rifles were test-fired it was clear that there had been a foul-up, but it wasn't to be until months later that the truth was discovered: in addition to the 149 weapons shipped directly to Australia by the Mossberg company, unknown numbers of the rifles had been imported by independent dealers, whose records were incomplete. The idea of tracing every Mossberg from import records was blown. Eventually, 353 Mossbergs were test-fired, more in hope than the expectation that something would turn up.

It never did. Firearms were not registered, and weapons were sold, swapped, won and lost in card games, taken to pay bad debts, borrowed and stolen. Of all weapons, the .22 calibre 'pea rifle' was as common as a pocket knife in the 1960s and as easy to buy new … with one important difference overlooked by the police.

Firearms sold by a registered dealer had to be entered in an official Gun Dealer's book, together with the name of the buyer. This was so that at any time the authorities could check who had bought particular weapons. Amazingly, this simplest of all checks was never done except at a few stores around Shepparton. One short telex request to police Victoria-wide would have revealed the name of the first owner of every new Mossberg sold in the State by dealers in the previous decade. From there, each original owner could have been traced and asked where the weapon was. If the rifle was available, it would have to be test-fired. If not, the owner would be asked for his fingerprints.

It was simple enough. But those in command didn't think of it. And the cowboy element among the detectives thought Ian Urquhart was guilty anyway, so their investigation methods lacked a key element. Commitment.

FROM the day the bodies were found the police had been swamped with information which threw up a bewildering variety of possibilities. Officially, this had been welcomed. On

March 9, Detective Sergeant Jack Ford told the newspapers: 'We don't expect all information to be exact and correct, but we are happy to receive a thousand wrong tips if at least one is a lead.'

But unofficially, given the handful of over-worked police available, it was clear there were more tips than they knew what to do with. The public outrage at the murders was a double-edged sword; it generated a mountain of material and put great pressure on the police to produce results. The combination made it difficult for detectives to work methodically through the rapidly swelling file. The inevitable result was that the most likely-sounding angles had been pursued vigorously, while others were skimmed over. From the start there had emerged from the mundane daily grind of inquiries a series of 'leads', which made good newspaper copy – and so fuelled public interest – but which were ultimately a hindrance. One of the first had been the 'black Holden' theory. A night-watchman who had driven down Wyndham Street just before 1am on the night of the murders was sure that he had seen Garry Heywood's car parked at the spot where it was later found by Senior Constable Frank Eyre. Near it, he said, was a similar early-model Holden, a black one.

The search for the mysterious black Holden was made public on March 7, when the *Shepparton News* ran a story describing it as a 'vital missing link.' Police were to discard the theory after being unable to substantiate it, but not before hundreds of man hours were spent tracing scores of examples of what was one of the most common vehicles in Australia. To further complicate matters, for months afterwards reports of black Holdens poured in from all over Australia, clogging the files with useless correspondence. It set the pattern for other abortive 'leads'. Next was the 'drag race' theory, which had it that the pair had been murdered after Garry Heywood had angered someone by out-racing them in his car. This possibility also made it into print, in the *Shepparton News* on March 9.

The black Holden and drag race theories had a common denominator: in accordance with what many Shepparton people wanted to believe, both implied foul play by outsiders. On March 11, as part of his campaign to keep the case alive, Laurie Sweet produced a story in the *News* which elevated the perennial animosity between locals and Queensland pickers into a 'jealousy war' bitter enough to cause the killings. This possibility was feasible enough that it clouded the case for years. There was a general assumption that if the murderer wasn't a local with a specific private grudge against either or both of the dead teenagers, then outsiders were to blame – which pointed an accusing finger at fruit pickers or one of the travelling carnival workers.

As the likelihood of extracting a confession from Ian Urquhart or other locals faded the police faced the needle-in-a-haystack proposition of tracing pickers and carnival workers who might conceivably have known something. This meant almost any of them. Not everybody was convinced that outsiders were responsible. One detective who later boasted to friends of the good times he had 'investigating' fruit pickers and carnival people interstate, still privately maintained that Urquhart was the killer, according to conversations he had with other police. The detective once told a local uniformed officer that he had 'belted and belted Urquhart, but he will not confess.' This upset the uniformed man, who believed Urquhart innocent. His recollection of the exchange was that he told the detective he was 'on the wrong track.'

It wasn't the first time the two had clashed over treatment of suspects. There had been a tense scene one day when the uniformed man stepped in to prevent the other, who outranked him, from threatening a youth with a truncheon. The uniformed man shielded the youth, who often behaved badly because of head injuries suffered in a car accident. He later recalled warning the detective: 'If you hit that kid in the wrong spot you'll kill him, and I don't want to have to give evidence about something I could have prevented.'

B Y the end of March, 49 days after the murders, 1000 people had been interviewed and scores of suspects eliminated. But the police were no closer to a solution than the day they had started. Without true bearings to steer by, the investigation yawed from one course to another, going nowhere. Nobody was saying so, but the process of elimination was not narrowing the field so much as widening it. If the killer, or killers, were not among the most obvious suspects, nor among the second rank of suspects, then who was he or they? The daunting thing for the police, leaving aside the preoccupation of some of their number with Urquhart, was the growing evidence that the murders were random and motiveless. In such circumstances all the detective work in the world was not worth as much as a little luck.

And this time the luck was all on the side of the killer. For among the 'thousand wrong tips' Ford had spoken of was the lead they so desperately needed.

But they missed it.

I T was one of the biggest murder investigations in Australia's history and it was being run from a backroom in a country police station. It was inevitable that in the first frenetic few months some things would go wrong; that exhaustion, frustration, and carelessness would cause mistakes to be made, loopholes to be left open. It was extraordinarily bad luck that the killer wandered through one of them.

It happened some time after April 1, 1966, probably in May

or June. The policeman concerned would be unlikely to recall the date afterwards, because at the time there was nothing to distinguish what happened from any of the countless routine inquiries that had been every Shepparton policeman's lot from the day the bodies were found. If that policeman later remembered what it was that caused him to visit Gawnes' farm at Ardmona, he never disclosed it, even to colleagues. But it was clear that among the hundreds of letters, telephone calls and furtive visitors that swamped the police station in early 1966, he intercepted one which was never recorded on the master file. It could have been a tip-off about a man known to own a Mossberg rifle, or a report of the registration number of a car seen acting suspiciously. Whatever the information was, it clearly identified Gawnes' recently departed sharefarmer: when the policeman went to the farm he asked for Ray by his full name.

Reg Gawne was working in the packing shed when the policeman arrived. After a brief conversation about the sharefarmer, Mr Gawne walked to his office in the house to look up his farm records. The policeman, a big man, followed closely and strode across the office to peer over Mr Gawne's shoulder as he leafed through a wages book, looking for the forwarding address he had written down. The farmer found the address and read it out: 'care of R. Clark, 'Sunny Plains', Mayrung, NSW.'

The policeman thanked him casually. 'We'll get the boys up there to pick him up,' he said. Then he left.

The Gawnes remembered that Ray had owned a Mossberg rifle, and assumed that the police wanted to test it. They didn't give the incident another thought for almost twenty years.

FIVE

Moving on, 1966-1968

IF a policeman came to Clark's property at Mayrung, Lesley didn't see him. Neither did Bob or Lorna Clark, whose wide-verandahed homestead stood across the yard from the cottage where Ray, Lesley and the three children were to spend the rest of 1966.

The probability is that no-one pursued the lead that took the policeman to Gawnes' farm. The reason for the omission can only be guessed at, but the answer lies in human error, laziness or jealousy. The most obvious explanation is that the Shepparton policeman simply forgot to relay his request to 'the boys up there,' meaning the New South Wales police at either Deniliquin or Finley. Because, presumably, he did not record his inquiries, once the incident slipped his mind there was no tell-tale note left on a file somewhere to alert those who were later to rake over the case for buried clues.

A second possibility. That the Shepparton man did contact New South Wales police but the latter, in a fit of petty interstate jealousy, ignored the request from south of the Murray. Such lack of co-operation was not unknown, although not openly acknowledged by either force, which officially kept up a polite fiction of fraternal loyalty and mutual helpfulness. Privately, however, Victorian detectives working on the Madill-Heywood case often voiced their uneasiness about leaving distant inquiries to interstate police.

A third possibility. The faint one that police did visit Clark's property and after a few questions went away satisfied that they had been through the motions of 'routine inquiries'. Although neither Lesley nor the Clarks saw any sign of police on the place, it was conceivable that Ray could have intercepted them before they reached the houses and sent them away content that they had drawn a blank.

Unlikely though the scenario was, circumstances made it possible. Bob Clark was often working on distant parts of the property. The cottage where Lesley spent most of the time between milkings was screened from the farm's entrance by a thick hedge. And the stockyards where Ray often worked with cattle during the day were closer to the road than the houses, which would usually allow him to be the first to see any visitors come.

Not that many did come. Ray had been keen to work at 'the back of nowhere', and he got his wish. It didn't make him any easier to live with. Although Lesley had been relieved to leave behind the 'creepy' old house at Ardmona, the isolation of the new place seemed to intensify the tensions on her disastrous marriage. Gradually the hold Ray had over her was weakening, although she didn't realise how much until about a month after their arrival.

How the fight started she could not later recall. It hardly mattered, anyway; such was the simmering violence of Ray's temper that each morning she would wonder what trifle might cause him to erupt in a volcano of abuse and blows. Whatever the argument was, it led to him raining punches on her in one of the bedrooms. For Lesley, it was all too brutally familiar. But this time, from some hidden crevice of her subconscious, she found the words to fight back. They came out like bile. 'You're sick, you bastard,' she screamed. 'Why don't you kill me and get it over with ... you probably killed those two kids in Shepparton.'

The accusation hung in the sudden silence. Lesley was shocked by her outburst, but no more than her husband. He stopped hitting her and, wordless, walked away. He never beat her again.

MONTHS passed. A few weeks before she turned 21, in the July of 1966, Lesley's subconscious yearning to escape from Ray was showing through the threadbare cloak of outward appearances. The Clarks were good people, and their apparent contentment contrasted sharply with Lesley's own miserable existence. Lonely, starved of affection, dispirited by the daily drudgery of farm and housework, she was likely to become infatuated with anybody who was kind to her.

As luck had it, that person happened to be Bob Clark. The farmer was pleasant to Lesley, and she was smitten by his casual compliments. Naive, for all her three children and errant husband, she imagined herself in love with a man almost old enough to be her father.

A harmless enough daydream, it might have evaporated without trace if it hadn't been for an argument she had with Ray late one night. For the first time in her life she had resisted his advances. Seeking to wound him the way he had so often hurt her, she drew on her fantasies. There was another man, she blurted, and she wanted to run away with him.

For one so blatantly unfaithful himself, and considering his past violent reactions to any opposition from Lesley, Ray seemed strangely disturbed. Gone was the foul-tempered basher, replaced by a stricken husband and father whose fear of being left had a desperate edge. It was midnight, but Ray got out of bed and left the house. He returned two hours later, still visibly upset. He told Lesley that he had rung his parents. They were driving straight from Chiltern. On the way they would pick up her parents at Yarrawonga.

The two sets of parents arrived just before dawn, faces drawn with strain and lack of sleep after the overnight drive across country. There followed a bizarre scene in the early morning light. Standing outside the homestead the six started a heated argument which drew the Clarks outside. Of the bitter accusations and counter-accusations hurled that morning Lesley was later to recall only Ray's father shouting at her that no matter what happened, she could not leave Ray because of the children. In light of the man's treatment of his own wife, it was a revealing glimpse of the character which had moulded Ray's attitudes as a child. It seemed to Lesley that regardless of how a man wronged his wife, she was expected to obey.

By the time the shouting died down that morning at Mayrung she had discovered that her passing infatuation was wishful thinking, not a passport to another life.

Meanwhile, she had to make the best of living with a man who both frightened and fascinated her. Ray was taking more notice of her because of her new-found streak of independence, because of the possibility that another man might take her. As had happened before, they papered over the widening rift between them. They left Clarks to milk the cows for a week, divided the children between their respective in-laws and went for a holiday in Melbourne.

They were driving the new station wagon Ray had bought about the time they moved to Mayrung. For some reason unclear to Lesley he had decided to trade in the red Falcon sedan bought in Shepparton only eighteen months before. Lesley was pleased. There was more room for children in the wagon, which made its purchase a thoughtful gesture on Ray's part. Unusually thoughtful, for him.

Ray had already lost Lesley, although it was to take more than a year for them both to face that fact. Back at Mayrung after their holiday, they called a truce. They rarely referred to the earlier incident, but each sensed that the pendulum of power in their marriage had swung Lesley's way. One day, discussing the situation with Mrs Clark, Lesley was surprised to find herself sticking up for Ray. Mainly out of pity, she later realised, but she had to admit to some tattered remnants of her teenage love for him as well.

The young brute who had been so careless of his family responsibilities started to affect great concern for his children. Lesley knew that he was using them as bargaining chips to keep her, and it troubled her. She was being manoeuvred into a position where she would have to choose between the children and freedom from a man who, if she was honest with herself, she knew was certainly unbalanced and probably dangerous. She was becoming convinced that Ray would go to any lengths to find her if she left with the children; that her only chance of getting away from him was to go alone.

The unspoken thought of having to make that choice agonised her.

In the event, it was Ray who made the first move.

It happened just before Christmas, 1966, starting as just another of their many arguments. It ended with Ray forcing the children into the car and driving off. Lesley, obliging even in a crisis, milked the cows before packing her belongings into their second car, a utility Ray had bought to use around the farm. She told Clarks what had happened, apologised for the inconvenience, and then headed for her parents' place at Yarrawonga.

Lesley guessed that Ray would go to his parents at Chiltern. Knowing his mother would take good care of the children, she made up her mind not to give in and took a Christmas holiday job at Cypress Gardens, a local caravan park.

The emotional scars of the previous six years had left Lesley tough enough to keep away from Ray. But when he came looking for her, as she suspected he would, she gave in. He told her he had a job in a meatworks at Wodonga, and that he would look for another share farm. Lesley was missing her children, and she knew she could not stay with her parents forever.

They were re-united at his parents' new cream brick house in Chiltern, the house the ageing couple had built to mark the end of years of buying and selling farms and small businesses. Twenty years later, with Ray's mother long dead, the house was to look ugly and unloved. But in the new year of 1967 it was the pride of that woman's sad and barren life.

Ray was still working at the meatworks as a slaughterman. Raised on farms, he had always been handy at butchering animals.

Lesley remembered how he had stolen and killed one of Gawnes' pigs two years earlier, and a yearling heifer on another property. The meatworks job required him to buy his own killing knife. He left the job after a few weeks, but he kept the knife.

They moved to Kevin and Dana Goode's farm at Tallandoon, in the heart of north-east Victoria's mountain country, at the end of January, 1967. It was the start of their last year together. The week after they moved in, the daily newspapers carried stories marking the first anniversary of the Shepparton murders. The police had questioned more than 2000 people, but there were no leads.

GOODES' farm straddled a creek meandering through a hidden valley in the hills. It was beautiful. The type of farm, Lesley thought wistfully when she first saw it, that you couldn't buy, only inherit. The tranquil setting did nothing to heal the open wound of her marriage. Ray, always brutal and demanding in matters of sex, had begun openly to exhibit tendencies that disgusted and frightened her. His increasingly aberrant behaviour was not confined to the bedroom. The ugly moods and unpredictable violence had become so common that Lesley found herself often referring to his 'split personality'. Her family agreed with that description. After six years of giving Lesley and the children refuge every few months, Ray's behaviour often upset but rarely surprised them.

Not that the family knew everything he did. Lesley, habitually apologetic and often ashamed, hid some things from them. And from herself, as if blocking his worst excesses from her mind would mean they hadn't happened.

It was a nightmarish existence. One day she called her parents from the farm at Tallandoon to beg them to come and get her. But when they arrived she was waiting in front of the house, and assured them effusively that everything was all right. It had all been a mistake, she said. She didn't want to go back to Yarrawonga with them after all. Lesley's parents drove home, puzzled by the girl's behaviour.

They didn't know that Ray had been inside the house nursing a shotgun, and had threatened to use it if Lesley left. The incident numbed Lesley's memory. Years later she was to recall the affair only hazily after being reminded of it by friends she had confided in soon after it happened.

Reaching for the gun was a symptom of Ray's increasingly disturbing ways. One of the many times Lesley left the two oldest children with her parents in Yarrawonga, Ray turned up to claim them. The children were frightened, and when

Lesley's mother refused to let him in he abused her. She rang her husband, who was playing bowls in a nearby town. He drove home to find Ray stalking the garden, in a black rage. When the older man tried to remonstrate with him Ray grabbed the shotgun from his car and menaced him. Lesley's father, too embarrassed to call the local police in a family matter, and frightened of what Ray might do, reluctantly agreed to let the children leave. As Susan and little Raymond climbed tearfully into the station wagon, their grandfather watched sadly, then drove slowly back to the bowling club. It was almost the last time he saw them.

L ESLEY'S escape, so long contemplated, happened quickly. On the night of New Year's Eve, the final hours of 1967, she ran away. Whether this apparently symbolic timing was accidental, or whether the calendar had inspired some dramatic impulse, Lesley could not later recall. What she was never to forget, however, was the overpowering sensation of guilt she felt that night.

It was two-fold. She felt guilty about making the long-dreaded decision to leave her children with Ray in the hope he would not follow her. And she was guilty of persuading another woman's husband to take her away. His name was Bernie. He also worked on the farm, and lived in one of the two other houses on the property with his wife and several small children about the age of Lesley's own.

But Lesley was desperate for a way out, and a man, any man, could provide it. The straying husband from next door would do as well as any other. She talked him into waiting for her in his car.

When she was sure Ray and the children were asleep she crept out of the house and walked quickly down the rough track to where her unlikely Galahad was waiting.

S HIRLEY Hughes hadn't seen Lesley for longer than either of them cared to remember. They had been best friends as teenagers, but Ray's tyrannical jealousy of anybody Lesley knew had forced them apart. When Shirley had married almost two years earlier, Ray had stopped Lesley from going to the wedding at the last moment. Lesley had telephoned to make a lame excuse about having to milk, but Shirley knew that it was Ray's way of humiliating her, a juvenile display of power. Once he had got 'the noose around her neck,' Shirley was to recall, 'he wouldn't let her out of sight'. The incident disappointed Shirley deeply because Lesley was the only close friend she had invited. They had written to each other regularly since the wedding, but Lesley had never confided anything which prepared Shirley for the strange visit she got early in the new year of 1968.

Shirley and her husband, Keith Hughes, were living in Hannah Street, Benalla. She was still clearing the breakfast dishes, when there was a knock at the door. On the step was Lesley, pale and tired. With her was a man she introduced to Shirley only as 'Bernie'. He didn't say much. Lesley did most of the talking, but her feigned cheerfulness was at odds with the hunted look in her eyes. Shirley sensed that her friend was almost as frightened of the unknown problems ahead as of the misery she was running from.

Shirley made coffee and listened sympathetically to Lesley's desperate chatter. She knew Lesley was worried about what she would think of her for leaving the children behind, but it wasn't until the man left them alone together to drive off on an errand that Lesley unburdened herself. She poured out the stories of how Ray had bashed her, and hinted at the bent side of his personality. 'I just couldn't stand it any longer,' she finished. Her lips quivered and she blinked back tears.

Shirley had never liked the flash youth who had married her

best friend. What Lesley told her that morning set her against him forever. But when he turned up looking for Lesley a few days later she couldn't help being a little intimidated. She admitted Lesley had been there, but said she didn't know where she had gone. This was true, as Lesley and her companion were camping in his car.

Ray looked at her with thinly veiled contempt, then turned on his heel and walked back to his car. 'I was just glad that he believed me and went,' Shirley said later.

T HE next fortnight was a bizarre chapter in Lesley's life. For the first few days the runaways stayed together in the car. Then Bernie, who had left home with only a few dollars, started work on a Country Roads Board gang. This meant Lesley was left to spend each day in the car alone. A forlorn brand of freedom for a woman with nowhere else to go.

At night they drove around, seeking camping spots. One fragment was to snag in Lesley's blurred memories of those two weeks. That was the evening they drove to Shepparton, cruised down the main street past Lake Victoria then turned across the river to find a quiet spot among the gums on the opposite bank. They were talking and smoking when a police car pulled up beside them. The policeman's message was courteous, but chilling. There had been a couple abducted and murdered while parking in just such a quiet spot two years before, he said. Perhaps it would be wiser to move on.

R AY could be charming. When he went to Lesley's parents' house in Yarrawonga there was not a trace of the evil-tempered bully who had pulled a shotgun at his previous visit. He told a 'sob story', as Lesley's mother described it, about how he was missing Lesley and how the children were fretting for her. When they heard the news the family was anxious about Lesley. She had left Ray before, but every time she had come home to them. This time there was no sign of her. After Ray left Lesley's mother said to her husband: 'We'd better start dragging the dams ... he's probably shot her and dumped her somewhere.' It was a strange joke to make about her own family. No-one laughed.

As the days passed without a sign of Lesley her parents grew distressed, as she found out when she came across a friend of her brother's in the street in Benalla one day. The friend told her that her parents were 'worried sick', and when he returned to Yarrawonga that evening he went around to see them. As luck would have it, Ray was there again, hoping to find out where to look for his suddenly valued wife. As soon as the friend told his story Ray headed for Benalla to track her down.

He succeeded. Lesley was sitting alone in the car beside the lake in Benalla when she heard the sound of a familiar motor. She looked around and saw the green station wagon pull up behind her. She was numb with fright. Bernie was working at Katamatite several kilometres away. He might as well have been in Kalgoorlie.

Ray looked angry, but he didn't hit her. 'What the hell are you doing here?' he grated.

'I dunno, Ray,' she said wearily. 'I dunno.'

LESLEY should have known better than to believe Ray, but he had unerringly picked her most vulnerable spot, her fears for the children. When he found her in the car by the lake he had told her that Susan was fretting, and cajoled her into making a compromise: to go with him to her parents' and see the kids.

So she went. When she got there she found that Susan was 'as happy as Larry'. Her relief at this defused her anger at being deceived, even though she realised then that Ray had set her up. She had counted on Ray not following her if she ran away with another man. The fact that he had found her and wanted her back did not destroy her resolve to be rid of him, but it weakened it. Reluctantly, she agreed to go with him to Queensland to visit her brother and sister in Townsville.

They set off a week before the Australia Day weekend in January 1968, on a trip which Ray seemed to think would re-unite them, an aim which Lesley knew was hopeless.

Behind were the children: two with Ray's parents at Chiltern, the youngest with Lesley's parents in Yarrawonga. Ahead was the final act in the sordid drama of their marriage.

The first scene was in the car. Ray had always driven fast; this time he seemed to have a death wish. Lesley was fright-ened, but powerless. For a few more days she would be tangled in the web of the man who had already wrecked what should have been the best years of her life. But she stuck to the promise she had made herself – that she and Ray were finished as man and wife. The car became a pressure cooker of emotion; in it Ray's split personality was bared. He would rage one minute, then plead the next, for Lesley to have sex with him. She refused, steeling herself against his mounting desperation.

The situation reached flashpoint when they stopped at Newcastle. In a rage, Ray threatened to drive away and abandon Lesley. Finally, her frayed nerves snapped. She screamed that she was going to kill herself, and tore the lid off a bottle of tranquillisers she had in her bag. Ray's reaction was bizarre. Instead of trying to stop her he shouted that he would kill himself too. After watching Lesley swallow a handful of tablets he snatched the jar and shoved the rest down his throat. And there, given a deadlier prescription, their bodies would have been found together. But the pills were not lethal, and neither died – although Lesley thought she was going to during the next few hours, in between spasms of vomiting.

They were on the road again that night, heading to the tropics and an uncertain future. As Lesley mustered her disjointed thoughts, she wondered at Ray's sudden willingness to attempt suicide with her. She flattered herself – and Ray – that it was a last desperate attempt to show he cared for her. Years later, she realised that he had deeper reasons.

Despite the attempt to kill herself, Lesley didn't like it when she saw a shotgun stowed in the back of the station wagon. The weapon had been in the same house with her for years, and she had never liked it. But this time she was touched by a fear far beyond her distaste for firearms.

'Get rid of it,' she said, catching Ray in one of his pleading moods. At the next town, somewhere in New South Wales, he stopped and hocked the gun for a few dollars. Lesley relaxed a little. She didn't think to wonder where Ray's other weapon was, the rifle he used for spotlighting before they'd moved to Gawnes' farm.

D ESPITE the strained atmosphere between herself and Ray, Lesley enjoyed Townsville. Her sister, Dot, and brother, Mick, and his wife Jan were on a working holiday, and Lesley was determined not to let Ray spoil the first real break she'd had after seven years of marriage and three children. As usual, where Ray was concerned, it couldn't last. A week after Ray and Lesley arrived, the group took the ferry to Magnetic Island for the Australia Day weekend. They rented a holiday cabin overlooking the sea. On the first night the others were outside when Lesley decided to go to bed. For the first time since the car trip the week before, Ray tried to force her to have sex. This time he succeeded. Lesley didn't cry for help, but as she struggled she kicked the wall next to her bed, making a noise which alarmed her brother. He rushed in to find Lesley sobbing with anger and trying to cover herself. Ray looked embarrassed and pulled the sheet over them both. Mick was slow to anger, but he had never liked his brother-in-law, an attitude which had hardened with years of hearing how he maltreated his sister. He glowered at Ray, and ordered him to leave Lesley alone.

Ray was sullen, but not defiant. 'It'll be right,' he said. 'She's my wife.'

It wasn't the first time that Ray had raped her, but Lesley made sure it was the last. She stayed away from him for the rest of the weekend. When they returned to Townsville, she moved in with her sister Dot at the home for underprivileged children where she worked. Ray stayed on at Mick and Jan's. She saw little of him for two weeks, until the evening he came to say he was returning to Victoria the next day, if she wanted to go.

Lesley was anxious to get back to see her children, so she accepted. Any qualms she had about being alone with Ray again disappeared when Dot decided to throw in her job and go home with them.

It was a fast trip and, apart from some floods, an uneventful one. But in the long hours staring at the bitumen Lesley couldn't help reflecting on her time with Ray, how it was finally over. There was something strange about the man at the wheel, something she'd always sensed but had never been able to identify. It was as if, she mused, his parents had spoiled him in an attempt to make up for something that other kids took for granted. But no matter what they had bought for him, there had always been something missing … affection, empathy, a sense of belonging.

And now he had grown up it was missing from his personality. Perhaps Ray sensed it himself.

Lesley's thoughts kept turning back to the day, a few months before, when he had begged her not to leave him. He had seemed as desperate as a wounded animal. Suddenly he had blurted: 'You know I'm adopted, don't you.'

SIX

The cuckoo, 1944-1960

THE baby was born at the Queen Victoria hospital, Melbourne, on March 12, 1944. There were no birth notices in the slim wartime newspapers, no cards or flowers from relatives and friends. The girl in the delivery room was not married, and her child was to be adopted.

On the original birth certificate the space for the baby's natural father was filled with a middle-European name, a rarity in the days before post-war immigration. It was, perhaps, an extra reason – during a war against Germany and Italy – for the shame and secrecy of the birth. There were 'enemy aliens', prisoners-of-war and internees, working on farms in the country in the 1940s. The stigma of a foreign-born father could only add to the stigma of illegitimacy.

A few days after the birth, according to the story told later by the woman who adopted the baby, the girl 'collapsed' in the hospital lavatories. Her listeners took this to be a physical collapse, giving rise to the notion that the distressed young woman had died soon after. In reality, it was more likely a mental breakdown, brought on by the horror of the impending separation from the child. The final act in the tragedy of the unmarried mother was played out in an Anglican baby home a few weeks later. The parting was inevitable, but no less painful for that. The baby home was a place of hushed voices and strained silences, and when the girl screamed with anguish the childless woman waiting nervously in a nearby room could hear every syllable, every sob, every gasp of breath echoing through the polished corridors.

The waiting woman's name was Mavis. She was kind-hearted, and the scarifying reality of adoption blunted her elation at getting a baby boy after seven barren years of marriage. The fact that her maternal yearnings were being satisfied at the expense of another's was reinforced, she told her mother and step-sister a few hours later, when she shared a waiting room with the baby's grandmother. While the staff carried out their bleak task with the impersonal efficiency of executioners, the grandmother confided to Mavis that she was sick at heart because she had refused the girl's pleas to keep the child. Torn between her own maternal instincts and the need to keep up appearances, she told Mavis she was blaming herself for the catastrophe. At the time she had thought the girl was too young to know what was best, but she couldn't help wondering if anything was better than the cold-blooded solution of the baby home.

There was a reason for the weary country woman to pour out her feelings to the stranger who was taking her grandchild away forever. She had no-one else. She told Mavis that not even her husband knew the real reason for the girl's long stay in Melbourne, away from the sharp eyes and tongues of her home district. It was a crushing load to bear by herself.

Mavis later often told relatives and friends that there was an extra dimension to the tragedy. The girl's sweetheart, she said, had been killed in action in New Guinea while the girl was pregnant, and so for months she had carried the child of a dead man. Whether this was true, or a convenient fiction to explain a vanished father, didn't matter. Either way, the baby was rejected from the moment of conception. It would have been better if his mother had miscarried.

M EMORIES fade and warp. Mavis's step-sister Joyce, sixteen in 1944, was to recall much later that Mavis brought the newly-adopted baby to their mother's shop in Richmond to stay before going home to the farm at Mudgegonga, near Myrtleford in north-east Victoria.

Much of what happened then and later became hazy, but some inconsequential details were etched in her memory, such as Mavis's defensive reaction when Joyce went to kiss the baby … Joyce had a cold, and the anxious new 'mother' did not want her baby to catch it.

The rebuff was enough to set the touchy teenager flouncing into her bedroom mouthing sarcasms about her big sister's precious kid.

The pique didn't last long, and Joyce grew fond of the boy. She had always been close to her step-sister, although her memories of being sent to live with Mavis and her husband Harold for most of the war years were not pleasant.

There was a touch of the bully about Harold, she was to say, which taken alone might have been bearable. But there were other things about the man that she didn't like. Things which caused her to rebel, to run away and, eventually, to return to Melbourne to live with her widowed step-mother. None of which would have surprised Mavis's father, although it would have made him angry had he lived to see it. His name was William McDonald, 'Son' to those who knew him. He had been a peppery little man who had taken a strong dislike to Harold from the time his eldest daughter took up with him.

The McDonalds had moved to Beechworth from Melbourne in the early 1930s when Mr McDonald had taken a job as a male nurse at the mental hospital in the old north-eastern gold town. Mavis had been in her late teens. She was, by the accounts of those who knew her then, a pleasant and demure young woman. 'A methodic, good girl who did her own sewing,' was the impression left with one contemporary. She was small, dark, pretty in an unspectacular way. And, being nineteen, she was impressionable, which explained why she fell for Harold.

He had been much older than Mavis, past 30 when she first met him, and well-known for his conquests around the country dances, pubs and tennis clubs. He had caught her eye while still in his prime: high, wide, and handsome, not yet bloated by a taste for beer. With his dark, curly hair and powerful square-built body he had cut a dash on the dance floor – and carved a reputation off it, according to those who knew him then. Harold had also been a strong tennis player, something of a local champion in the competition in the farming districts around Beechworth between the world wars. Mavis had also played tennis; it was this, recalls one of her friends, which sparked her interest in Harold.

As a new girl in town, Mavis had been at first unaware of Harold's reputation. Later, presumably, she chose to ignore the warning signals put out by those who knew him of old. For all his success with women, Harold had never been 'one of the crowd at all', remembered one woman who had watched the infatuated Mavis snub other, younger, men in his favour.

'He was good-looking, but I wouldn't have taken him home,' was her judgment half a century later. 'We all thought Mavis was a fool.'

As soon as Mr McDonald had discovered why his daughter was showing so much interest in tennis he ordered her to stop seeing the dashing farmer from Leneva West, the district near Yackandandah where Harold's forebears had been among the earliest settlers. He bristled whenever he heard Harold's name, and called him a 'skirt chaser'.

The family had moved back to Melbourne about 1935, but distance did not discourage Mavis. There was a touch of her father's obstinacy about the girl; she had set her heart on Harold, and the more obstacles that were put in her way the more determined. she was to have him.

She was working as a tailoress in Swanston Street in the city. One night she had come home to Preston wearing an engagement ring. If she expected to win over her father she was mistaken. As soon as he saw the ring he ordered her out of the house. It was the last time Mavis was under the same roof as her parents. She went to stay with relatives in Brunswick. And as soon as she had turned twenty-one, in March 1937, she went to Albury to marry Harold. Her mother took the train up to attend the wedding, but her father would have nothing to do with it. Mavis was hardly to see him again. William McDonald, man of principle to the end, died ten months later 'still hating Harold', according to one relative.

He was a good judge.

THE next seven years were to prove barren in more ways than one. Mavis stayed loyal to Harold, but others noticed the lonely life she led. She had no friends to confide in at Mudgegonga, the isolated district north-east of Myrtleford where Harold bought a farm soon after the wedding. The nearest neighbours were almost a kilometre away, and even had they found the time to get to know Mavis, Harold did not encourage friendships.

A charitable explanation might have been that his attitude was a legacy of growing up in a family of German background during the anti-'Hun' hysteria of the first world war. Whatever the reason for his behaviour, it didn't endear him to his neighbours.

'Harold,' one elderly farmer recalled almost 50 years later, 'was one of the few people around Mudgegonga that I took a set against.' Several neighbours were concerned about Joyce's welfare. One woman who had known Mavis in Beechworth lived on a nearby farm. At best, she was to say, 'there was something better a girl that age could have been doing than working on that farm for nothing ... I don't know why her mother left her there. She'd often clear off and you couldn't blame her.'

Away from home, Harold was a gregarious man, often seen in hotels anywhere between Mudgegonga and Albury. The district knew that when Mavis went to Melbourne to visit her mother, Harold would leave the farm for days. Mavis must have suspected what was happening – even in the first year of her marriage. But even in the rare chances she got, pride prevented Mavis from complaining about her lot. She made the best of it.

HAROLD was a shrewd man who prided himself on his eye for a deal, a trait that was to lead to many moves for the couple as he bought and sold farms and businesses over the following 25 years. He also dealt in livestock, and usually played the markets successfully.

Mavis bore the brunt of this. When Harold was away she would have to milk cows and feed the other stock as well as do the housework. When Joyce arrived from Melbourne soon after the war started, Mavis at least had some company. But, as time went on and Joyce grew from a child to a pubescent teenager, the presence of the young step-sister (in fact adopted and Mavis's first cousin by birth, though the girls didn't know this as children) made things even harder for the young wife. Although not, it should be noted, in the way of work. Joyce often said that she more than paid her board with unpaid labour.

Almost thirteen years younger than Mavis, Joyce was twelve when she came to Mudgegonga, almost sixteen when she returned to her mother in Preston. There were scurrilous rumours about the reason for her leaving the farm, still remembered more than 50 years later. But there was no sordid secret behind Joyce's return to Melbourne, she averred later. She was not pregnant, she said. She was rebellious and independent. Although they got on well, Mavis did not share her step-sister's mental toughness. As the flaws in her marriage became obvious she chose mostly to ignore them. There was little alternative for a poor but respectable woman in the early 1940s. But this passivity grated on Joyce, who was as game as a bantam, and never hesitated to call Harold's bluff.

A favourite ploy, when Harold was getting ready to go out – ostensibly to visit other farmers or stock sales on business – was secretly to read the mileage on his car's odometer. When he returned, often well after milking time at night, a quick reading of the mileage would reveal how far afield he had been. Occasionally Mavis struck out. One day, Joyce was to remember, Mavis lost her temper when she found Harold in the dairy with one of the Land Army girls who worked in the district during the war. She hit him with a jug she was carrying. But mostly she endured her troubles quietly, the victim of a lopsided relationship uncannily similar to the first marriage of the son she was to adopt.

By the time Harold entered his 40th year it was clear that he and Mavis had little chance of having a child. They decided to adopt. How they came to choose the baby from the Mission of

St James and St John is uncertain. There was supposed to be some family link with the child, but knowledge of it was buried with a generation already heading for middle age in 1944.

Mavis was the first to tell the tragic story claiming that the child's natural father had been killed at war. There was as much doubt about what happened to the child's mother, while some were led to believe she had collapsed in hospital 'and died of a broken heart' following her double loss, others thought she went to a mental institution following a nervous breakdown. As likely as either explanation was that she faded quietly back into country life with her secret.

The only certainty is that a male baby was born to a young woman in harrowing circumstances. A fair-skinned child with the promise of sandy or auburn hair. There is disagreement over how he was named. One relative thinks the baby had been called Anthony in hospital, and that Mavis had later changed the name to suit herself. But Mavis told others that the little boy had been named after his 'dead' father, and that out of respect she had changed only the surname. If she did, it was a thoughtful gesture, but a wasted one.

By whichever route, the baby was called Raymond. He was born on a Sunday. 'The child that is born on the Sabbath day, is bonny and blithe and good and gay.'

IF Harold had entertained any doubts about adopting the son that chance had thrust at him, they vanished by the time Mavis was ready to bring the baby home. For a man of his age and hard-bitten ways, he was visibly excited on the morning he was to meet the train. He milked his cows earlier than usual, rang one of his nieces from the Mudgegonga post office, then drove to Myrtleford to pick her up on his way to Wangaratta. Harold was at his charming best, and he wanted company and some help in choosing a new pram as a surprise for Mavis. The homecoming of a son – adopted or not – was a source of pride and pleasure. After picking out and paying for a pram, Harold told the shopkeeper he would be back to fetch it after he had met the train.

He waited impatiently at the station.

When the train pulled in he stood beaming as Mavis stepped onto the platform, cradling the baby self-consciously in her arms. She looked pleased. It was, in its way, one of the happiest days of their married lives.

Harold drove carefully back to the shop where he had bought the pram and fetched it out for Mavis's approval. It was one of the best that money could buy, the first of the indulgences that he was to shower on the boy for almost twenty years.

It was as if Harold was anxious to make up for the circumstances of the child's birth, to erase the stigma of illegitimacy and massage his own vanity by spending money. It was a mistake, and succeeded only in creating a gap between the boy and other children where there needn't have been one.

LITTLE Raymond showed early signs of selfishness. The circumstances made it inevitable. Like the baby cuckoo, hatched and raised in another bird's nest from which the smaller hatchlings have been heaved, he was alone. In his case, alone in the glare of attention from a middle-aged, egocentric man and a nervous, doting woman with failing health and years of turning a blind eye to things that would outrage many wives. It was not a good combination for any child, let alone one whose subconscious was sown from birth with the subtle emotional stresses of adoption.

Ray didn't stand out as an evil child. He didn't stand out at all, except in the way of being an indulged and lonely boy, neither of which was his fault. As a toddler and at primary school he was in all ways ordinary, although separated by the abundance of his toys and, later, pocket money, compared with the children of other battling country people. Harold, though notoriously tough in business dealings, had a Lear-like fondness for indulging himself by indulging the child.

Much later, when those who had known the boy dredged their memories for early signs of what was to come, there was little to find. He would throw tantrums, said one relative, 'until one day when his mother wasn't around I smacked him.' Another, just as impatient of spoiled behaviour, recalled that 'he was a bugger to bite until I bit him back.' Neither criticised Mavis and Harold outright, but both left open the inference that they were guilty of not disciplining Ray. A worse lapse, in its way, than their constant gratification of his appetite for sweets and playthings.

One relative, Harold's sister-in-law Ruby, once told Mavis that the child would come 'to a bad end.' It probably wasn't the startling prophecy it seemed in light of subsequent events. Aunty Ruby, explains a relative, took a set against Ray when he was small because once, when Harold and Mavis were visiting, he kicked a hole in the flywire of her screen door. The stern aunt didn't approve of children who did things like that. And the fact that her in-law's child was adopted might have whetted her disapproval with the righteousness of the fertile woman.

It wasn't so much what adults said to the child as what they didn't say that was calculated to affect a malleable young mind. Ray didn't know he was adopted – Mavis wanted to tell him, but Harold refused – and so the boy was to spend his pre-pubescent years sensing that he was somehow different, but not knowing why. Until, inevitably, in his teens he was confronted with the truth of his origins, a shock all the more devastating because of the realisation that everyone else had known all along.

But that came much later.

R AY was three when Harold and Mavis made the first of what became a series of moves. This was to a little property on the northern outskirts of Wangaratta. After turning the place over for a quick profit, they took over the Springhurst general store, then moved to a house in Beechworth where they stayed two years before Harold bought a bakery business at Mansfield.

About the time of the move to Mansfield in 1950, Mavis's mother fell ill and Mavis, with the boy, spent months in Melbourne caring for her. Already Ray was showing signs of being a loner, a legacy of his solitary upbringing. One of Mavis's cousins recalls seeing the fair-haired little boy from the bush during his first week in Melbourne. She asked Mavis if she was worried about him starting at a tough city school in Preston. 'Don't worry,' Mavis had replied, 'he can look after himself.' By the time Mavis's mother had been nursed back to health, Harold had sold the bakery and bought 300 acres near Chiltern, where Ray was enrolled in first grade in 1951 ...

Six years later, after selling the farm, Ray and his parents were to move briefly into a weatherboard house in the town. The previous occupants were called Chuck, and their boy was also called Raymond. The tiny coincidence of the boys' names foreshadowed a much bigger one.

R AY Chuck, although younger than the other Ray, had already earned a reputation as the wildest schoolboy in the district. He defied authority, and was fearless to the point of recklessness. One neighbour recalled the day he chased another boy to his home and when the frightened lad locked himself in a shed, Ray Chuck grabbed the axe from the woodheap and chopped the door down.

It was an example of the brazen attitude which led young Chuck, under the surname Bennett, to become one of

Australia's most notorious armed hold-up men. As a young tearaway he and another Australian criminal were to go on a spree of jewel robberies in England in the 1960s. They were arrested, but Chuck, alias Bennett, had the nerve to pull off a stunt which would sound contrived in a film script. He 'persuaded' a petty offender being held in the same court cells to exchange identities with him, spent a few minutes in the dock and then was turned loose on the street. By the time the British police realised the Australian had worked a switch, he had vanished.

The escape was the first step in a remarkable underworld odyssey that saw Ray Chuck weave his way back to Australia undetected. But he was to top that feat with another, according to police and underworld sources, when he masterminded the multi-million dollar heist of the Victoria Club in Melbourne in April, 1976. It was dubbed 'The Great Bookie Robbery,' and the word was that Chuck/Bennett had planned it while in prison in England. It was one of the most audacious crimes in Australia's history, taking just eleven minutes to strip Melbourne bookmakers of millions of dollars cash as they were settling after the Easter racing carnival.

The police didn't have any evidence to incriminate Ray Chuck. But the heavy division of the Melbourne underworld didn't need evidence. The robbery which was his most ingenious criminal venture was also his undoing. Its success started an underworld war which led to Chuck and two accomplices being arrested for the machine gun murder of a rival painter and docker, a standover man called Les Kane. Chuck and his friends were acquitted of the charge through lack of evidence, but while the other two went into hiding interstate, Chuck was kept in custody to face separate charges.

If he thought that being behind bars would protect him, he was wrong. On November 12, 1979, he was brought before the

Melbourne Magistrates Court for a hearing that would have taken only a few minutes. And there, while being escorted from one court chamber to another, he was shot dead by a hit man ...

None of which would have surprised those who knew him from his Chiltern boyhood. A lot of people in that drowsy little town had their memories of 'Chuckie' to recycle, and they still do. But few can say the same about the other boy named Ray. He seemed too ordinary.

A TEACHER at Chiltern State School from 1951 until 1956 glancing idly at Ray's class would see a dozen tiny signposts pointing to the likely course of adult lives. Here, a stolid girl who knits – one plain, one purl – at recess, rural wife and mother written on her placid face. There, in a quiet corner, the studious one of the bunch, bent over the second book borrowed that week and already dreaming of escape to the outside world. Out on the quadrangle the strapping boy with the strutting walk and the cocksure voice, perched on top of a pecking order that will make him a local hero on the football and cricket grounds, and later a bar room bore.

But Ray? He doesn't fit easily into any category but 'miscellaneous,' which might explain some things. Would it have been better if he were the budding sportsman of the group? Or the clever one with a bright future? Either would have given him a sense of identity that was missing, made him popular or admired. As it is, he is only ever pointed out for the wrong reasons: the accident of his birth. He is moderately big for his age, with the puppy fat that comes from gratifying a taste for ice cream and sweets, but he is not regarded as athletic. Nor especially inquisitive. Nor imaginative. He is strong enough and self-centred enough to dish out more punishment than he takes, but is not to be remembered as being the playground bully. Anybody looking for ominous portents draws a blank.

116

It is a biographical cliché that when old school mates are asked about a Prime Minister or a murderer, too often pieces are produced which fit obligingly into the jigsaw. The future statesman had said something which earmarked him for greatness well before he could even tie his own shoelaces; the future killer has been seen pulling the wings off flies.

But in this case the picture is not so conveniently clear. At schoolwork, he is average, in the sense that at least half the class get better results than he does. Not because he is dull, but perhaps because there seems less incentive, less encouragement at home, for him to do well at his lessons than for some children. He is, as most Chiltern adults and many of their children know, the adopted and only son of a man who clearly regards himself as prosperous enough to set up young Ray when the time comes, education or no education. Until then, the boy is marking time. Always, it seems, he is a little apart from the crowd. True, some families remember him bringing a selection of his many toys to play in their backyards, though it is the toys they remember better than the boy. And true, no one takes a violent dislike to him. But no-one really likes him, either.

THE child is father to the man. In six years at Chiltern state school Ray made no close friends, setting a lifelong pattern. Few contemporaries still living in Chiltern could later summon more than a hazy memory of the name and the face. One was Bill Plemming, 'Plemmo' to his mates, and for a few months in the mid-1950s Ray almost qualified as one. Knocking around with the young Plemming was the closest he came to making a friend at Chiltern – the district where, as it turned out, he stayed longer than any other place in his life.

'Plemmo' was to recall, 30 years later, the few times that he and Ray went fishing and prospecting in the old goldfields around Chiltern. Sometimes they went with Harold in his Chev utility, at others the two boys pedalled their 'treadleys' out to the old Magenta mine and panned for gold in the creeks. 'Plemmo' still has a memento of one of those dimly remembered days in the bush: a tiny glass vial holding a few specks of gold he panned with Ray.

One outing was to stick in his mind. They'd gone fishing ('Ray always caught more than me ... ') at Woolshed Creek, and somehow trapped a young kangaroo in an old mining trench, an adventure made more exciting because the boys were chased by older 'roos. While one boy guarded the animal, the other went home for a bran bag to carry it back to town. The kangaroo was a pet at the Plemmings' place for years after the boys lost track of each other.

Ray's parents were to move to a farm near Myrtleford in 1957, and 'Plemmo' joined the PMG, as it then was, and worked in Wangaratta, Bendigo and Melbourne before returning to his hometown as a telephone linesman. But he was to run into Ray again, in early 1965, eight years since their casual schoolboy acquaintance.

Better friends might have grown too far apart – noticed too many embarrassing differences in each other – but 'Plemmo' and Ray had never really been close enough for that. 'Plemmo' knew Ray was married but 'thought he must have been separated at the time'.

Ray was driving the red Holden sedan, he recalled later. 'An EK dolled up with spats, aerials, the lot.' A buck's car, good for 'pulling birds' ... even if the driver did have a pregnant wife and two kids. Telling his story, 'Plemmo' paused slightly, flicked a glance at his wife, and framed his next sentence with studied nonchalance. 'I went to the drive-in with him a few times, took a couple of bottles. After a while we drifted apart again.'

And women?

'Plemmo' became coy. 'Like,' he said jokingly, 'if Ray got a chance to get in bed with a woman he wouldn't knock it back … Who would?' There was a touch of defensive bravado about this. 'Ray,' he said, 'always struck me as decent. Never struck me as odd in any way.'

Subject closed.

A NOTHER was not so generous. Bob Douglas, outspoken and gregarious, did not hoard any vivid memories of Ray which earmarked him as a monster in the making. But he claimed to have noticed 'something different'.

At school, he recalled, 'you could always tell which kids were to be coppers or crims.' They take the same path for a while, sharing a willingness, even a desire, to be different from the herd, only later choosing which side of the law to follow their destinies.

'The kids who are going to be coppers are the kids who often didn't seem to worry about getting on with anyone … and this bloke Ray was a bit the same,' Douglas said. 'He seemed to be a bit one out. When you start a job you get a bit of a ragging from the others, and after that it's all right and you're one of the mob. But there's that sort of bloke who will sort of dwell on it for years afterwards … and that's what I reckon Ray was going to be like. He was an odd sort of a bastard, not the sort of bloke you'd want to go and have a beer with.'

Shrewd character reading? Or an example of hindsight posing as psychology?

Either way, it seemed Ray the schoolboy was ordinary, and average. But not quite normal.

H AROLD'S reputation preceded him. Reg Brine had never met him, but when Harold turned up to look over Brine's farm at Rosewhite, tucked in a valley between Myrtleford and Mudgegonga, he knew to expect hard bargaining. Harold first inspected the property shortly after the Brines had tried to auction it. Reg had been born on the farm, which his father had taken up under the soldier settler scheme after returning from the first world war. Like most of the farms in the valley, it had once been part of a big grazing property owned by a pioneer family, the Woodsides.

THE old Woodside homestead, shorn of all but its house paddocks, stood next door to Brines' place. The family that lived in it were to regret the day that Harold decided to buy into the district.

As usual, Harold was out to drive a hard bargain, but in Reg Brine he came close to meeting his match. After days of haggling, Brine dropped his original price by £1000 on the condition that he save agent's commission by making it a private sale.

This suited Harold admirably – until he found out that Brine was going to take the farm's stock of superphosphate and hay unless he paid for it separately. Grumbling, he paid up.

And so, early in 1957, Harold and Mavis and their son moved to Rosewhite, their sixth shift since Ray's adoption. Once more, they were 'the new people next door,' and their boy was an outsider.

Ray was thirteen when they got to Rosewhite, and fast approaching the crossroad where the signs point to different directions.

Puberty.

WHEN a teenage boy is interested in neither books nor games, there is potential for trouble. Ray, a little older than the average first form student and big for his age, was soon headed for it.

His first year at Rosewhite was also his first at secondary

school, which meant a long, slow bus-trip to Wangaratta Technical School, where he had enrolled while at Chiltern. The unremarkable talents displayed at primary school were submerged even more in the bigger classes of the 'Tech.' As Ray entered the emotional minefield of sexual awareness his behaviour – until now merely spoiled, selfish and introspective – took an anti-social edge.

No single transgression was to stand out 30 years on, but the sum of them was enough that at the end of 1957 he left the Wangaratta school, under a cloud following what Harold later described as a 'dispute with the headmaster'.

The headmaster's presumably poor opinion of the moody boy from Rosewhite was no doubt more significant than the boy's opinion of the headmaster. The bus driver who ferried the district's crop of children into Myrtleford didn't like Ray either.

The driver, Rex Millen, was a reasonable man considering the trials of his job. He was, for instance, always ready to give locals a lift if they waited by the road.

One day a woman from Myrtleford caught a ride to Rosewhite with him. Along the way they exchanged the usual commonplaces of their place and time: the weather, the crops, land and stock prices, the swirls and eddies of small town politics and gossip.

But among the idle chat they touched on the arrival the year before of Harold and Mavis, and it prompted the driver to pass an opinion so pointed that it was to stick in his listener's mind for three decades.

'Rex said that the kid was spoiled rotten,' she recalled. 'He said that Harold had given him the world, and that he was utterly ruined.'

One of the presents Harold bought Ray around that time was a rifle from a sports store in Myrtleford. An automatic Mossberg .22 with a fold-down grip.

S EX and guns … all teenage boys are interested in the first. And in country Victoria in the 1950s, most were interested in the second. There should not have been, then, anything unusual about Ray's preoccupation with either. But there was – though few realised it. His was the sort of devious nature which easily camouflages its motives.

By the time Ray transferred to Myrtleford Consolidated School in 1958 to start second form he was eying girls speculatively, and some started to return the sly looks and clumsy innuendos: an early sign that despite his unpopularity with most other males, he was attractive to some women.

Physically advanced for his age, he began to shed the childish plumpness and to cultivate the tough 'rocker' look of the older youths in the town. By that year Elvis Presley had touched Rosewhite together with the rest of the Western world, and the depression generation of hard-working, God-fearing country people were faced with the first wave of baby boomers, a generation engrossed in itself and an imported culture whose icons were rock 'n' roll, Coca Cola, fast cars and tight jeans.

Even before he'd heard of James Dean, Ray fitted the stereotype of the rebel without a cause, a tendency aggravated by being the only child of middle-aged parents for whom he provided the only common bond in a barren marriage. That alone didn't make him different from many another troubled teenager. But under the surface of adolescent angst, Ray was disturbed.

A N early and constant sign of Ray's inner turmoil was his bedwetting, a nervous affliction which continued until his early teens. Harold and Mavis went to great lengths to break him of the habit, without success, which indicated psychological rather than physical causes. After exhausting the list of patent 'cures', such as mattresses with inbuilt alarms, Mavis took the boy to a doctor in Wangaratta.

The doctor confirmed that there was no physical fault causing the bedwetting. But during his examination he did discover that Ray had only one testicle, a fact Mavis and Harold hadn't known, and which Ray was to keep secret until he entered hospital 25 years later.

The other thing that worried Mavis, she later told relatives, was that the doctor admitted to her that he had given Ray the 'wrong' drug.

A drug, Mavis reported, which the doctor told her was normally used 'to accelerate puberty'.

Many years later, it was unclear whether the doctor was referring to a single dose or to a series of doses. A single dose of the hormonal derivatives used to accelerate puberty would probably not have a marked effect on behaviour, according to experts. But what if several doses were administered before the doctor discovered the mistake? And what if the dosages were too heavy?

By the 1980s it was an accepted fact of sports medicine that some athletes given courses of steroids – which are derived from male hormones – became aggressive, and developed unnaturally powerful sex drives. And this was using steroids which had been refined to maximise the growth of muscle and minimise psycho-sexual side effects on adults. What, then, were the potential risks of the crude hormonal derivatives available in the 1950s? Could they affect the balance of psychological and physical elements undergoing change during puberty?

The implications of the drug mistakenly administered by the country doctor are beyond investigation. The doctor is now dead, and his records lost. He treated the teenager from Rosewhite in an era when babies were born deformed because their mothers had been prescribed a drug called thalidomide. It, too, had been considered safe.

FOR the first time in his life Ray had some mates. He was still at school and they were working on farms around Rosewhite, but they hung around together on weekends.

One Ray had known earlier. His name was Bob Newman, he had worked briefly for Harold some time before, and now worked on a dairy farm owned by Bill and Jack Browne at Rosewhite. He was a quiet, hardworking boy well-liked by his employers and, left to himself, unlikely to get into any sort of trouble.

There were two brothers, Frank and Doug McGrath, knockabout farm labourers who had worked all over the north-east of the state. Frank worked for a farmer called Washington Briggs; Doug, later a drover, worked anywhere he could pick up a casual job.

An occasional fifth member of the gang was a youngster named David, who, by a neat irony, was later to become a prison officer. He worked for a farmer called Kelvin Walker. These four hardly qualified as evil companions, but they were all older than Ray. And Frank McGrath had a car, which made him valuable in the eyes of a fifteen-year-old who looked seventeen and was out to impress girls. From the night they first met a local dance at Rosewhite, Frank noticed that Ray was 'always real keen on girls,' he was to recall. 'He went to all the dances and that. He was as good as gold, never got into much trouble, although he liked to drink.'

At that first casual meeting Frank divined something different about Ray. Something more than the fact that he was younger and, unlike Frank, 'given everything he asked for' by prosperous parents. But geography and a shared interest in shooting, cars and girls dictated that Ray be tolerated as one of the group. He had his new automatic rifle and plenty of ammunition to waste; the others had the car, firearms and easy access to the pubs.

There was another attraction for Ray. Like him, the farm workers were outsiders, not members of the families who had lived in the valley for years, even generations. He shared their distaste for going to the football and cricket matches, which dominated the social lives of the locals. Even in company his were essentially solitary amusements, like the prospecting and fishing of earlier days at Chiltern.

'There was nothing to do,' said Frank McGrath later. 'Everyone knew what everyone else was doing. If there was a football match everyone would go ... except us.'

On those days, in between morning and evening milkings, they would have the district almost to themselves. Much of the time they spent shooting kangaroos and rabbits, which were thick.

They were all handy shots, which was nothing unusual, but with more time to waste than the others, practice made Ray a good marksman.

A neighbour, Ian Browne, once saw him shoot a snake in a creek bed from a bridge about ten metres away. It was sharp shooting, but that wasn't what impressed the scene on the watcher's memory.

'Even when the snake was dead he just kept firing,' he recalled. 'He most probably emptied the whole magazine into it, which was a lot of shots.' It was frenzied and senseless. But within a few seconds Ray seemed normal again.

Normal, for Ray, had become by his sixteenth year the habit of wearing a leather jacket with chrome studs and his sandy hair brushed back in a rocker quiff. It was, Ian Browne noted, 'a bit rugged for Rosewhite'.

Taken altogether, the emerging picture was of trouble

waiting to happen. But Mavis was too close, too fond, to notice the transition. So it was a shock to her the day she answered a knock at the door to face a sight that every parent dreads.

A policeman on the doorstep.

IT had happened the previous Saturday night. After milking, Ray and three of the others had crammed into Frank's old Holden ute and driven to Wangaratta. For no particular reason other than the universal teenage one, 'it was something to do.' For the same reason, while driving home about 11pm, they pulled up at the garage at Everton, a hamlet on the Ovens Highway between Wangaratta and Myrtleford.

But before the battered ute rolled to a halt the idea must already have taken shape. 'We decided,' remembered Frank McGrath, 'to have a bit of a look around the joint.' Ray, although the youngest, led the way. He tested the windows, found one that was easily forced and squeezed through it. Inside, he headed for the till and rifled it. He pocketed some change and grabbed a few tools which were lying around and handed them through the window. Half an hour later they were home, each creeping quietly to bed at a different farmhouse.

And that could easily have been that. But it was a country district, and people took notice of anything suspicious. Someone must have seen something which connected the Rosewhite boys with the break-in, and reported it to Beechworth police.

The police called during the afternoon milking. Shrewd timing. Each boy was hard at work and had no idea what was happening until the tap on the shoulder. There was a touch of drama about the episode which was also shrewd, because it had deterrent value. Despite the pettiness of the crime, people were shocked. It was a long time since police had come to Rosewhite for anything even vaguely criminal. At Beechworth police station the routine motions were gone through. The young bucks had got their scare; the police saw no point throwing the book at them.

Frank McGrath and Bob Newman, being the oldest, were charged with the bare minimum, and subsequently given good behaviour bonds by the local magistrate. Ray and the other boy were let off with a warning.

Afterwards, Ray treated the episode as a great joke. And well he might have. It was the first time his budding delinquency had resulted in an arrest, and it hadn't even gone on his record.

An hour's drive away, in New South Wales, they all would have been fingerprinted.

HAROLD and Mavis were mortified. They had always been sensitive and defensive about Ray, especially Harold. Mavis was devoted to the boy, and gentle compared with her husband's overbearing way, but she could see Ray's faults more clearly than Harold. He obstinately refused to concede that the boy was becoming wayward, just as he refused to tell him he was adopted.

'He'll be right,' he would insist. And because Mavis nearly always obeyed him, Ray stayed both undisciplined and unaware of his origin. Two time-bombs stored away for a time of reckoning

Despite his age – 55 in 1959 – Harold still gave gossips something to talk about. Neighbours later recalled that he was a regular at the Happy Valley hotel, a short drive away on the main road towards Myrtleford. He was regarded by some drinking mates, in the euphemism of the day, as a 'man's man.' Whether his deeds matched his boasts is a matter for speculation, but one former Happy Valley drinker claimed later that 'Harold used to hunt at night, like a fox.'

Whether Ray was affected by his father's example or reputation was a moot point. Mavis had reason to confide to at least one friend in Myrtleford than she was worried because the boy seemed 'too highly sexed'. She knew that Ray was hanging around a girl who lived nearby, and it made her anxious.

Always a solitary and secretive boy, Ray was developing the loner attitude that was to be the most distinguishing feature of an otherwise undistinguished man. He would often disappear between milkings and then again in the evenings. Sometimes he would be with his mates, and sometimes with the girl. Strangely, for a teenager, he chose to keep his two activities separate, not telling the boys anything about the girl. As if he already had two personalities. A hidden sexual one, and the mask that he turned towards the world.

THE girl was pregnant. The gossips, promoters of a vicious double standard, tended to blame her for her predicament because she was a few months older than he was; to say she 'led him on'. But, as Ray was to prove elsewhere, there was little doubt he was most at fault.

At best he was merely tolerated by other males, but he seemed to fascinate some women. And, even at sixteen, he was prepared to ruthlessly seduce them.

Somewhere on the journey between an unwanted baby and lonely, spoiled youth a barrier had formed between Ray and other people which made him incapable of giving or receiving the affection he needed to be normal. It meant he didn't have a conscience.

Perhaps it was this which stung the girl into striking back at him the only way she knew: she told him the truth about his adoption. It explained the unsettling feeling of being different which he had sensed for so long, but it cut him to the quick. The gap between him and others was suddenly a gulf.

None of which helped the girl. It was she who had to confess her predicament to her shocked parents; she who had to run the gauntlet of gossip during a pregnancy followed by a furtive birth; she who had to endure the knowledge that the child would be taken from her to be brought up by strangers.

History was repeating itself. Ray had condemned the girl to his mother's fate, the baby to his own. They were his first victims.

E ARLY 1960. One shame on top of another was too much for Harold and Mavis. Their boy had been branded in the minds of their neighbours as bad company. Harold's pride was not the sort that weathers adversity. He could not cover up Ray's notoriety, so he took an easier way out. He put the farm on the market, and started looking at properties all over the north east and the Murray Valley.

After selling the Rosewhite farm, Harold rented a house in Yarrawonga, and Mavis and Ray went to stay with Mavis's mother in Preston. Harold had bought and sold on rising markets since the war, and had done well enough that he was now after a top-class irrigation farm. His idea, he told agents, was to get a property on which to set up Ray, and then retire. But he was hard to please. By the time he approached Bill Elligate, a Cobram stock and station agent, he said he'd inspected eighty farms without finding the one he wanted. Elligate, then with the New Zealand Loan company, had good connections with farmers on soldier settlement blocks at Yarroweyah, near Cobram. He took Harold to inspect a farm owned by the Stewart family. It didn't suit him. But on the way back they drove past a property in Kokoda Road which took Harold's eye.

The farmhouse had a well-established orchard, shade trees and garden, and white-painted fences. The dairy was clean, the rushes that infest much irrigation land had been kept under control, and the milking cows were well-bred and in good condition. It was, as one neighbour described it later, as neat and natty as a stud farm. The only problem, as far as the agent knew, was that it wasn't for sale. But there was no harm in asking, he decided. He pulled into the driveway and went inside.

It seemed a long shot, but Harold's luck was in.

The property-owner was a returned soldier called Ray Northausen. He had worked hard for thirteen years to establish the place from scratch. He and his wife had lived in an old wagon before the house was built, all the while clearing and draining land, milking cows, feeding pigs and calves and raising a young family. Seven days a week, with no holidays. On top of serving in the New Guinea jungles, the battle had affected Northausen's health; a few days before Harold and the agent chanced to pass, his doctor had warned him that he should rest because his asthma was getting worse. His widow was to note sadly years later that few of the soldier settlers 'made old bones.' If war wounds didn't get them, turning rough blocks into farms did ...

So when the agent spied the farmer in the paddock and walked across to him, he did not get the rebuff he half expected. By the time Ray Northausen walked slowly back to the house, the deal had been struck.

W ITHIN days of getting to Melbourne with Mavis, Ray found himself in a sordid episode straight from the pages of Truth. The woman was verging on middle-age, and known to the family, which made it easy for her to get her hands on Ray's willing body without causing suspicion. She lived in Melbourne with another woman in her 30s. They were, as Ray was dimly aware, lesbians. But the older one had a voracious bisexual appetite. After the first encounter, when she caught him looking at her in the shower, she seduced him many times, destroying the few inhibitions that he had, showing him things he hadn't imagined.

It grew more deviant. Ray was invited to watch the two women in bed together before coupling with the older one while the other applauded. Each time she seduced him she encouraged him to be rougher. Until the day came that she resisted him, and he forced her to have sex. It was a turning point. 'That was when my problem started,' he confided to another man 25 years later.

The women had taken an introverted, egocentric and highly-sexed farm boy, his mind ready to soak up any experience like blotting paper, and made him a rapist and a voyeur. By the time he left his grandmother's, Ray's sexual proclivities were twisted into a knot he could not unravel, his imagination filled with gross fantasies he could not satisfy.

SEVEN

Shotgun wedding, 1960-1964

Y ARRAWONGA, mid-1960. Boy meets girl. Two girls, in fact, killing their lunch break on a Wednesday chatting outside the bakery where one of them works. But only one – the tall, pretty one called Lesley, with the blonde hair and the friendly smile – likes what she sees. She sees a strongly built youth, suntanned and fit, with the capable look of one who works outdoors.

Her friend is not as impressed. Shirley Martin, small, shy and dark-haired, is a natural observer less inclined than Lesley to take people on face value. And she instinctively distrusts the stranger who has come sauntering up the footpath and opened a conversation with them. He is insinuatingly bold and confident, as if he has 'a high opinion of himself,' she is to recall.

Just as Shirley and Lesley are opposites in looks and temperament, they have different tastes in men.

By the time Lesley runs back up the street to her job as an

apprentice hairdresser, the boy has arranged to take her to the pictures the following Friday night. She is, Shirley knows resignedly, keen on the cocky stranger.

In the six months the two girls have been working in Yarrawonga they have met lots of boys, and there are 'some roughies around'. But never before has Shirley taken such an instant dislike to one. There is something about him she never forgets. 'His weird eyes.'

T HE Friday night at the pictures was the beginning of Lesley's romance with Ray. He was sixteen; she had just turned fifteen. In the few weeks that he was to stay in Yarrawonga before Harold took over Northausen's farm, they had plenty of opportunity to see each other. Ray wasn't working, and had never been prevented from doing whatever he fancied; Lesley was boarding with an aunt who let her go out.

Despite Shirley's misgivings about Ray, she did not criticise him in front of Lesley, and the two girls remained close friends. Shirley had grown up in unhappy circumstances on a farm beyond Mulwala, which helped explain her reserve. But with Lesley she felt comfortable, and spent most of her spare time with her during the week. At weekends she almost always visited Lesley's family, who had a shop at a small town called Lowesdale an hour's drive away. For Shirley, Lesley's people were like a surrogate family; Lesley had two brothers and three sisters and they always made her feel welcome. The bond had been strengthened when she went out for several months with Lesley's brother John.

As Lesley's infatuation with Ray went on, Shirley sensed that her private opinion of him was shared by most of Lesley's family. The parents were easygoing people, prepared to see the best side of Lesley's boyfriend when she started to bring him home at weekends, but her sister Dot and brothers Mick and John disliked Ray.

'He was always a fast sort of a feller,' was the impression John formed. 'He drove too fast for my liking and was hard on cars. When he pulled up the motor would be creaking and groaning from being so hot. He was sort of sly looking ... and he had everything given to him.'

Dot thought that Ray was polite enough when he chose. But not pleasant.

YARROWEYAH, late 1960. Before leaving their farm the Northausens, knowing that Harold and Ray had not worked an irrigation farm before, offered to have Ray stay with them and learn the ropes. He came, reluctantly, and stayed only a few days. He left, Mrs Northausen was to recall, saying 'he knew everything there was to know about irrigation.'

The Northausens moved out just before Christmas. They left the new owners two workers. One was a teenage English lad, Graham Sweatland. The other was 'Teddy,' a red kelpie dog. The pair were good mates.

The dog was noted for his devotion to the Northausen girls. If anybody, even their father, spoke to them harshly the dog would spring to their defence, growling.

From the day Ray took over in the dairy the dog took a dislike to him, a feeling Graham Sweatland shared because of what he regarded as the arrogance and laziness of his new employers.

This simmering antagonism boiled over one day when Ray kicked the dog. It growled at him, and he went into a rage. He grabbed an iron bar and smashed its skull, killing it.

Graham was outraged. He sprang at Ray, and in the following brawl produced a knife and stabbed him in one arm, inflicting a wound that later had to be bandaged by a doctor in

Cobram. The doctor, Lesley was to discover, took a dislike to Ray and later warned her about him, but it came too late to help her.

Towards the end of 1960 Lesley broke up with Ray, who had been driving to Yarrawonga to see her in the Chevrolet ute his father let him use, although he had no driver's licence. But she was flattered when he came back to see her a few weeks later, and resumed where they had left off.

It was her downfall. Before that she had resisted Ray's insistent demands to have sex. But now she gave in. She was a kid who thought she was in love, and she was frightened of losing him.

Lesley's sixteenth birthday fell on July 12, 1961. Ray visited, bringing two presents. One was the green twin-set in a parcel under his arm. The other turned up a few weeks later ...

She was pregnant.

YARROWEYAH, late 1961. The woman was an acquaintance of Mavis's family, one of the few people to visit the farm at Yarroweyah. She had been born in the country, and after years of working in the city she liked to wander alone around farm buildings when she got the chance, savouring the sights and smells of her childhood. Absentmindedly, this day, she wandered into a shed ... and came face to face with young Ray.

He started guiltily, and she automatically began apologising, then stopped as her mind registered what he was holding. It was a gun. And even in the gloom she could tell the barrel had been sawn off.

Ray got in first. 'It's only an old gun,' he said with feigned nonchalance. 'Don't tell Dad, will you.' The wheedling friendliness of the words were belied by his eyes, which avoided hers. The woman considered herself an intimate of Ray's, but she was troubled by the implied menace of the weapon, the suggestion of premeditated crime. She told him she knew it was illegal to saw off guns. Later, just before leaving, she told his parents what she had seen. Mavis waited until Ray was out of sight and then searched the Chev ute he drove, but without finding the weapon.

The visitor left for Melbourne. Hours later, she was parked at the side of the highway near Kilmore having a cup of tea, when a car pulled up. It was Harold, and he looked upset. He told her, she was to remember later, that he had asked Ray for the weapon, and that Ray told him he'd 'thrown it in the dam.' Her impression was that Harold wasn't sure if the boy was telling the truth.

She had never thought badly of Ray. But the pang of dismay she felt that day lingered. She did not speak of the incident for 25 years. Not even when the police interviewed her.

SOON after Northausens had left the district, the local garage man, Jim Sutton, was called to the farm. The new owner's son was having trouble with his Chev ute. When Sutton arrived, he noted that a crude attempt had been made to adjust the carburettor; he knew this because it was leaking fuel all over the manifold. But when he asked Ray what he had done the teenager flatly denied touching the vehicle. There was no good reason for the lie, but he persisted with it, even after the mechanic pulled the carburettor apart, showed that the needle and seat was gone, then looked on the ground underneath until he found the missing part. Having proved his point, Sutton worked in silence. He knew that Ray must have dismantled the carburettor and then not known how to reassemble it properly. It seemed a trifling thing to lie about so vehemently. The mechanic shrugged it off. Maybe it was the nature of the beast.

136

KEVIN Kirby did not suspect Ray's propensity for secrecy until the day Ray offhandedly announced that he had to go and 'see this bird because she tells me she's pregnant and we've gotta get married.'

'The bird,' as Kevin was to find out that night, was Lesley. It was the first time in more than six months of playing in a local dance band with Ray that he had heard she existed. Ray had sometimes 'skited' about sex and girls, but Kevin had dismissed most of it as hot air. From his position, playing saxophone almost as badly as Ray played the trumpet at country hops, Ray seemed a quiet bloke. Not shy, the way Kevin was – more of a loner.

Kevin had met Ray through their shared interest in music, although in both cases it was more the dabbling of restless teenagers than an expression of latent talent. The Kirbys farmed another block in the soldier settlement area, on Labuan Road. Kevin, skinny and red-haired, was taking saxophone lessons, and somehow he found out that the new arrival in Kokoda Road could play the trumpet a bit, the legacy of a brief spell in a brass band at Myrtleford.

Soon after Ray had arrived in Yarroweyah they joined a dance band run by a Mrs Jackel in Cobram, then switched to a breakaway group of younger musicians. They called themselves the 'Melodees', and they spent as much time practising – often in Ray's parents' living room – as they did playing at dances.

Kevin thought Ray's mother a 'nice sort of a lady.' But Harold was 'a sulky sort of a bugger.' He rarely greeted the boys with anything but a grunt when they came around to practise.

Typically, Ray's association with Kevin was more the result of geography and a shared lack of interest in football and cricket than any real friendship, and it was consolidated by the fact that Ray had a car and Kevin didn't. Like the others who had known Ray at Chiltern and at Rosewhite, Kevin was never to crack the surface of Ray's self-absorption. Kevin realised that most people didn't like him, and that this was a reaction to the contemptuous edge in Ray's attitude.

'A lot of young blokes knock around together, even three or four carloads at a time,' Kevin was to ruminate. 'But Ray never went in for that sort of thing.' What he did go in for was music, driving fast, and sex. The latter perplexed Kevin: 'You never saw him in action but from what he said he never seemed to have much trouble getting women. Half the time I thought he was bullshitting … but it turned out he wasn't.'

Kevin was astounded when Ray told him about Lesley. That night he went with him to visit her, invited by the calculating Ray probably to share the burden of an embarrassing situation with the pregnant girl's family. Kevin was impressed by Lesley, but shocked by Ray's offhand attitude towards her. 'She was not only good looking but she had a nice personality. I thought she was terrific,' he was to say. 'If you had to get married then you couldn't get much better than her – but Ray wasn't keen.'

Kevin didn't protest at Ray's cavalier treatment of Lesley, but he never forgot it. Nor how Ray manipulated the feelings of his parents. It seemed to Kevin that there was a chip on Ray's shoulder, and in his actions an implicit threat that if Harold or Mavis dared curb him he would leave home.

Ray got away with things that nobody else in Kevin's circle would dream of. One Sunday when his parents were out, Ray took him on a joyride to Melbourne in Harold's new car. That Ray would do this without a licence surprised Kevin; it was far-removed from driving around local roads in the old ute. But the reason for going also disturbed him.

On the way Ray told Kevin that he was looking for a girl he'd met on an earlier visit. When they arrived they drove around the northern suburbs looking for an address Ray had, but they didn't find the girl.

Then, as carelessly as if he'd been to the local store for a loaf of bread, Ray headed his father's new car back to Yarroweyah. Fast, as always.

Kevin worried about what Harold would do if he got home first and caught them in the car. Harmless though the outing had proved, there was a smell of delinquency about it which troubled Kevin.

But the silent youth at the wheel didn't show any sign of sharing such misgivings. Even when he had company, Ray was alone.

AFTER her sixteenth birthday Lesley had 'broken up' with Ray for some trifling reason which, she knew, should have left her feeling downcast, if only for a few days. But she wasn't. In fact, she had confided to her father that she felt 'sort of free.'

The first tiny seeds of doubt about him had already been sown. She found it hard to put into words, but there was something intense about Ray that rang a faint alarm bell. But the sickening sensation of finding herself pregnant swamped such subtle misgivings.

Panic-stricken, Lesley telephoned Ray and asked him to come over to see her. He was unenthusiastic. When she told him she was pregnant he 'more-or-less said we should get married.' He said he would tell his parents if she told hers.

Lesley took him at his word. She screwed up courage and poured out the truth to her sister, Dot, begging her to break the news to her mother.

Lesley waited in her bedroom, her mouth dry, the blood pounding in her ears. She heard Dot hesitantly talking to her mother, then a stunned silence.

Her mother came in, shook her like a naughty child and

sobbed: 'You're the one I had faith in.' Over the next few days Lesley made her peace with her parents. She started to worry because she hadn't heard from Ray.

One lunchtime she went to a telephone box and rang his parents' number, hoping Harold wouldn't answer. Ray's mother came on the line. Lesley's heart sank when Mavis said brightly: 'Oh, hello. I'll get Ray; he's just gone out.' Lesley knew then that her fears had been accurate: he'd been 'too gutless' to tell his parents.

'It's all right,' she said bravely. 'It's you I really want to speak to anyway ... '

FOR Lesley, the first mistake was getting pregnant. The second was allowing herself to be forced into marrying Ray. The irony was that her parents did not insist on marriage. Kindly people; they offered to help her if she wished to go it alone: to support her and the child while she finished her hairdressing apprenticeship. But these good intentions weren't enough to overcome their wish to keep up appearances when Ray's father made empty promises that Lesley 'wouldn't want for anything' if she married Ray.

Harold often argued with Ray, but usually gave in. Unfortunately for Lesley, the marriage was one issue Harold wasn't prepared to sidestep. His pride could not stand the prospect of another disgrace like the one left behind at Rosewhite. Harold exerted his strong personality, and got his way. This put Lesley and her parents in the humiliating position of having to appear grateful for what Harold clearly considered was his honourable and generous behaviour.

Ray sullenly acquiesced. Lesley, sunny-natured and ready to think the best of people, cherished a vague teenage dream of wedded bliss. The wedding date was set. Saturday, September 23, 1961.

140

TWO weeks before the wedding Lesley's brother John started going out with a girl called Carol, eventually to become his wife. The first time she met Ray she had heard nothing of him, and so saw him with the clarity of fresh eyes.

He wore sharp clothes: the pointed shoes, stovepipe pants, narrow ties, and brushed back hair of the rocker uniform. But underneath the veneer of working-class fashion Carol saw not the friendly farm boy she might have expected, half embarrassed and half proud about imminent marriage and fatherhood, but a supercilious youth who looked her over as speculatively as a butcher appraises a lamb.

Carol's impression hardened into distaste when she knew Ray better. 'He didn't believe in females having a say, and that irritated me,' she was to recall. 'But at that stage I didn't think he was strange or creepy. He wasn't anything, really, except a spoilt boy who liked his own way.'

Had she been pressed, Carol would have guessed that Lesley was making a mistake. But, like the rest of Lesley's family, she kept her own counsel. None of them had anything against Ray that went beyond personal whim, and on the surface he appeared quite a catch ... the only son of a prosperous landholder and in line to take over a good irrigation farm. Many a strong marriage had been built on less.

There was one problem. Ray wasn't interested in a successful marriage. Kevin Kirby wasn't the only one to realise that Ray regarded the whole thing as a black joke, an inconvenience that wouldn't stop him doing what he pleased. A middle-aged member of Mrs Jackel's dance band, who had always considered Ray a pleasant youngster, was surprised at his reaction when the marriage was mentioned at band practice one evening. Ray had scowled and said, 'I'm getting married – but I'm NOT going to stay married.'

The omens were all bad, but the wedding went off well at the little Presbyterian Church in Corowa. The sun shone. The groom was handsome in his navy blue suit, the bride pretty in the cream satin dress borrowed from Mavis's step-sister, Joyce. Kevin Kirby, smiling and lanky, was best man. Not because he was 'all that matey' with Ray, he explained much later. It was just that there was no-one else.

Outside the church, cameras caught Lesley and Ray in opposite moods: she smiling shyly; he deadpan with his eyes squinting into the bright spring sunshine. At the reception, held nearby at a little hall, Ray drank steadily, becoming boisterous, then drunk. He delighted Joyce's adopted son Phillip, then a small boy, by sitting him on his knee and playing with him. A bond had grown between Joyce, Ray and Phillip perhaps because each was adopted. They made an odd trio in an odd family, the secrets of their births hidden from them for years.

When the time came for Ray and Lesley to leave, little Phillip caused great hilarity by asking if he could go with them. 'Of course you can come, kid,' Ray slurred, 'course you can come'.

Lesley's brother and one of his mates drove the newlyweds to Albury, dropping them at a guest house where her father had booked them in. Ray was still drunk, and the landlady threatened not to let him in until Lesley pleaded that they had just been married.

Next morning, Ray carrying their single suitcase, they walked to the Albury station and caught the Melbourne train.

That was Sunday. The following Wednesday they stepped off the train at the Yarroweyah siding. Ray was due to milk that evening. It was one of the few nights that Lesley didn't have to work with him. The next day Harold made it clear Lesley was expected to work in the shed, pregnant or not.

The honeymoon was over. Lesley was sixteen years and two months old, and hadn't even finished growing.

K EVIN Kirby knew Ray and Lesley were back, so he decided to drop in and see how they were going. He was walking up the drive when he looked up to see Harold striding towards him, barrel chest thrust out, jaw set.

It seemed an unfriendly way to approach the best man of his son's wedding, but Kevin kept walking. Harold blocked his path, and made it clear he wasn't welcome, 'in such a way that he made you feel a bastard for coming around.' Ray was married now, Harold said, and had 'to be responsible.' Which was true, Kevin thought, but it had hardly been a case of him leading Ray astray. 'It seemed to me he was blaming me for any problems Ray had.'

Kevin shrugged and walked away. He never went back.

I T was Sammy Smith's first real job. The day he had turned fourteen, in June, 1961, he'd left school in Yarrawonga and started looking for work, but it wasn't until a few months later that he'd come out to the farm at Kokoda Road on the recommendation of a local stock agent.

Harold picked him up from Yarrawonga and drove him out to the property. The boy kept quiet, subdued by Harold's brusque manner. But when they arrived and he carried his case inside to meet his employer's family, he cheered up because he saw a familiar face. Sammy had known Lesley for years; his elder sister had been friends with her at school. Lesley seemed almost as pleased to see him, a reaction which did not please Harold or Ray. Harold was hostile to anybody in the family mixing with hired help. Ray's attitude mirrored this churlishness, but it was also tinged with jealousy; irrationally, he seemed to resent the fact that the lad had known Lesley before he had. In the few weeks that Sammy was to put up with such treatment, Ray once even accused the youngster of 'making eyes at Lesley,' and told him to 'stay away from her.' The ridiculousness of the idea stung Sammy into retorting: 'Cut it out!' But Ray's insecurities were too deeply entrenched for it to have any effect.

Sammy was to remember Ray as 'a quiet sort of a bloke, but a cocky sort of a bloke,' who would unhesitatingly use him as an excuse to get away from the farm as often as possible. A few times Ray took Sammy to dances where he was playing the trumpet in the band. On one of these excursions the boy saw a flash of Ray's uncontrollable temper.

Sammy was too young to be engrossed in girls or to be included as an equal among the older unattached males in the crowd, so he was one of the few looking at the band. Suddenly, something upset Ray, and he threw his instrument on the stage in rage in the middle of a song. Seconds later, 'he switched off,' picked up the trumpet and joined in as if nothing had happened.

This streak of spontaneous violence frightened Sammy, but it wasn't the only reason he started secretly looking for another job. Outside, apart from milking, he was usually left to do all the farm work himself while Ray and Harold amused themselves elsewhere. Inside, he found the atmosphere in the family unbearable. 'Everything seemed to be hushed up around the place. As soon as I had breakfast, dinner or tea I was shunted out to work or to my little room at the side.'

It seemed to the boy, later, that he was an innocent bystander in a three-way war of nerves between Ray, his parents and Lesley. He rarely heard anything, but the pregnant silences weighed on him. 'Ray's mother was a frightened sort of a woman,' he was to recall, 'as if she was a prisoner in her own home. There was something missing in that family.'

To escape, he went home to his parents at weekends. For the first three weeks he hadn't been paid. He told his father, who insisted that he ask Harold for the missing wages. He did, but

Harold fobbed him off for another few days with an excuse about not having been able to get to the bank. When the money did appear, it was less than the wages he'd been promised. It was the last straw. One Friday he got a message from the Yarrawonga post office offering him a new job. He went home that day and never came back.

Later, trying to explain to his father why he had quit, he said: 'It was so tense in that house, it was like sitting on a time bomb.'

Lesley could not escape so easily.

By Christmas, 1961, after three months with her in-laws, she was becoming disenchanted. The other side of the tense silences endured by the hired hand was Harold's relentless belittling of her, aggravated by Ray's dark moods and the fact he often left her marooned on the farm while he went off to play at dances and whatever else he felt like. Mavis was usually pleasant enough while they were alone together, but if Harold were there she would side with him.

For reasons difficult to fathom, given Ray's record, Harold often needled Lesley with insinuations that Ray was not the father of her unborn child. This once boiled over into an open accusation that she had 'trapped' Ray, which reduced Lesley to tears of anger and hurt. 'I didn't trap him – he didn't have to marry me!' she screamed at Harold. But the denial, like her distress, had little effect on the man she grew to hate even more than the husband who was to abuse her so badly.

Despite Ray's offhand treatment, Lesley harboured romantic feelings for him. Soon after the wedding she went to the doctor in Cobram who had stitched Ray's arm following his fight with the English farmhand. After examining her he asked who she was married to. She told him, and was surprised at his reaction. The doctor warned her that Ray would 'think of himself first, last and always,' Lesley recalled.

'I thought it was a bit of a cheek. But he was right.'

E ARLY 1962. Tommy Pavlovsky was fifteen when he arrived from Mulwala to work at the Kokoda Road farm. He was to stay longer than Sammy Smith had, but not because he liked the family better.

For small wages he worked seven days a week with every third Sunday off, ate what he was given and no second helpings, and was banished outside or to his room immediately after meals.

Like his predecessor, he usually worked alone except at milking time in the morning and afternoon. It was a lonely life for a youngster; he spoke more to the cows than he did to his employers.

Harold went to the hotel each afternoon, and after a token gesture Ray 'would often bugger off somewhere in his old Chev ute, saying he had to go to band practice,' leaving Tommy to feed the pigs and calves and do any other chores.

This worried the boy, because Ray knew more about dairy farming than he did, yet Tommy was often left to cope with treating cows for bloat and milk fever. It seemed a careless attitude towards valuable livestock, but it reflected the fact that the prize farm was rapidly going downhill.

Despite Ray's habit of dodging work when he could, Tommy got to know him well. The more he saw, the less he liked. Being two years younger, and away from home for the first time, he was jarred by Ray's thinly veiled appetite for sex and violence.

Some incidents were to stick in his mind, like a handful of snapshots salvaged from an old photo album ...

O FTEN a neighbour's schoolgirl daughter would ride past on her bike or on a pony, and Ray would stare at her and 'say something like, "Aww, I wouldn't mind getting into that",' Tommy was to remember. Sometimes, when Ray employed his old trick of using the boy as an excuse to drive into Cobram, he would cruise the streets 'perving' on girls.

This mildly embarrassed Tommy, although it didn't worry him. But one afternoon he was shocked by something Ray said. It happened when they were sitting in the ute outside a shop where they had each bought a pie. Ray, who had been covertly gazing at the shop assistant as she served them, seemed perturbed.

Suddenly he poured out an obscene and explicit description of what he would do to the girl if he could force her into bed with him. It wasn't so much the depravity of Ray's fantasy as its intensity that fascinated Tommy Pavlovsky. A quarter of a century later he could still quote Ray's outburst. Word for dirty word.

If Ray's sexual bent surprised Tommy, his temper frightened him. Once, in the dairy, a cow kicked Ray in the head. He grabbed a shovel used to clean up manure and flogged the cow with it for what seemed, to the horrified boy, like quarter of an hour. 'It was just shitting itself with terror … I couldn't get it into the shed for weeks,' he was to recall.

Another day they were picking up firewood from the back paddock and bringing it up to the woodheap near the house. As they unloaded the trailer Ray started throwing the wood aggressively towards Tommy, who was on the ground. He hit him in the leg and Tommy, irate, called him 'a bastard.' It was an innocent enough expression, for the farmhand didn't know that it was uncomfortably close to the truth. Suddenly Ray threw another lump of wood, but it was the look on his face that scared Tommy. It was the same as when he'd attacked the cow in the bail.

'When he got angry he got a very mean look … his eyes would sort of glaze over. It wasn't anger, it was hatred.'

Tommy felt sorry for Lesley, 'a striking looking girl, but they weren't warm towards her.' At night, alone in his room, Tommy sometimes heard Ray's raised voice, and Lesley crying. One night he heard thumps and slaps and cries of pain. Next morning, while they were working, Tommy told Ray what he'd heard and that he didn't like it. But when Ray looked at him he recognised the danger signals, and fell silent. Ray had a pitchfork in his hand, and Tommy knew he was capable of using it. In broad daylight and sober.

One Friday night in Cobram Tommy got a glimpse of what Ray could be like when he was drunk. Ray drank for effect, not socially. 'If you want to get high quick,' he'd boasted to the youngster, 'you buy a bottle of wine.' This night, Tommy had gone to a cafe while Ray went drinking. When they met to go home Ray was swaggering drunk, and truculent. He swayed provocatively into one of two other youths walking up the footpath. The youth said something, and Ray seized on it. He king-hit him, knocking him over. When the second teenager tried to help his friend Ray 'flattened him too.'

Tommy didn't want to get into trouble with the police, and neither did Ray. When they got to where the Chev was parked, he thrust out the keys and said: 'You'd better drive.' Tommy took a deep breath; he had never driven a car in his life. They covered the thirteen kilometres to Yarroweyah in first gear. Ray thought it a great joke, but he had a strange sense of humour. Something Tommy found out the hard way.

There was a horse on the farm which had been there before Tommy arrived. It was a rogue, but Tommy didn't know that when Ray persuaded him to ride it. Predictably, Tommy had a heavy fall, winding him. 'Ray just stood over me, laughing. Anybody else would have picked me up.'

Ray always kept a rifle on the back ledge of the ute. Sometimes Tommy went with him to the back paddock to have a shot. Years later, when he joined the Army and earned the crossed rifle insignia as a marksman, he was to remember Ray's prowess. 'I realised how from 25 to 50 yards he was pretty good. He often shot pigeons and galahs with that rifle. Always in the head.'

Sex and guns.

DRUNK or sober, day or night, pregnancy or not, Ray always wanted sex. And always had it, regardless of Lesley's feelings.

In March, 1962, the month before the baby was due, he disappeared. Lesley did not know where he'd gone, except that it was probably to Melbourne. After a week Mavis went to visit her mother in Preston where she obviously suspected Ray was staying. When she came back, she brought him with her. At the time Lesley did not know that the attraction was another girl. All she knew was that when he returned he was sulky and hostile, and slept in the spare room for two or three nights, as if to make the point that he didn't need her.

Where an older woman would have been angry, Lesley was bewildered, hurt and lonely. One night after Harold and Mavis had gone to bed she stayed up, watching television in the living room with Ray, who pointedly ignored her. Tentatively, she asked him if he would come out to their room to sleep. He didn't answer. She asked again. Ray leapt from his seat and started to punch her.

Lesley, eight months pregnant, crouched instinctively to protect the unborn baby, and took the blows on her head and shoulders, calling out with pain and fright.

Ray hailed her with blows, then stopped as quickly as he'd started. Lesley crept off to bed alone and sobbed herself to sleep.

Next morning she did not help with the milking. Significantly, nobody asked her why, even though she had worked right through the pregnancy to that time. Lesley plucked up courage while Harold and Ray were outside, and asked Mavis if she had heard her calling out the previous night. Mavis looked uncomfortable, and said she'd heard something, but 'thought it was the television.'

She added that she couldn't 'stand a man belting a woman,' and promised to 'talk to him about it.' But nothing was ever said or done. Mavis, in her way, was trapped as hopelessly as Lesley.

APRIL 17, 1962. Lesley's waters broke at 4.30am, but she didn't realise how close she was to giving birth until Mavis told her late that morning. After lunch, the contractions started. Ray, who'd been outside all morning, hung around long enough to say goodbye, but left it to Harold and Mavis to drive her to Cobram hospital.

The baby was born about six hours later, at 7.15pm. A girl, brown-eyed and fair, weighing seven and a half pounds. There was no-one but the doctor and the nurses to share the moment. Ray and his parents had stayed at the farm, and didn't know until the hospital rang with the news. Lesley called the baby Susan Maree, a name she'd had picked out months earlier. Ray had taken no more interest in names than he had in the birth.

The doctor was relieved that Lesley's youthful resilience had seen her through what he suspected had been a trying pregnancy. Six weeks before the birth he had been called out to the farm to look at Ray when a cow jammed him against the bail. Ray had been bruised, winded and shaken but otherwise all right. The doctor had been more concerned about Lesley; to his disgust she was still working in the milking shed. He ordered her to go to the house. It was no job for a heavily-pregnant girl, because it required much bending, and there was always the risk of the sort of accident that had happened to Ray.

150

The doctor's misgivings were reinforced the day after the birth. Mavis, looking a little shame-faced, turned up early to visit Lesley and the baby. But there was no sign of Ray. He had gone off somewhere, probably Melbourne, Mavis admitted. Lesley was disappointed, but not heartbroken. Already her attitude was tempered with resignation.

Mavis was delighted with the baby, and volunteered that she looked a lot like Ray, picking a resemblance that was to become more striking as the girl grew up. Lesley was pleased. She knew it was impossible that anybody else could have fathered the child, because he had been her first and only lover. At last, she thought, 'Harold might leave me alone.' But she was wrong. For years Harold was to accuse Lesley of Ray not being Susan's father and even taunted the child about it.

Lesley stayed in hospital for six days. She and the baby were fit, but her doctor seemed reluctant to let her go back to the farm. When she asked if she could leave, the doctor said he would much prefer her to go to her parents. He knew that Ray had not visited, and although he tried to reassure Lesley that it was probably just because he was young and overawed, she could tell he didn't think much of Ray. By that evening she was settled in at her parents' place, a milkbar they had taken over at the nearby town of Wahgunyah.

Lesley was rapt in the novelty of being a mother. The baby gave her life a meaning it had lacked for months, made her feel proud and important, and was an outlet for her frustrated feelings of affection. All of which pushed thoughts of Ray into the background …

Two days later, on a Wednesday night about 8pm, the family was relaxing in the living room attached to the shop when the bell on the shop door rang. Lesley's father wandered out to serve the late customer. He stepped back with surprise when he saw who it was.

Ray strolled in casually, his face deadpan. 'You'd reckon,' Lesley was to marvel much later, 'that with Dad there he'd at least be sheepish, but you couldn't say he was.' Lesley herself, by contrast, 'nearly died of shock, but I was as happy as Larry that he'd turned up.'

Ray had run his eye over Susan with the disinterested politeness of a distant relative, pronounced her 'a lovely baby,' and said he'd come to take them home.

All as casually as if he'd spent an afternoon in Cobram, and not eight days and nights with another woman.

HAROLD'S dream had turned sour. The farm he had chosen so carefully to hand over to Ray was already starting to run down. Ray did not seem interested enough to do more than the bare minimum of work, and he would vanish if something upset him. Instead of improving with age, he seemed to be getting more wayward. Harold swung to the view that Ray had jeopardised his future by marrying unwisely and too young.

The neighbours had noted another reason for the farm's decline, one which Harold's pride might not have admitted. For all his shrewdness as a livestock dealer on grazing land, Harold was new to the specialised business of milking cows on irrigation country. He knew little about it, and Ray had brushed off the opportunity to learn from Northausens. Ignorance was not the only problem; neither Harold nor Ray was willing to devote the hours of extra toil needed to keep the place as lovingly as Northausens had. The neatly-painted white fences around the house yard were beginning to peel and sag, the fruit-trees in front of the weatherboard farmhouse needed pruning, the rushes were creeping back into the flat, low-lying paddocks, the cows not as well-husbanded.

Harold was getting old and no doubt regarded the farm work

as Ray's responsibility. But though Ray was capable of working hard and fast, his was essentially the mercenary attitude of the pieceworker: do the work, get the money. He was never any good at caring for anything, whether it was farms, animals or other people.

Ray's restlessness brought matters to a head soon after Susan was born. Harold and Mavis decided to go ahead with their plans to build a new house at Chiltern and retire. Ray had been given his opportunity, and rejected it, so he would be free to make his own way. The farm would be sold.

There must have been discussions which led to this decision, but Lesley never took part. If she entered the room where Harold, Mavis and Ray were talking, they would fall silent. Almost, she was to say, 'as if they had a conspiracy against me.'

THE farm was auctioned on July 19, 1962. Bill Elligate, the agent who had acted for Harold less than two years earlier, was sorry it hadn't worked out better for his client. He felt less sympathetic after the sale, which had included the milking cows.

Dairy cows, while in production, must be milked daily, or else they suffer pain, possible illness, and eventual loss of milk. It is therefore an unwritten law of dairy farming that when a milking herd is sold the vendor does the right thing by the cows and the buyer by milking them as usual that night. In a lifetime of auctioneering Elligate had never known anyone to break that code.

But by 4pm on the day he auctioned the cows on the Kokoda Road farm, he realised that the vendors had gone, and that if he didn't milk the cows himself, no-one would.

The auctioneer told his assistant the bad news, and rolled up his sleeves. Strange people, he thought ...

That evening, mulling over the day's events, the couple who

had bought the farm mentioned how the owner's son, the reddish-haired youth, had mustered the cattle from the paddock in his bare feet. In mid-winter.

R AY had said he wasn't going to stay married, and this seemed to be his opportunity to escape. Two weeks before the auction he told Lesley that she should take the baby and go back to her parents. Lesley 'was a bit shocked,' but she had little choice. She arrived at her parents in time for her seventeenth birthday on July 12. A lot had happened in a year. For her previous birthday Ray had brought her a present, pregnancy and marriage. This time he didn't even ring her.

He didn't need to. Lesley didn't know it then, but Ray had a new girl. He had met her at a cafe in her home town of Numurkah on one of his frequent night-time outings, just before he sent Lesley to stay with her parents. The connection between the two events was significant: Ray was never likely to separate himself from convenient sex.

While his wife and baby were crammed in a back room with Lesley's two younger sisters, Ray swiftly established a sexual liaison with the Numurkah girl. He had never shown much interest in his child, but now he used her to snare the girl into feeling sorry for him as an aid to seduction. She was to recall how he produced a snapshot of the baby and told a pathetic story of how he was separated from his wife and planning divorce. 'He was so young to have a baby girl,' she was to say. 'It was sad, and I think this caused me to fall into a relationship with him.'

Soon after they met, Ray invited her to go to a dance to see him play in the band. It was the first of several outings – including a day trip to Myrtleford – that they were to have over the next few months. By this time Ray had turned eighteen, and was driving the new red Holden Harold had bought him. The girl at first thought him a 'quiet, well-spoken, well-behaved person who was sensitive.' But she wondered why he could not see her more regularly, why he did not take her home to Yarroweyah where he and his parents were still living pending settlement for the sale of the farm.

When he did take her home one day, she received a surprise that made her suspect his motives. Ray's parents were out when they got to the farm, but arrived home unexpectedly, and Mavis greeted the girl frostily. When she offered to help Mavis wash up, she was rebuffed. Mavis was upset; after an uncomfortable silence, she asked the girl if she knew Ray was married.

The girl was sure of herself. 'I explained that I did know that, but that Ray was getting a divorce,' she said later. 'She told me he was not getting a divorce and this shocked me.'

Soon afterwards Ray made an excuse and they went. Driving away, he calmly assured the girl that he was separated and that his mother had over-reacted. She accepted the explanation, and continued to meet him for another couple of months, but she grew suspicious again because of the irregularity of his visits.

One day she decided to ring the farm to see if she could find out the truth about Ray's marriage. A woman whom she took to be his mother answered the call and was very short with her. About three weeks later Ray suddenly turned up. He told her he hadn't been in touch 'because he'd been on holidays.' They talked over their relationship for an hour, then parted.

She didn't see him again for more than two years.

LATE August, 1962. Luck, all of it bad, led Lesley back to Ray. When she had fallen pregnant the previous year her parents had offered to support her and the baby if she chose not to marry. The same option, a year later, was probably still open. But only if she could swallow her pride, and purge herself of the notion of getting back with Ray.

The trouble was that Lesley, at heart, was a romantic. And she was still naive enough not to suspect what was happening behind her back.

She was not to discover for years that the real purpose of Ray's absences in the month leading to the baby's birth was to see the girl in Preston.

Lesley trustingly assumed that Ray had simply wanted to visit Mavis's mother and his 'aunt' Joyce.

The first step on the road to a reconciliation was when Lesley went with her parents to visit her elder sister Barbara, who was married and living in Melbourne. By chance, Lesley had heard that Harold and Mavis were visiting Mavis's mother in Preston. Kind to a fault, she felt sorry that Mavis and her mother had not seen Susan for a long time, so she asked her brother-in-law to drive her and the baby to Preston to visit them.

When they arrived, Harold was unusually friendly. He told her that Ray was staying at Joyce's place, not far away, and suggested that she should go and see him. Lesley was surprised and pleased at this apparent change in Harold's attitude towards her and the baby. So she went.

Even at this stage, it wouldn't have taken much to save Lesley from disaster. Ray could have been out, or he could have had another woman with him, or he could have been in one of his surly moods.

But chance played Lesley a dirty trick that day: Ray felt like company. While Harold drank beer in the kitchen with Joyce, he spent an hour with Lesley and the baby. She said she didn't want to live with his parents any longer. He said he would be able to get a job on a farm somewhere so that they could live their own lives.

Lesley took the bait. So completely that she got Ray to drive her to her sister's place immediately to tell her family and to pick up her luggage. That night they slept together at Joyce's. Next day they drove to Benalla, to stay for a few weeks in the house Harold and Mavis were renting while their new place was built at Chiltern. Ray started looking for a job.

The trap was sprung, but Lesley couldn't yet feel its jaws.

THE first pang of fresh doubt about Ray struck Lesley even before they left Benalla. She was looking for something in his car when she noticed a name and address scrawled on the back of the sun visor. A woman's name, a Numurkah address. Pricked by jealousy, Lesley recalled the evening two months before when her father and brother John had come home from working for the State Rivers at Numurkah, and told her they'd seen Ray sitting in a car with a teenage girl. At the time Lesley had tried to dismiss it, but now she was furious.

In the glove box, she found a letter Ray had written to the other girl but not posted. The letter not only made it clear how intimate he'd been with the girl, it was more than he'd ever written to Lesley.

As soon as she caught Mavis alone, Lesley told her the name of the girl, and asked if she knew anything. Mavis admitted that Ray had brought the girl to the farm at Yarroweyah, and told Lesley how she had warned her that Ray was married and not about to be divorced.

It was the best Mavis could do, but cold comfort for Lesley. She found it hard to handle the first obvious evidence of Ray's infidelity.

STANHOPE, late 1962. It was a lousy way to spend a first wedding anniversary. Ray milked, the same as any other evening in the seven-day working week of a dairy farm labourer. Lesley looked after the baby, and did the cooking and washing.

The anniversary wasn't mentioned. Ray didn't care; Lesley didn't dare bring it up.

Within weeks of Ray getting the job at George Varcoe's farm Lesley's optimism about a fresh start away from his parents had trickled away, replaced by the depressing thought that his strange behaviour around the time of Susan's birth had not been left behind. It seemed an unnatural and virulent jealousy. When they had first married she and Ray had 'got on really normally and well most of the time,' she later recalled. But as her stomach had started to swell and her thoughts and conversation had turned to the baby, Ray had become disturbed, had 'started to belt me and started disappearing.'

At Stanhope, with the novelty of the reconciliation worn off, the beatings and the disappearances resumed, setting a pattern that was to last for the next three years. It wasn't made any easier when, just before Christmas, Lesley found she was pregnant again. Often, after milking, Ray would say he was going spotlighting. Other nights he would not bother with excuses, but would silently get cleaned up, change into sharp clothes and drive off. He would come home after midnight; usually Lesley could smell perfume on him or found lipstick on his shirt. When she spoke to him about this, he told her to mind her own business.

Even though she 'loved him and accepted it,' Ray's infidelity hurt. Her bruised feelings were stirred into rebellion one night when she saw the Varcoes' son pick up Ray at the farm's front gate and drive away for the evening. Lesley was angry; she picked up the baby and walked to the Varcoes' house and there, choking back tears, told them she would prefer it if their son didn't go out with Ray. She didn't tell them she suspected Ray was chasing 'tarts' in nearby towns when supposedly spotlight shooting. But Mr and Mrs Varcoe took Lesley seriously, and spoke to their son before he went out to milk next morning.

As soon as Lesley caught sight of Ray walking back from the dairy that day she knew he was angry, and braced herself. He kicked open the door, abused her and hit her, although 'not as bad as he had on other times.' It made no difference; he kept going out.

On the farm Ray established a reputation as a hard worker, but he was restless. Once, Lesley's brother John visited them, and described a job interview he'd had with the Victoria Police a few weeks earlier.

Ray was fascinated with the prospect of uniforms, handcuffs, guns and fast cars. He questioned John closely about how difficult the entrance test was, and said he was thinking of recruiting.

'One thing,' John was to comment later, 'in those days he wouldn't have had any trouble passing the physical.'

TONGALA, late 1963. The Varcoes had thought well enough of Ray's work to put him in charge of their other property, at Tongala, with their son and another young man, Keith Trezise, working under him. Trezise lived in another house on the Tongala farm with his wife Moira. He got to know Ray well over the following months, during which time he and young Varcoe often accompanied him on shooting trips. Both Trezise and young Varcoe noticed that Ray was often quiet and sometimes moody, but each put it down to 'domestic trouble.'

Neither suspected how much trouble there was, nor all the causes of it. Since moving from Stanhope Ray had gone out at night less often, but he distressed Lesley in other ways.

It was a big farm with several staff houses. In one of them lived a couple with two teenage daughters. One of the girls flirted constantly with Ray, and Lesley suspected them of having an affair. One night the two girls called in and, while one talked to Lesley in the living room, the other slipped into the kitchen with Ray. A few minutes later Lesley, suspicious and angry, walked into the kitchen to find Ray with his arm around the giggling girl. For once, she took the initiative. Shaking with rage, she yelled at Ray to 'wake up to himself' and slapped him on the face. Then she turned to the embarrassed girl and ordered her out.

As the sisters went out the door, Lesley's control of the situation evaporated. Ray abused her for embarrassing him, then he hit her. That night he forced her to sleep on the floor. She was eight months pregnant.

On August 6, only weeks after her eighteenth birthday, Lesley gave birth to a son. This time Ray took a little interest in the child. He called him Raymond Harold.

R AY had to have other women, one was never enough, Lesley often reflected later. 'But he was still jealous of me, sort of like a kid. It was as if I wasn't allowed to have any friends … '

New friends, even casual acquaintances, weren't much for Lesley to want, in circumstances which tied her to looking after two infants in a farm house in a district where she had no relatives. But the flaw in her husband's personality made it impossible. He treated Lesley's feelings as brutally as he did the cows, which he thrashed with a leg chain if they upset him in the dairy.

Geography and shared circumstances made it natural that Lesley would strike up a friendship of some sort with Moira Trezise, the wife of the other farm hand, even if they had little in common otherwise. When Moira was due to have a baby, Lesley lent her a baby bath, which little Raymond had outgrown. It was worth next to nothing, it was of no use to Lesley at that time, and she knew she could get it back later if she needed it. But when Ray happened to notice that the bath was gone, he ordered Lesley to get it back immediately. She was too frightened not to obey.

There was a worse humiliation in store.

A middle-aged couple, Joan and Leo Collins, lived nearby and visited them one evening. Ray rarely drank at home, but this night a bottle was produced and he had a couple of beers with the other man. The four were seated at the table chatting when Ray got to his feet as calmly as if he was going to fetch a bottle opener or a piece of firewood. Instead, he walked around the table to where Lesley was sitting and deliberately poured his glass of beer over her head.

She was devastated. Ray had made her look 'an absolute idiot.' And, worse, he had revealed himself in front of other people as frighteningly, bizarrely unpredictable. Lesley burst into tears, and ran to the bathroom, where she sat on the edge of the bath and sobbed. Mrs Collins followed her in and tried to console her. 'Don't worry about it, Lesley,' she said soothingly over and over, patting her head. After Lesley calmed down, the Collins left. They didn't visit again.

TONGALA, early 1964. Apart from losing his temper with cows, Ray rarely revealed the dark side of his nature to those he worked with. To Neville Varcoe he was 'a loner' with whom, according to other staff, he sometimes clashed over the running of the place, despite their earlier night-time outings together at the Stanhope farm.

'I worked virtually side by side with him seven days a week,' Varcoe was to recall grudgingly, 'and he could go a day without saying anything. But he did his job okay.' Apart from his quietness, the only faintly odd thing Varcoe was to admit noticing about Ray was that he often worked in bare feet, to the extent that his soles would crack.

Trezise, a keen shooter, occasionally went with Ray after

ducks on a nearby swamp, when Ray used an old shotgun. But he noticed that when they went spotlighting for rabbits and foxes Ray was a good enough shot that he swapped the gun for a rifle, an automatic .22 with a telescopic sight.

One night Ray, Trezise, Varcoe and his girlfriend went spotlighting over the border at Deniliquin. The others remembered, years later, how fast Ray drove. And how, at one stage, he steered with one hand and took pot shots out the window at signs and posts as they travelled.

KEITH Trezise knew Ray too well to like him. Despite often being taken into Ray's confidence during his disputes with Varcoe over running the farm, and despite a common interest in shooting, Trezise did not mix with Ray socially. There was something about him Trezise instinctively distrusted. But even he under-estimated Ray's deviousness.

Farmhand wages were notoriously low, and Trezise started to cast about for something better. He heard of a share-farming position on a farm at Ardmona, a district closer to Shepparton. It would be more demanding and responsible than a wages job, but with payment being a share of profits, it promised a lot more money. Trezise had a wife and new baby, and he was ambitious. He drove to Ardmona for an interview. He returned that night full of enthusiasm. It would pay twice his existing wages, and although there had been at least a dozen others interviewed, Trezise reckoned he was odds-on to get the job.

And he would have, if he hadn't talked so eagerly about his prospects in front of Ray next day. Nothing in Ray's manner signalled more than a passing interest, but when he knocked off that night he told Lesley the plan he'd quietly hatched. She thought it was a dirty trick, but her feelings had never worried Ray. He rang the farmer at Ardmona and persuaded him to interview one more applicant …

162

THE Gawnes were pleased with their last-minute choice. They had been on the verge of hiring Keith Trezise when the other fellow from Varcoes' had rung up. It had been a tough choice between the two; each was a keen, young married man with experience, and looked as if he would work hard and stay longer than a few months. But in the end they'd decided to take on the last applicant, Ray, because he seemed the 'less stroppy' of the two, Stewart Gawne recalled later. This impression was confirmed, a few days after Ray got the job, when Gawnes received a furious call from Trezise, who abused them for letting Ray 'cut under his neck.' Just before hanging up he warned: 'You'll be sorry when you find out what he's like.'

Gawnes dismissed it as sour grapes.

EIGHT

The accused, 1966-1972

S INGAPORE. February 11, 1972. It was six years to the day since Abina had died, and the bitter memories must have come streaming back to haunt Ian Urquhart as he sat on the plane from Sumatra, lulled by the whine of the jet turbines. The memories, he'd told his sister on his last visit home, he managed to block out most of the time, but they were never far away, even in the good times.

It was dark outside. Tiny lights flickered and winked in the ink below. From this height and distance, Singapore looked like an explosion of fireflies.

That morning, Ian had been ferried by helicopter to the mainland from the offshore drilling rig where he had worked for several months. Helicopter rides were no longer a novelty for the farm boy from Shepparton. As a maintenance specialist with a Canadian exploration company, he was flown from rig to rig, trouble-shooting.

It was a top job, and the money was three times that he would have been making in some garage back in Australia. Like a wattle seed that germinates after a bushfire, adversity had brought out the best in Urquhart. The knocks he'd taken in Shepparton after the murders had hardened his resolve not to waste the potential his family and friends had seen in him. With his Scottish instinct for making things work – including himself – he had made his name on the drilling rigs of Asia.

His engineer's ear would have caught the subtle change of pitch in the engines as the captain eased back the throttle ready to scythe off height in the approach to the runway. Below, in the airport's long-term car park, was the sports car he'd bought not long before. Ahead was a pleasant week with the friends he'd made in Singapore, then a quick trip home to Shepparton to see the family. After that, he was going to Canada: the firm had invited him and his mate on an all-expenses-paid trip to train for a promotion. It wasn't bad for a bloke three days short of his 25th birthday. Maybe even good enough to get married on, now that he had mustered the courage to tell his girl, the first one he'd been really keen on since Abina, about the nightmare he'd left behind.

At first, he hadn't known how to broach the subject, but after talking to Bob Dowdell on his last trip home, he'd realised that the best way was to tell her the whole story quietly. He had nothing to be ashamed of, and none of the Urquharts ever wanted sympathy from anyone.

Pride and toughness was bred into them. He just wanted her to understand the truth, he had told Mr Dowdell, the one policeman who had taken his part, who had believed absolutely in his innocence. Who, the Urquharts believed, had resigned from the force rather than tolerate some of the abuses of police power at Shepparton in 1966.

It wasn't easy telling anyone, let alone the girl you love, that you're the number one suspect for a double murder. That you've been tried, convicted and sentenced by rumour and innuendo ... even if the whole thing was started by a couple of standover policemen who had played the wrong hunch, but wouldn't admit it.

The trouble with the truth was that to an outsider it sounded no different from the cries of innocence from every criminal ever accused. No wonder he was bitter. He was trapped. No matter what he said, or didn't say, it would be taken as evidence against him. Nothing was going to change that unless the real murderer accidentally wandered into the police's arms. Until then, he was an exile ...

The plane taxied to the terminal. The sun-tanned Australian and his Canadian friend strolled down the gangway with the indifference of seasoned travellers, and set off to find their luggage, then the car park. The cream MG was in good order, the way Ian had always kept cars. The difference was that now he could afford the sort of machine he had coveted when he was eighteen.

He'd come a long way in six years. The Canadian settled into the passenger seat. The high-compression motor stuttered to life, roared, then dropped back to the sweet burble that made its owner's heart sing. Ian Duncan Ross Urquhart eased the car into gear, and drove out onto the highway to face his destiny. It was just on midnight.

S HEPPARTON, mid-1966. The longest journey starts with a single step, goes the proverb. For Ian Urquhart the road to Singapore and prosperity began the day he decided to leave his hometown. The two most senior policemen involved in the murder investigation in Shepparton, Matthews and Ford, had officially cleared him. They had come to the home of his sister, Heather, to dole out a few insincere platitudes about the necessity for tough investigating in such a terrible case. They did it grudgingly, it seemed to the Urquharts. And in the end it was meaningless, because it didn't make any difference to what people were saying about Ian.

'It was no use telling US!', Heather often said later, her eyes bright with emotion. 'We knew he was innocent. What they should have done was tell THEM,' she would add fiercely, sweeping her arm to take in all of Shepparton outside her own spotless cream brick house. The house where Ian had spent most of his time after coming in off the little fruit block at Lemnos where the six Urquhart children had been raised. The house which had become a refuge from gossip which held that he was a murderer.

Ian, his brother David was to say, 'could take it on the chin.' But he was tired of taking it. He had given Shepparton plenty of opportunity to grasp that he'd been cleared, that there was not a scintilla of evidence against him, but most of the townspeople ignored the facts.

The mob wanted someone to blame for the murders; until somebody better came along Urquhart was it. Everybody knew someone who knew a policeman who was positive that the murderer had 'already been interviewed,' but 'they just don't have enough evidence to charge him.'

These roundabout accusations even made it into print, not surprising considering the warm working relationship between certain policemen and a local reporter who confused gossip and facts.

Ian didn't make a fuss about it. One day after work he told the family that he'd given notice at Smith's and was leaving town to work in a garage at Wangaratta, more than an hour's drive to the north-east. But Wangaratta wasn't far enough. One weekend, Ian was visiting his family in Shepparton when one of his friends produced a newspaper that mentioned his name in connection with the murder.

Two decades later Heather couldn't remember the date. But she could remember the look on Ian's face, and what he said. 'That's it,' he had said quietly. 'I'm going.' He left a few days later, heading north-west. He travelled light: spare jeans and tee-shirts, a couple of tools, a blanket. And in his pocket, scrawled on a piece of paper, the Perth address of cousins he'd never met.

WITH Ian gone, his mate Peter Hazelman lost one of the few people who knew he was innocent of implication in the murders. He stood condemned by gossip as Urquhart's 'accomplice'. The malevolence of public feeling was astounding, and did not abate. Hazelman, too, felt the urge to leave town, but was reluctant to go too far because of family ties. He took a live-in job in the machine shop of the Dookie Agricultural College which, although not far from Shepparton, kept him away from town during the working week. And weekends as well, if he felt inclined to stay in his quarters or visit elsewhere.

But Dookie was too close. 'The whole bloody town thought I was guilty,' he was to say. After a year he took a job on one of the Bass Strait oil rigs off the Gippsland coast. He started as a rigger, and finished as a cook. The hours were long and the conditions tough, but the money was good ... and no-one knew who he was. Almost two years later he took his last helicopter ride from the rig into Sale and went home to Shepparton. But nothing had changed. Peter Hazelman, like the Urquharts, had to endure the sting of gossip, ostracised by people he'd once thought were friends.

Of the two youths, Peter was more vulnerable than Ian. Once, driving home from Dookie, he accidentally ran over a hare and killed it. Because he knew his mother fancied hare soup he picked it up and brought it home, but she noticed tears in his eyes when he brought it into the kitchen. 'I'm sorry I killed it,' he said to her sadly, looking at the blood-matted fur and glazed eyes of the little body.

Years earlier, as a young apprentice, his mates had pestered him to go shooting with them on duck opening day. When he came home, his mother recalled, 'he was absolutely disgusted to think people could kill birds like that.' He never went shooting again.

Such a gentle personality did not have the stubborn streak that guarded Urquhart's feelings. Peter's sheltered upbringing in a comfortable, law-abiding family had left him ill-prepared for treatment calculated to break down the resistance of hardened criminals. Because he had been brought up to expect justice from the law, he was shocked by the fact that the system he had believed in could persecute the innocent. Whereas Ian and his family were left simmering with silent anger, Peter was too bewildered even for that. 'Let sleeping dogs lie ... the police were just doing their job,' he was to mumble whenever the subject was raised in the next twenty years.

Only those who knew him knew how deeply the false accusations had scarred his soul.

WESTERN Australia, late 1966. Ian reached Perth the long way round. The details of his odyssey were hazy to those at home; he had never been a letter writer. But he talked later of gouging opals at Coober Pedy, and working a few casual jobs as he threaded his way to the north-west corner of Australia. There, he took a job looking after the motor on a water-drilling rig somewhere between Roebourne and some of the hottest, most desolate country on the continent. But that suited Ian: it was as far as he could get from Shepparton on Australian soil. Later, he was to go further. But first there was the trip south to Perth, and a visit home for Christmas.

Ian's uncle, Andrew Urquhart, was incredulous, then proud

that his brother's boy had crossed Australia with no more than 'a blanket and a spanner.' There was a touch of wanderlust about the lad, but hadn't Andrew himself migrated when he wasn't much older? It was in the blood.

In the weeks that followed that summer Ian formed a lasting impression on the uncle and cousins he'd never met before. He was resourceful, self-reliant and helpful. He checked and worked on every car in the family without being asked, repaired his uncle's lawn mower, then looked for other odd jobs to do around the house.

He hated being idle. With his faded jeans, his motorbike, his desert suntan and his nomadic existence of the past few months he seemed 'a bit of a harem scarum' in the staid suburban world of his cousin Bess.

'But he had a heart of gold. He was a capable boy who could stand on his own two feet, and he never said he'd do a thing and then not do it,' she was to say.

The family was aware of the trouble which Ian had left behind; his sister Heather had sent them letters and newspaper clippings. But it was never mentioned until one day when Ian was alone with Bess.

He said to her quietly: 'I was supposed to have been in strife – but I had nothing to do with it.' No fuss. No anguished explanations or complaints. He was, as his brother said, taking it 'on the chin'.

Ian left as suddenly as he had come. His relatives waved goodbye and watched the motorbike clatter to the end of their street. They didn't see him again.

SHEPPARTON, December 1966. Ian rode into town, tired, dirty and pleased to be home in time for Christmas. He went straight to his brother's place and surprised him when he came home from work, still at the tractor section at Smith

Motors. Then his brother rang everybody with the news. That night the family gathered to eat together, welcome their little brother, and hear the tales of his travels.

A memorable homecoming. But beyond the warm glow of the family hearth Shepparton gave the 'accused' an icy reception. He had, according to the slander-mongers, proved his guilt by leaving town in the first place. By coming back, of course, he was showing his contempt for the law.

Ian couldn't win. He was resigned to that, and shrugged it off. Besides, he had developed a taste for travel. Within months he was to be working on a drilling rig working off the West Australian coast. It was the first of a series of jobs which were to lead him to Sumatra and Singapore.

SHEPPARTON, July 1970. This time Peter Hazelman was going further than Bass Strait. It was more than four years since the murders, but the pressure hadn't eased. He was going to Mt Isa and maybe overseas. It didn't matter, as long as he was a long way from Shepparton.

He knew there were other innocent victims besides himself and Ian Urquhart who felt the same way. Max Hart and Jan Frost were justifiably bitter about how they had been treated by the police, the media and the public.

They were to be married that October, and later to spend five years in New Guinea.

There were others who couldn't as readily avoid the casual cruelty of gossip. Peter's mother had suffered in silence, as she was to for years. When Peter had gone to Sale to work on the oil rigs his mother had confided to a woman she thought was her friend that 'he couldn't stand the insinuations.'

To which the woman had replied tartly: 'Well, that's something you and Peter have to live with for the rest of your lives.'

Mrs Hazelman never spoke to that woman again. But she couldn't stop speaking to everybody who slandered her son; it would have cut her off from almost everyone she knew. Every week someone would assure her blithely that Ian Urquhart had killed Abina Madill and Garry Heywood, regardless of the fact that by saying so they were accusing her son of complicity in murder. The stricken mother's usual answer was: 'Well, my Peter was with Ian all that night, and I know he didn't do anything.'

Mostly, her tormentors would shrug this off with a scornful look that might have sparked hatred in a less generous spirit than Mrs Hazelman's. But she was a Christian woman who tried hard not to hold grudges.

'If it had been their children accused perhaps I would have been the same,' she mused later, 'although I like to think I wouldn't judge them like that.'

When Peter left for Mt Isa she wasn't to see him for another six years, and rarely after that, because he married and moved to Darwin. But time didn't heal the wounds for either mother or son. Each day Mrs Hazelman was to recite the prayer which had already helped her through the worst time of her life:

God give to me for just this day,
That calm serenity for which I pray,
That I may say 'Thy will be done,'
When I must accept things as they come.

S HEPPARTON, late 1971. Heather was serving a customer at Fairley's clothes store when a flash of lemon-coloured silk caught the corner of her eye. 'What a beautiful shirt,' she thought as she bent over the parcel she was wrapping. It wasn't until the customer walked away that she realised the man in the silk shirt was still near the counter.

She looked at his face, and gasped with joy. It was Ian. He loved surprise visits. But not long ones. As with Ian's other rare trips home, it was brief; he came to Shepparton only to see his family.

He had decided on a whim to jam a flight home in to a week's shore leave from the rigs. He had stepped off a plane at Tullamarine, hired a car and driven straight to Shepparton without pausing even to make a telephone call. He had gifts for everyone in the family.

They gathered at David Urquhart's place to celebrate the homecoming with a chorus of excited questions. 'None of us had been overseas – Ian was a bit of a hero,' his brother-in-law, Bill Halsall, said later.

Heather always made pavlova for family events, and at the end of the week she made a huge one for Ian's farewell at David's place.

Late in the evening Heather's two young sons were tired, so she ushered them out to the makeshift bed rigged up in the family station wagon.

She asked them to say goodbye to Ian, explaining that they wouldn't be seeing him again because he was leaving early next morning. The younger boy started sobbing; he could not be convinced that Ian would ever come back. In the end, Ian himself went out to the car and talked to the child for half an hour, lulling him into a restless sleep. But the little boy's instinct was right.

S HEPPARTON. February 12, 1972. A drowsy, summer Saturday afternoon like any other, except that in Shepparton people remembered it was the sixth anniversary of the week Abina Madill and Garry Heywood were murdered. Heather Halsall had been playing tennis. When she got home she sensed something wrong even before her husband spoke.

His voice was carefully controlled. 'Come in and sit down,' he said, 'I want to tell you – ' Before he could finish she was yelling: 'What's wrong? What is it?' There'd been an accident, he said haltingly, groping for words to soften the stark facts relayed by the police.

A car accident in Singapore. Just after midnight, near the airport. Ian and his Canadian mate. Both killed.

SHEPPARTON. February 17, 1972. The mourners gathered in knots outside the Scots Presbyterian Church, where Abina Madill's funeral service had been held six years earlier. Bob Dowdell sat in his car and watched, his mind drifting back to the last time he'd seen Ian … it had been the previous year, during Ian's last trip home. Each time the boy came back to Shepparton he had made a point of coming to see Bob. But this time he had wanted more than the pleasure of seeing an old friend. He'd been anxious, and wanted advice. So badly that he had waited for hours in the reception lounge of Dowdell's motel while the former policeman attended to urgent business. When they finally had a chance to speak privately, Ian had come straight to the point.

He said he'd fallen in love with a girl in Singapore, and he would like to ask her to marry him. But he was worried about whether he should tell her of the accusations levelled at him in Australia. Bob Dowdell had been unequivocal. 'You must tell her exactly what happened,' he had said. 'The truth. That you've been accused, you're the prime suspect but that you are innocent. If she loves you, she will marry you.'

It was what Ian had wanted to hear. They'd shaken hands and parted, Dowdell joking that the next time they met would be at Ian's wedding.

And here it was his funeral, he thought morosely. Just when things were going so well for the boy.

174

Dowdell's reverie was broken by approaching footsteps. He looked up, and stared hard at the well-dressed former detective walking towards him. He was a man he'd never had any time for when they worked together, and one of several unwelcome faces at the funeral service. Not just detectives but a reporter who'd caused the Urquharts a lot of grief. The retired detective stopped beside Dowdell's car. He bent down to speak. He oozed feigned friendliness, but there was no mistaking the triumph in his smile.

'Well, that bastard got his just deserts,' he said.

Bob Dowdell just shook his head in disgust. They couldn't even let the kid be buried in peace, he thought. One day they might get it into their heads that he was innocent.

Dead innocent.

NINE

The invisible man, 1968-1982

MELBOURNE, February 1968. There is nothing to distin-guish applicant number 5671 from countless other aspiring tram conductors. Nothing, that is, that reveals itself in a routine scanning of his application form. The primitive spelling and the sudden shifts from clumsy lower case to even clumsier capitals, often in the space of one word, hardly raise an eyebrow among those whose job it is to push through the fresh intake of recruits. The list of personal details on the form could have come from any one of sheafs of them stacked in some obscure in-tray at the Tramways Board ...

'Address: Preston. Age, 23. Birthplace: Melbourne. Height (without shoes): 5 feet 10 inches. Weight: 11 stone 3. Education: third form. Have you at any time been employed in the Board's service? Have you previously applied for employ-ment in the Board's service? Have you at any time been charged with an offence? War service?' No, no, no, and nil. As a profile of the average conductor it seems hard to beat. But on the reverse side of the application form there is a falsehood woven into the simple answers, a clue to the applicant's secret fears and motives which is to be hidden in the archives of the Tramways Board for seventeen years.

The clue lies in the answers supplied to a section of the form, under the heading: 'Particulars of previous employment during the last 5 years:'

Here, the applicant has laboriously printed the names of three previous employers, and the place and duration of employment with each. Only the particulars of the first entry are anywhere near truthful: 'K. Goode, Tallondoon (sic), March 1967 (to) Dec 1967.'

The second employer he gives as 'D. Clark, Mayron, 2½ years (to) Dec 1966.' This not only gives the wrong initial of a man whose first name the applicant knows well, but mispells Mayrung as 'Mayron'.

Both are convenient slips for someone trying to make it hard to check how long he really did work for the Clarks, but the mistakes could conceivably be genuine.

What cannot be accidental is the substitution of two-and-a-half years for the correct period of only eight months. The falsehood is reinforced in the details provided for the third employer: 'R. Gawne, Ardmona, 18 months (to) July 63.'

In a few strokes of the pen applicant 5671 places himself some three years and many kilometres from Ardmona in 1966. None of which is of any interest to the personnel section of the Tramways Board in 1968.

He starts training as a conductor on March 5, sells his first ticket ten days later. A month later his driver's licence expires. He does not renew it for almost ten years and as many changes of address, none of them recorded in electoral rolls. It is as if he wants to disappear from official records. To become invisible.

FOR Lesley, the nightmare of living in fear of Ray was over. But he and his parents were determined to punish her for leaving him by cutting her off from her children. Raymond junior and Mandy had stayed with Ray's parents while Lesley and Ray had visited Townsville. As soon as they got back to Victoria, Ray had taken Susan from Lesley's parents and sent her to stay with his cousins at Rosewhite, while he went to Melbourne to look for work. He had also filed for divorce.

When Ray came to take Susan the little girl was terrified. 'My Daddy doesn't love me,' she sobbed, cowering behind a chair. 'I want to stay with Nanna and Pop.' It was the last time Lesley was to see any of her children for more than four years.

Lesley stayed with her parents at Yarrawonga for three months, working in a milk bar. She felt powerless, as she'd always done, against the combined wills of Ray and his father. Even Mavis, with whom she'd once got on passably well, had hated her for running away from Ray at the beginning of the year. Harold, to Lesley's everlasting chagrin, refused to acknowledge Ray's abominable treatment of her. She was often to torment herself later with fears for the welfare of her children.

But at the time she faced a dreadful choice: either she stayed away from Ray and was persecuted by not being allowed to see the children, or she let herself be cowed into a life of degradation and fear. She decided not to be blackmailed, and resolved to establish a new life for herself.

In the middle of the year Lesley moved to Melbourne and took a job with the motor registration branch. Had she stepped on the wrong tram during her first couple of months in town, she might have come face to face with Ray, but she didn't know that. She thought he was still working on the farm at Tallandoon.

Lesley went home to Yarrawonga for Christmas, 1968, and

returned to Melbourne in the new year with the new man in her life, Gerald. A kind man who was the opposite of Ray in every way. The man she was to marry.

SHEPPARTON, late 1968. Colleen Knight, with two children, no husband and no money, had no choice. That was the way her mother saw it, anyway. After several months of having her strong-willed daughter and two infants under her roof the mother was enthusiastic about Colleen taking the house-keeping job she had found in the *Weekly Times*.

Colleen herself was not so sure; Tallandoon was a long way from anywhere. Besides, the advertisement said there was no objection to one child, and she had two.

But her mother was persistent. Reluctantly, Colleen answered the advertisement.

The farmer arrived on the doorstep a few days later, after calling to say he was coming. He introduced himself as Ray, and said he'd gone back to share farming after working in the city for a while.

Despite her doubts, Colleen was almost as impressed as the rest of her family. Her prospective employer was a strong-looking young man, dressed in a suit and driving a good car. He agreed to stay for a meal, and chatted pleasantly with the family. Later, he drove her to Tallandoon to see the farmhouse and to meet the Goodes, who owned the property. Then he took her back to Shepparton, and said she could have a week to think it over. She had given him the impression she had only one child.

During the week Ray's parents came from Chiltern to visit Colleen's family. They, too, impressed Colleen's mother as 'nice people' – and prosperous ones. She took Colleen aside and said meaningfully: 'You won't get a better chance than this.' Colleen decided to take the job.

TANGAMBALANGA, early 1969. Colleen wasn't sure how it had happened, but Ray had gained a hold over her. It was something that was to puzzle her for years, the way he could fascinate women and yet be so disliked by men.

In her case it had started when she admitted to him, early in the short time they'd stayed at Tallandoon, that she in fact had two children and had left one with her mother. That she had lied didn't seem to worry him, but as soon as her second child arrived, he stopped paying her the agreed wages. This worried Colleen, but she didn't leave. She was twenty, she was lonely, and she was 'naive,' she said later.

Whatever the reason, she was sleeping with him.

MELBOURNE, January 1970. Four years after the Shepparton murders, the mystery still fascinated reporters. On January 20 the Melbourne *Sun* carried a prominent story revealing that police in all states were looking for a man falsely reported drowned the previous year.

Detectives believed that he was alive and that he was a likely suspect for five murders, including that of Garry Heywood and Abina Madill.

The newspaper reported that homicide detectives had been interested in the man since early 1968. They had been told that he was absent from work in Melbourne on the day of the murders, and that several people had seen a man like him in Shepparton the same day. Early in 1969, police had been told that the suspect was missing, suspected drowned, at a beach resort. The man had dived and allegedly failed to surface, and a subsequent search had found no sign of him. The 'drowning' was viewed sceptically by homicide detectives, who launched a new hunt for the suspect after reported sightings of him in Geraldton, Western Australia, in late 1969 around the time of a sex murder there, and in Sydney a few months later.

The new lead, like all the others, soon died: detectives found a man and cleared him from the inquiry through finger-prints. But the publicity about the 'faked' drowning had been considerable. Enough to have reached a dairy farm in a mountain valley in north-east Victoria.

S HEPPARTON, June 9, 1970. The Heywood-Madill murders were front page news again. After endless delays, the inquest had finally begun. Sixteen witnesses were called to recite the depressing litany of facts police had gathered within days of finding the bodies.

Despite thousands of hours of investigation there was nothing new to add. All the proceedings could do was re-open wounds for the Heywood and Madill families and the young people who had been with the murdered couple on the night they died.

Predictably, next day's headlines highlighted evidence that Abina and her friend had been drinking vodka and orange in Garry Heywood's car on the night of the murders. The evidence was of no more consequence than any other tendered that day, but it titillated the notions of teenage excess that had dominated gossip about the case.

Evidence was also carefully led to put on the record that Ian Urquhart was 'very annoyed' when told that Abina had gone with Garry. Urquhart, then in Singapore, might have been 'officially cleared', but it was plain that the trail was being blazed to charge him if a sliver of evidence turned up.

Senior Constable Peter Parkinson told the coroner that 3478 people had been interviewed, and that investigations were continuing. An inquest was no place for innuendo, gossip and speculation; so there was no reference to newspaper stories the previous year quoting unnamed police sources as saying they believed 'they have already interviewed the murderer – but can't act because of insufficient evidence.' In answer to questions put by former homicide detective Henry Morrison, who was assisting the coroner, Senior Constable Parkinson explained that the four-year delay was because of the hundreds of leads that had been followed.

'On many occasions we had hoped to solve the case, but without result,' he said.

The coroner, Mr H. E. McCallum, SM, found that Abina Madill and Garry Heywood had been murdered by a person or persons unknown, in the early hours of February 11, 1966.

It was beginning to look like the perfect crime.

TANGAMBALANGA, January 1971. Colleen thought herself lucky if she got away from the farm once a month. When she wasn't in the house cooking and cleaning for Ray and the five children, she helped outside, where there were 150 cows to milk and 200 pigs to raise. Unpaid drudgery, she was to complain later.

With each passing week the web of circumstance had made it a little harder to extricate herself and her own two children. First she had fallen into a de facto relationship, then she had fallen pregnant. Even that, she was to say, was Ray's way of making sure she stayed under his control.

After two years Colleen knew the viciousness of Ray's temper, and had been on the receiving end of it several times. But she had missed one of the worst exhibitions; the day he cornered a dog and, frenzied, kicked it until its ribs were smashed. The animal was so badly injured it could barely crawl. Ray then picked up something and clubbed it to death. The savagery of the attack seared itself in the memory of a child who was watching. That child never trusted Ray again.

But Colleen trusted him, in a way difficult for some people to understand. Her hardy nature tolerated Ray's violent streak where a more vulnerable woman might have fled. Ray worked hard, earned good money (though she saw little of it) and on his good days was pleasant enough company. All of which made the events of January 15 the harder for her to comprehend ...

There was nothing in Ray's manner to betray his intentions. The night before, he had said to Colleen that after the morning milking he would go fishing on the Hume weir, then return to pick up the family and go for a picnic in the afternoon. She had been pleasantly surprised.

Next morning, Ray put his rod in the green Falcon station wagon he'd bought two weeks earlier, and drove off. Colleen went inside to prepare the picnic lunch. She wouldn't to see him again for three months.

When Ray hadn't returned at lunchtime, Colleen was annoyed. By the time she and the children did the afternoon milking she was fretful. After serving a hurried meal, she rang the police. They found the new station wagon just on nightfall, then the boat Ray had hired moored to the branches of one of the many drowned trees in the reservoir.

When the police relayed this to Colleen, she was unsure about what might have happened. Ray was a strong swimmer, but with hidden branches under the water there was a chance he had got into trouble.

The search lasted two days. While police dragged the weir around where the boat was found, Colleen waited on the bank, fearing what they might find. One officer had warned her that after 48 hours in the water 'a body isn't a pretty sight'.

Days passed. The mystery excited local interest. Then a story in the Albury *Border Mail* prompted a taxi driver to tell police that he'd picked up a man matching Ray's description near the weir and driven him to Wodonga railway station. The story was picked up by the Melbourne newspapers.

Colleen was stunned. It was the first time he'd left her. For a few days the neighbours were sorry for the woman stranded with five children, and helped with the farm work, while Ray's parents came and looked after the children. It was during this time that Ray's first wife, Lesley, arrived to collect her three children, but she went away empty handed. Colleen's step-father came to stay for a couple of weeks while the farm owner looked for a replacement share farmer. Then she packed five children and their meagre belongings into the new station wagon and went to stay with her family.

Lesley was in Yarrawonga visiting her parents when she heard that Ray was missing, feared drowned. Her first thoughts were for her children. She rang a solicitor, and on his advice set out to retrieve them from Crosthwaites' farm at Tangambalanga.

One of her brothers drove her to the district, but Lesley didn't know where the farm was. They stopped at the local police station for directions. It was a mistake.

Lesley worked out later that someone – probably Harold – had spoken to the policeman first, and persuaded him that she should not be helped.

'He wouldn't let me move,' Lesley said later. 'He made me sit outside his office for more than an hour. I think he rang up Colleen and warned her so she had time to hide my kids.' The long wait made Lesley's brother suspicious. He came into the police station, motioned Lesley outside, and asked around until they found directions to the farm.

But it was too late. When they got to the farm Harold met them, agitated and blustering. He insisted that Lesley's children weren't there. Lesley knew that they couldn't be far away. Colleen, the housekeeper she had heard that Ray employed, was there with her two children. Colleen's swollen stomach testified that there would soon be a sixth child to add to the collection.

Mavis ran out to see her. She was so distressed about Ray's disappearance that her bitterness towards Lesley over leaving the children was temporarily forgotten. She was crying. But not, strangely, because she was sure that Ray had drowned. She threw her arms around Lesley and said, sobbing, that there was a rumour someone had seen Ray on the Melbourne train at Wodonga wearing nothing but his underpants.

'He wouldn't do that, would he, Lesley?' Mavis appealed desperately, more in hope than conviction.

Lesley comforted her as she would a child. 'No,' she said, 'of course he wouldn't.' But she didn't believe her own words. She thought Ray capable of anything.

MELBOURNE, early April, 1971. Colleen's brother-in-law, Ken, was driving east along Barkers Road on his way to work when, from the corner of his eye, he saw a familiar figure. A burly man with sandy hair and a match sticking from the side of his mouth. He was stepping out from an old private hotel a few hundred metres past the Kew tram depot.

For a few seconds Ken was perplexed. Then he realised. It was Ray, the farmer Colleen had been living with, the one who'd disappeared. The match in the mouth was a habit of Ray's which Ken had noticed when they'd visited the farm at Tallandoon.

Ken waited for a break in the traffic, swung his car into a U-turn and drove back towards the city for a second look. There was no mistake. He did another U-turn, pulled up at a tram stop and waited.

When Ray came in sight, walking slowly along the footpath, Ken stepped out and leaned on the mudguard. Ray didn't notice him until he spoke.

'Howya going?' Ken said sardonically. For once, Ray looked startled. Ken was running late for work in Croydon, so he arranged to meet him at the Beehive Hotel, opposite the tram depot, at five o'clock that afternoon. 'And if I'm late, wait for me,' he warned.

Ken had good reasons for wanting to talk to Ray. The main one was that his wife, Winnie, Colleen's step-sister, had spent weeks helping Colleen to cope ever since Ray's disappearance. Ken couldn't see why the rest of the family should be saddled with Ray's responsibilities because Ray chose to run away.

He said as much when they met after work, but Ray was unrepentant. 'If you tell anyone where I am I'll just disappear again,' he said.

Ken knew he meant it, so he changed tack. He told Ray that his parents should be told he was safe because his mother had been diagnosed with terminal cancer, and her fears for him were accelerating her decline. This was true, as Ken had driven Mavis to Melbourne for treatment after visiting Colleen at the farm. Ray grudgingly agreed. He slept on the couch at Ken's house in Richmond that night. Next day Ken rang Ray's parents with the news.

Harold answered the telephone. He sounded relieved but not surprised that Ray had turned up. He'd done it before, he grunted. Ken didn't expect any thanks from Harold.

During the confusion after Ray's disappearance he had got to know Harold well enough to dislike him.

Although Ken had used his own car to move Ray and Colleen's belongings from the farm, Harold had never offered to pay for petrol.

It was pretty tough, thought Ken, considering that Harold had immediately claimed Ray's new Falcon station wagon, leaving the pregnant Colleen and five children without a car.

The police knocked on Ken's door a day after he rang Harold. They wanted to know where Ray was. Ken told them Ray had slept on the couch that morning, but that he didn't know where he'd gone. It was no use chasing him, he explained, because he would only disappear again. The police seemed to accept his explanation, and went off to pursue more urgent matters than a runaway husband.

Colleen was not so easily deflected. She was almost ready to have the baby, and needed money. She turned up next day asking if Ken would contact Ray for her. Instead, he drove her to the private hotel in Barker's Road where Ray had been boarding, 'and left her to it.' She found him. They were reunited on April 5, 1971, and she gave birth seven days later. A son. They called him David.

Two months later Colleen's mother gave them the deposit on a house in Goodwin Street, Richmond, just across a back lane from Ken and Winnie's place.

S HEPPARTON, July 21, 1971. The divorce, after all Lesley's waiting, was an anti-climax. Her solicitor had telephoned her at short notice to say that the case would be heard the following day. Lesley had taken the train from Melbourne to her parents' place at Yarrawonga that night, then asked her father to drive her to court at Shepparton next morning.

Lesley, her father and the solicitor were standing on the footpath near the courthouse when Ray and his parents, and Colleen and her mother, pulled up next to them in Ray's car. There was an uneasy silence as the group alighted and found a spot to wait.

The hearing was late in the afternoon. Lesley was surprised at how quickly a decade of marriage was dissolved. All she could remember later was signing some affidavits and listening to the drone of routine legalities from the bench and the bar table.

She hardly noticed that her Brunswick address was read out as part of the proceedings.

DONVALE, July 26, 1971. *Susanne Y states: 'I am a married woman with three children. I am 25 years of age ... at about 10pm in the evening I was in my home with my children. The children were all in bed and my husband was out visiting friends. I was washing the kitchen and dinette floor. I was leaving the dinette area and going to the laundry to get some clean water in a bucket.*

'As I went into the hall I saw a person walking along the passage towards me.

'At first glance I thought it was my husband because he was wearing similar type clothes. When I first saw this man he was about twenty feet from me. The lighting in the hall is not a bright light and the hall floor is three steps higher than the floor I was on. As soon as I looked up I realised it was not my husband. This man was wearing a stocking type mask over his head.

'I immediately became frightened and could feel my heart thumping. I screamed a couple of times but I think it was more from surprise and shock than an effort to attract any attention.

'He then lifted his right hand and I saw that he was pointing a knife at me. The knife was about a foot long. When he produced the knife he was about ten feet from me. I heard him say something like: "Keep quiet. Don't scream. I don't want to hurt you."

'He spoke quietly and seemed to be asking me to be quiet rather than telling me. I also noticed he seemed to have a slight accent. English or Scottish.

'I backed away from him into the dinette and then into the kitchen until I had backed in the corner at the pantry door. He followed me as I backed away from him and continued to hold the knife up in my view ... I was scared of the knife. When I backed into the corner, I screamed again. He again said: "Be quiet. I don't want to hurt you," or similar words.

'I then asked him what he wanted and he said: "Have you got any money in the house?" I said: "No. My husband hasn't been paid yet." Then he said: "You had better get undressed then." I said: "Oh no. I have just had a baby." He said: "Yes, I know. Come on, I won't hurt you." I said: "Yes, you will. I have still got stitches in."

'When he first told me to get undressed, he put his hand between my legs, but took it away immediately. I then started pleading with him to leave me alone. I don't remember what I said. I remember that he appeared to be a bit nervous and unsure of himself but I was still very frightened of him.

'He asked me again if I had any money in the house, and I said I didn't. I did have about $40 in the dressing room beside the bedroom but as the children were up in that area of the house, I didn't want to take him there in case he did something to them.

'Then he told me he was going to tie me up. I said: "No, don't do that." He said: "Yes, then I'll go." I said: "Are you sure you'll go?" He said: "Yes, cross my heart."

'He then crossed his heart. He told me to hold my hands out and I put my hands together and held them out. He started to tie them with a stocking. I don't know where the stockings came from, I didn't see them in his hand before this.

'After he had started to tie my hands in front he changed his mind and said: "No, I had better tie them behind your back." He then told me to turn around and then tied my hands behind my back. Then he said: "Come on. I'll tie your feet." I asked him not to but he said: "Yes, otherwise you will run after me. You had better sit down somewhere."

'I then sat on the floor in the dinette with my back against the wall. He then tied my feet around the ankles with another piece of stocking. When he had finished tying my feet, he put his hands over my breasts ... '

MRS Y screamed again and her attacker ran from the house. She freed herself and rang police. Within four minutes an unmarked car arrived. In it were two detectives, John Levielle and Ken Mansell. Inside the house, Mansell saw bare footprints on the polished floorboards in the hall. Outside, he shone a torch in the garden. A plumbing trench had recently been filled in alongside the house, leaving the ground freshly dug. In it were dozens of muddy footprints, grouped under each window.

Mansell called his partner to show him. The offender had obviously studied his victim for a long time as she moved from room to room.

Later, after speaking to the woman, Mansell was struck by her statement that the attacker had understood when the woman told him she had been stitched after childbirth. It was almost certain, deduced Mansell, that they were looking for a married man with children.

Next day, Sergeant Dennis Hanna, stationed at Ringwood, came to interview Mrs Y and inspect the scene. He immediately noticed the similarity of the attempted rape to a rape in the same suburb eleven days earlier. Both Hanna and Mansell were later transferred to Shepparton.

It was there, eleven years later, that the pair realised the significance of the fingerprints found on a window ledge at the Donvale house that night. And of the fact the rapist carried stockings to tie up his victim.

RICHMOND, late 1971. The girl was fourteen, just old enough to mind Ray and Colleen's children after school. She was from a broken home, and had been forced to leave it. Being an unpaid babysitter of six children was not easy, but it seemed better than the misery of being rejected at home. Even the arguments and the undercurrent of violence between Ray and Colleen were bearable if she kept out of the way. One night the girl saw Ray beat Colleen until she was screaming with pain, fear and anger. Colleen's step-sister Winnie came running from her house across the street when she heard the noise. Winnie and her husband were tired of breaking up fights between Colleen and Ray, so she called the police. When Ray saw the blue uniform he controlled himself. He made no trouble, and for months afterwards was noticeably less inclined to belt Colleen.

The nightmare began, for the teenage girl, when Colleen weaned the baby and was able to go to work full-time. Because of changing shifts on the trams, Ray was often at home alone with her and the children.

The girl had never liked the look in Ray's eyes when she caught him watching her. With Colleen out of the way, he did more than look.

One night, ignoring the children, he calmly walked up to her and ran his hands over her body. She shrank with fear and loathing, but Ray took no notice. He picked her up, carried her to a bedroom and wrenched her clothes off.

She struggled, but it was an unequal contest. He was 27 years old and fourteen stone. She was fourteen and weighed seven stone. Besides, she had nowhere else to go, no-one to tell.

B RUNSWICK, late 1971. Lesley and Gerald were living in the same rented two bedroom flat they had at the time of Lesley's divorce hearing a few months before. They had one bedroom, and Lesley's aunt had the other. She was staying with the couple to offset their rent while they saved to buy a house for when they married.

Lesley's aunt was not usually nervous, so the night that she knocked on the couple's bedroom door to say there was a prowler outside, they were surprised and alarmed. While she was undressing she had seen someone looking in her window. Gerald rushed outside, but the intruder was gone. Lesley did not suspect then that she might have known who it was. Only later, when she remembered how her address was read out in the divorce hearing, did she begin to wonder.

A few weeks later, just before Christmas, Lesley asked her solicitor about obtaining access to her children. To her surprise, he told her she should have arranged access with her former husband immediately after the divorce hearing. She contacted Ray. They met in a car park in Flinders Lane near the Government offices where she worked.

Lesley was struck by his flabby appearance, and asked him if he had been drinking a lot. As she sat warily in the passenger seat of his car to discuss, as she thought, the children, she did not suspect she was to spend the next three hours fending off increasingly insistent proposals that they get back together. He told her that he 'didn't accept the divorce,' that he would be good to her if she returned to him. He even offered to buy her a new engagement ring, to replace the one she had lost when they had lived at Ardmona.

Lesley was incredulous. They had parted almost four years earlier, and each had started a new life with a new partner, but Ray seemed oblivious to reality. Obsessive, like a kid who wanted everybody else's toys as well as his own. There was something bizarre about it, Lesley thought. She was right. He married Colleen four weeks later.

SHEPPARTON, January 25, 1972. The wedding seemed to please both sets of parents more than it did Ray or Colleen. It was as if a pact had been made to match them the day more than three years before when Harold and Mavis had visited Colleen's mother to urge that Colleen become Ray's housekeeper. Colleen's memory of the events leading to the wedding was that Ray had visited his parents for a few days at Chiltern while she stayed at Shepparton with her mother. When he rejoined her he had suddenly announced that they should get married right away.

Colleen had agreed, to the delight of her mother. But her sister, Winnie, vehemently disagreed. Colleen persuaded her to be matron of honour for the wedding, but until the last moment she warned Colleen against the marriage. Winnie claimed to have a sixth sense, and she often told Colleen she sensed something wrong about Ray. Colleen was never to forget that, even walking down the aisle of the church, her sister whispered: 'It's not too late to get out of it.' When the service was over, she said to Colleen that the marriage wasn't binding if she didn't sign the register. Colleen signed it.

Outside the church, it was a warm summer day, and a happy one for Mavis, but she would die of cancer before the year was out.

MELBOURNE, November, 1973. Ray had been working full-time on the trams for more than two years, but it wasn't enough. He took a job with a security firm as a night patrolman using his own car. He was assigned a patrol route taking in most eastern suburbs. A few days after starting the new job, he called Lesley's older sister, Barbara, at Mooroolbark, an outer eastern suburb, and asked for Lesley's latest address and telephone number.

Barbara was worried about his motives, and warned him to 'leave Lesley alone,' because she had remarried and was pregnant. But Ray, calmly spoken and plausible, assured her that he wanted to talk to Lesley about the possibility of her taking custody of the children, which had been legally granted to him the previous year. Barbara agreed to give him the address and telephone number he wanted, but she was still anxious.

Lesley and Gerald spent the Melbourne Cup holiday visiting Gerald's sick father in the country. Soon after they got home that night Barbara rang to warn them that Ray had their address, by this time a house in Harold Street, Thornbury. Lesley's telephone rang at 10am next day. It was Ray. He was pleasant, but when he asked Lesley if it were true she was pregnant, she could tell he was jealous about it. 'He said he thought I'd never have got married again, after him,' she was to recall. 'He offered to bring the kids to me because he said he had split with Colleen, and didn't want to let her have them.'

Lesley's heart leapt, but she hid her emotion. She would agree, she said, only if Gerald approved and if they consulted a solicitor and had a binding custody agreement drawn up. After talking it over with Gerald, Lesley decided to go ahead with the proposal. Ray telephoned that night and promised he would bring the children to the house the following day. Lesley was excited. The last time she had seen the children was on an abortive access visit the previous year, when the children had been 'brainwashed into not having anything to do with me.' After that crushing experience Lesley had decided not to cause the children any more confusion, or herself any more unhappiness, by continuing to visit them. She was upset by the memory of standing on Colleen and Ray's doorstep and hearing her son Raymond ask: 'Who's that lady?'

This time, she thought, she would have a chance to win back her children's trust. She rang her parents, and asked them to come down from Yarrawonga to give her support when Ray brought the children. They arrived early next morning, pleased at the prospect of seeing the grandchildren they hadn't spoken to for almost five years. But their hopes were broken. No-one came. By nightfall they all knew it was just another example of Ray's cruelty.

After the evening meal, Lesley's father walked over to the

window to close the venetian blinds. He glanced outside into the evening gloom, then stepped back in surprise. There was someone outside, looking in. Gerald ran to the back door, but again he missed the intruder.

This time Lesley was certain she knew who it was. The coincidence was too great. Their second prowler in two years ... within 48 hours of Ray discovering her new address. Some coincidence.

MELBOURNE, February 1974. Ray was still driving without a licence. It hadn't prevented him from getting the security job four months earlier, nor from being issued with a permit to carry a pistol on February 15. The same week he bought a .32 calibre Webley and Scott automatic pistol and a set of handcuffs.

He did not have to be fingerprinted to get the permit – unlike police, who were automatically fingerprinted when joining the force. Ironically, later in 1974, police were to press for mandatory fingerprinting of all applicants for pistol licences, a recommendation that was still to be gathering dust in 1977.

It was sixteen years since he had last owned a new firearm, the rifle his father had bought for him in Myrtleford around the time he left school.

But in 1974 the gun dealer's book recording the transaction with Myrtleford's only gun dealer was destroyed in a flood. With the book went the last and best chance of tracing the rifle's owner.

MELBOURNE, March 1974. Lesley knew something was wrong as soon as she got up. It was about 11am, and her aunt and Gerald had gone to work hours earlier. Lesley, heavily pregnant, was returning to the bedroom from the bathroom when she again caught a whiff of the smell she had detected when she woke up. She wrinkled her nose, puzzled. Then she doubled back to the kitchen to check if the stove were leaking gas. It wasn't. Lesley walked to the front of the house again, and the pungent smell hit her nostrils. She went into the living room.

The stench of gas made her feel sick. Holding her breath, she went over to the gas heater. It had been turned on, but not lit. She flicked it off, then opened the windows and doors. It took an hour for the smell to clear.

Lesley was worried. The heater had not been used since the previous winter. There were no children in the house, and it was inconceivable that it could be turned on accidentally. If it wasn't Gerald or her aunt playing some sort of stupid joke, she thought numbly, there was only one explanation. That night Lesley told Gerald and her aunt what had happened. They were astonished. Neither had been in the living room that morning, let alone near the heater.

Lesley was convinced; someone must have climbed through one of the windows, and turned on the heater. Someone who had been watching the house, and knew its layout. Someone with a grudge. Ray.

G REENSBOROUGH, January 31, 1975. *Mrs M states: 'I am 23 years of age. I live with the man I am going to marry. Also my two children from my first marriage. I am a widow and have been for two and a half years.*

'I went to bed tonight at about 11pm. It was not long after my fiance had left to go to Sydney …I had my son sleeping in my bed with me and my daughter was in her cot in her room.

'About ten past four this morning, I woke up when I heard a noise. I didn't know what the noise was, but I did think that perhaps it was my little girl rattling the side of her cot, as one side is loose and makes a rattle … I waited for about five

minutes, then decided that the noise was coming from the laundry part of the house. The laundry is opposite my daughter's bedroom.

'I put the light on and saw a man standing in the doorway of the bathroom. He had his right arm raised above his head with a knife in it. The blade was pointing down ... the blade was about twelve inches long. When I saw the man I screamed as loudly as I could, about three or four times. Then he said to me: "Don't scream. I don't want to hurt you." He kept saying all the time that he didn't want to hurt me. I think he might have said once that he loved me.

'I said: "I have a girlfriend staying with me down in the end room and when she heard me screaming she probably got out the window and went down the street to get the police." I think he said: "It's a lie, no-one will see you for a couple of days until your husband gets back."

'I looked from the man's feet and knees up to the knife and noticed that his fly was undone and his "business" was hanging out. By "business" I mean penis ...

'The man walked towards me and put his hand on my shoulder. He still had the knife and I thought he was going to stab me. He forced me back towards the bed. His pants were already undone and he pulled them down with his left hand. Then he pulled my pants down.

'I was wearing the bottom half of my bikini. When they were round about my knees they just fell the rest of the way. He then undressed completely.

'He forced me across the bed. My son, who was sleeping with me, was sitting up in bed petrified. I think the guy said to my son to lie down and go back to sleep and he put a blanket over his head. He was lying on top of me when he put the blanket over my son. He put the knife down beside the bed on top of his clothes ... '

THE intruder raped Mrs M. She struggled and tried to push him away, and he said: 'Don't be scared, I won't hurt you. I have been waiting for this for a long time.' The victim thought she heard a noise and asked the rapist if he had someone with him. He said: 'No, this boy works alone.' Chillingly, he added that he'd been in the house before.

When the police came they found fingerprints. These were found to match fingerprints of an unknown person discovered at a rape scene in Donvale in 1971. It seemed certain he was the unknown offender the fingerprint people called the 'Donvale rapist.'

The victim described the rapist as in his late twenties, stout, with sandy hair and wearing dark shorts, blue singlet, blue tee shirt, and no shoes.

Much later, when re-interviewed, she was to add something else. He had an odour she couldn't identify.

OFFICER, mid-1975. Ray could not stay in one spot, and he preferred to have more than one job. After four years in the city he was share-farming again, renting out the little house in Richmond. Officer, in West Gippsland, was close enough to the eastern suburbs that he was still able to do night patrols for the security firm.

The farm had two houses. Ray and Colleen lived in the new house as part of the share-farming agreement. The old one was rented by tenants who were causing trouble, stealing milk from the bulk vat and cutting hoses used in the dairy. Ray had complained to the owner, Don Miriklis, saying he'd been forced to padlock the cowshed door to prevent thefts.

Miriklis tried to have the tenant's family evicted. A few days later, he visited the farm. Miriklis was standing in the yard talking to Ray when the tenant saw him and came out of the old house yelling abuse. 'You. I want to see you!' he shouted.

'You're kicking me out of the house. I'll get a gun and shoot you, you bastard.'

Miriklis was angry, but not frightened. He said sarcastically: 'Well, get a gun and shoot me,' thinking that would end the exchange. Suddenly, Ray butted in. He jabbed his finger at the tenant and snarled: 'Back off, or I'll get a gun and blow your head off … I've done it before.' The tenant retreated to the house without any argument. 'Ray sort of smiled,' Miriklis was to recall, 'and he said: "I've got a gun in there. It's the gun I had when I was a security guard." '

Seconds afterwards, Ray was his usual quietly-spoken self. To Miriklis, his savage outburst sounded like a counter-threat, the bravado of a man out to show he isn't to be trifled with. Except for the last bit, about doing it before. Miriklis didn't attach any significance to it, but he didn't forget it, either. He was grateful that Ray, the man he already judged the best share farmer he had hired in years, had been staunch enough to back him up.

G REENSBOROUGH, July 30, 1975. *Mrs G states: 'I am a married woman and I reside … with my husband and my daughter, who is eighteen months old. I am 25 years old.*

'On Wednesday, 30th July, I was sitting knitting in my lounge room. It would have been about quarter to ten or ten o'clock in the evening. It was blowing a gale outside and I heard what I thought was the passage door slam. This door divides the kitchen from the laundry and bedrooms.

'I was sitting with my back to the passage door. When I heard the door slam I immediately turned around to face the door. I then saw the man standing in the kitchen. He started walking towards me. I got up from the sofa and asked him what he wanted. I think he said: "I don't want to hurt you." I was scared stiff and I kept pleading with him not to hurt me, and to

leave. He started to walk down the stairs and into the room where I was.

'As the man came down the stairs from the dining room, I made a run for the front door which I found to be locked. I think I opened the door a little but the man came from behind and pushed it shut. I had intended to call out to a neighbour.

'My husband wasn't home because he works part-time ... He left home at six o'clock in the evening. My daughter was sleeping in the bedroom. While we were still by the front door the man produced a knife from his back trouser pocket. It was about ten inches long including the wooden handle. He said: "I don't want to hurt you."

'I was frightened to say anything to him about my daughter in the bedroom because I thought he might do something to her. I don't know if he said to go into the lounge but this is where we both ended up. I was pleading with him not to hurt me, and to go. I was so upset I said to him in the end: "What do you want?"

'He said: "I just want to make love to you." By this time he had put the knife back in his pocket ... When he said he wanted to make love to me I said: "Why me?" He said: "Because I like you." He came towards me and I just stood there ... I was too scared to move. He then put his hands on my upper arms and came closer towards me. He then gave me a kiss on either my right cheek or right side of my neck. He said: "I've been watching you." I said: "How?"

'He then said: "Haven't you been seeing me?" I said: "No." He then let go of my arms and began undoing the buttons down the front of my shirt.

'I said: "Please don't, please don't." I didn't move because I was thinking of my daughter being in the other room, of the knife he had. He pulled my shirt down over my shoulders ... he said: "You get undressed." I undid the sleeve buttons and he *then took my shirt off me. He undid my bra while he was standing in front of me. I know he was saying something, but I can't remember what ... I kept talking all the time, pleading with him to let me go.*

'*He then undid the press stud and fly down the front of my jeans ... in the end I had my jeans, my pants and my socks and slippers off. He then came towards me ... I said: "Don't you know any girls."*

'*He said: "Yes, but I like you."*

'*He then began to get undressed. I tried not to look at him because I was too scared ... the next thing I knew he was hugging me with his left hand.*

'*I was so scared I didn't know what to do ... I couldn't even cry.*'

THE intruder raped the terrified woman. This time the police found no fingerprints. But in the victim they found an observant person who provided a detailed description of the rapist.

He was at least five foot eight and eleven stone weight, she said, podgy and flabby, with brown hair tending to red or auburn. Hazel or brown eyes. Sandy complexion, few freckles. Smooth hands. Did not have an accent; spoke in a soft Australian voice and did not swear. Clean shaven. Broad shoulders but not athletic. Not wearing shoes.

Afterwards, shaking with delayed shock, she remembered something else. Something she would never forget. How, when she had lied to the rapist that her husband would be home soon, he had coolly and confidently replied: 'He won't be home until later.'

Wednesday evening was the only night of the week that her husband worked until midnight, and her attacker obviously knew it. He must have watched the house for weeks.

S HEPPARTON, November 1975. Suddenly, Ray had decided to get away from the Melbourne area. He had thrown in his job as a security guard and given Don Miriklis notice on the farm at Officer. By now Colleen was used to Ray's inexplicable urge to change jobs and houses.

This time he had chosen another share farming job, on a property at Kialla, just south of Shepparton. Of all the short-lived jobs Ray took, this was the shortest; they were to stay only three months.

It was an irrigation farm, which meant that Ray sometimes had to check the water at night. This gave him an excuse to be absent at odd hours. Colleen knew little about irrigation, but she wondered sometimes why Ray spent a long time absent from the house. One night, when he stayed away for several hours, she asked him why. He told her he had fallen off the farm motorcycle in the dark and winded himself. She accepted the explanation.

The farm was only twenty minutes drive from Murchison East. When the family drove past the hamlet on the highway Colleen often referred to the murdered teenagers whose bodies had been found there years before, when she had been a teenager in Shepparton.

It was a warning, she told the children, of the dangers of going out late, drinking and talking to strangers. At which Ray would nod in agreement. He remembered the murders too, he said.

On a weekend trip from Shepparton they visited Colleen's sister at Tecoma in the Dandenongs. While there they saw a rundown roadhouse for lease at Ferny Creek. Ray, unpredictable as ever, was keen to take the business on, and negotiated on the spot. Colleen went along with the idea.

They left the Shepparton farm on February 22, just three weeks after the children had started new schools. The papers were full of the Madill-Heywood murders again. It was the tenth anniversary of the mystery.

FERNY Creek, late 1976. The roadhouse business improved, but the patchwork family started to come apart under the strain of Ray's outbreaks of perverted behaviour. There had been unsavoury incidents between Ray and Colleen's daughter Laura and his own daughter Susan, but the girls had not confided in Colleen. When Susan – by this time fourteen – finally grew desperate enough to tell her step-mother what was happening, Colleen was 'devastated,' she was to say later.

Like many women in her position, Colleen found it hard to go straight to the law. Eventually, she did speak to the police, but in circumstances which made it look as if she had a grudge against Ray.

It happened when she went to the local hotel to have a drink with a young man who was a regular customer in the shop, and started to pour out her troubles to him. 'Somebody must have told Ray where I was, and I was frightened he would kill me, so I went to the police station,' she was to recall.

'I told them what the kids had told me. They got a police-woman from Boronia up to talk to me, but nothing was done. They probably thought I was having an affair and was frightened of Ray and making it up. They said something about kids often telling wild stories to attract attention.'

Susan's version of events, backed up by a relative who clearly remembers the series of incidents, was that her step-mother abused her when she made the accusations against her father.

'She whacked me over the head with a broom and told me not to lie, and I threw a plate at her,' Susan was to recall. 'No police came to see me. If they had I would have told them what had happened.'

Either way, Ray was not spoken to. And so his deviant tendencies were not noted, let alone charges laid or fingerprints taken. The same set of circumstances in any other state might have resulted in both the complaint and the prints being put on file for future reference.

Ray's name came up once more at Belgrave police station, but again he was not spoken to. The permit for his security guard pistol had expired, and the police sent a demand for the weapon to be handed in. To Colleen's puzzlement, Ray asked her to take the pistol to the station. For someone who had once thought of joining the force, Ray was shy of police. And astonishingly lucky at avoiding them. He was still driving without a licence, and was never picked up for it.

By the end of 1976 it was clear the roadhouse venture was doomed. Colleen found it hard to manage the business and the children while Ray was working shifts at a factory in Ringwood. They sold the lease of the roadhouse and arranged another share farming job, this time at a small property in Wells Road, Chelsea Heights, on the fringe of the bayside suburbs.

Before starting at the farm, the family went for a month's holiday to Airlie Beach in northern Queensland. It was 'a good holiday,' Colleen noted later, except that Ray 'was strange. Very distant.' The hold he'd exerted over Colleen was loosening, but – oddly, given the evidence of his depravity – she stayed with him. She was even to admit hoping that the holiday would 'bring a bit of romance.'

It didn't, a fact which underlined Ray's growing inability to have normal sex with Colleen. He rarely managed to have sex with her from the time their son David was born. Colleen worried about this, and spoke of it to relatives and friends, sometimes in front of Ray. He would 'lie in bed as though he was in a different world,' Colleen was to say. Sometimes he made sexual suggestions she found even more disturbing than his usual lack of interest. 'Things so disgusting I couldn't even repeat what they were.'

CHELSEA Heights, February 14, 1977. *Mrs D states: 'I am a married woman aged 37 years ... I live with my husband and my three children. On Monday the fourteenth of February, 1977, my husband went to work at 9pm. He always works night shift. My daughter had gone to the city and I was home with the two boys. I went to bed between 2am and 2.30am after my daughter came home. All the children were in bed when I went to bed. My three-year-old son was in the double bed with me.*

'I had been in bed a while and dozing when I was disturbed by something. I thought it was my other son rather restless in bed, which he often is.

'I stayed in bed and dozed off again. I woke a short time later and the bedroom light was on and I saw a man coming towards me with a stocking mask on his head ...

'As he came towards me he said very quietly: "Don't make a noise, I'm going to rape you." He also said he had been watching me for some months. I kept saying to him: "Who are you? Who are you?" and he was saying: "Keep quiet, don't wake the little boy up."

'I noticed he was wearing a dark blue knitted top like a tee-shirt. He came over to the bed and told me to take my nightie off. He started to pull up the bottom of my nightie, and I told him that I had my period.

'He said: "That's all right. Take everything off." I was so frightened of him and what he might do I took my nightie, pants and pad off. He laid on top of me and was kissing me and touching my breasts and stomach. He pulled the mask up over the top of his nose. He said again he had been watching me for a few months and that I was sexy ...

'I did as he said as I was terrified for myself and for the children, especially my son who was on the bed. I thought he might have done anything to him.'

WHEN it was over the rapist told Mrs D. to close her eyes. She heard him go out the front door. She did not hear a car. Dazed with shock, she stumbled out of her bed and mechanically made a cup of coffee and agonised over what to do. Then she rang friends, who rang the police when they arrived shortly afterwards.

Tim McLean, the fingerprint expert called to the scene, dusted powder on the living room window where the man had entered the house. He was pleased to find some prints, which he recognised immediately. He telephoned the office to tell them the news ... the 'Donvale rapist' had moved south.

Meanwhile, local police were taking the victim's statement. In describing her attacker she overlooked one thing she remembered later. He had an odour.

CHELSEA Heights, early 1978. It was the first time that Susan's friend Jenny had stayed at the farm in Wells Road. The two girls slept in Susan's bedroom. Jenny found it hard to sleep in the strange surroundings, and to make it worse there was too much light in the room.

Enough light that when a naked male figure walked silently through the bedroom door and stared at her, she recognised it as Susan's father. He was 'playing with himself,' as she later described it.

Jenny started with fright. Ray turned and padded out the door and towards his own bedroom, quietly for such a heavy man. Jenny reached over and shook Susan awake, embarrassed at what she had to tell her, too nervous not to.

Susan was upset, but she accepted the story without any hint of disbelief. Not pausing to get dressed, the two teenagers grabbed some bedclothes and climbed out the window, so that they wouldn't risk being seen walking through the house. They sneaked out of the yard and into the paddock, and spent the rest of the night huddled under a tree in the far corner of the property.

Next day Jenny told her mother what had happened. Her mother was outraged. She questioned the girl closely to make sure she wasn't hiding anything. Eventually, satisfied that Susan's father had not touched either girl, she decided against calling the police. Instead, she gently asked Susan what had been going on. Susan, acutely embarrassed and ashamed, haltingly revealed some of the secrets which had tormented her for years.

Jenny's mother rang Colleen and told her what had happened. She was prepared for any reaction but the one she got. Colleen, she was to remember, defended Ray. 'Raymond wouldn't do that, Raymond wouldn't do that!' was the woman's recollection of what Colleen said to her. Colleen also described Susan as an uncontrollable 'delinquent' who fabricated stories about her father to try to break up the marriage.

Jenny's mother wasn't convinced. She knew Susan as 'a quiet and lovely girl.' Besides which, she knew Jenny wouldn't make up a story which had been so obviously embarrassing to tell.

CHELSEA Heights, May 1978. Two weeks before, on Susan's sixteenth birthday, Ray and Colleen had taken her and some friends to the 'Les Girls' cabaret act in St Kilda, for which Ray had come by some free tickets. It was, by most standards, a tawdry enough treat, but the fact Susan was to remember the outing as an almost pleasant interlude showed how bleak her life was.

Within days the peace was shattered. Again, her father did something that sickened and frightened Susan. Again, the nightmarish quality of her predicament was compounded because she didn't get on well enough with Colleen to convince her of what Ray did behind her back.

So Susan ran away. It wasn't the first time, but this time she was determined never to go back. She went to her friend Jenny's house, which wasn't far from the farm. Jenny's mother, mindful of the earlier incident, was sympathetic and agreed that she could stay.

That evening, about 8pm, Susan and Jenny walked to a milk bar nearby. They were sitting on a seat outside the shop when Colleen drove past and recognised Susan. She pulled up, according to Susan, and abused her. But Susan was past caring. She was out of reach of her father, and that was all that mattered to her.

Colleen ended the tirade by saying that she was going to take Susan to the police station to have her arrested as 'an uncontrollable child.'

Susan wasn't intimidated. 'Good,' she said defiantly, 'let's go. And I'll tell them what's really happening.'

She got in the car with Colleen, leaving Jenny to run home to tell her mother. Colleen drove to Mordialloc police station. There, she demanded that Susan be locked up, to the bemusement of two policewomen who tried to calm them down. Susan, incensed at Colleen's accusations, said she was 'mad.' Colleen then slapped her face, Susan said later.

The policewomen guided Susan to an interview room so that she could tell her story uninterrupted. She told it. When she had finished they took her to Frankston police station. Susan said she had nowhere to stay, so the police arranged for her to go to Winbirra, the remand section of the Winlaton home for wayward girls. She arrived about 2am.

Peter A. was shocked by the telephone call. It was a Presbyterian deaconess whose work included counselling inmates of Winlaton. The gist of a one-sided conversation was that Susan was marooned in the remand section; the police had put her there for her own protection because of what she'd said about her father's sexual deviations. She was desperate for somewhere to go.

Peter told his wife, Margaret. She set off on the short drive to the home to talk to Susan. Peter stayed home, unwilling to believe the implications of the deaconess's world-weary revelations. Susan had often babysat for Peter and Margaret over the previous ten months, and she seemed a normal, happy teenager. And they had never noticed anything strange about her father. Peter had met him the previous July when Ray had started work for the Australia Seal Company bottle-top plant in Moorabbin.

Peter was an experienced production man, and in the burly, quiet farmer he'd recognised someone else of some natural ability. After years of self-dependence, Ray had a quality that was rare in run-of-the-mill factory hands. He was a quick learner, he was a hard worker and he had initiative; 'Show Ray something once and he knew how to do it.'

Ray seemed to appreciate Peter's kindness, and had invited him and his family to the farm in Wells Road for a barbecue. Peter's children, younger than Ray's, had been fascinated by someone who lived on a farm so close to the city.

The barbecue had been a success, in its way. Colleen had obviously gone to a lot of trouble to cater for it, and Ray seemed to take pleasure in showing the kids how to milk cows.

From there, the acquaintance had become a casual friendship. For Peter it was a doodle in the margin of his workaday life, a reflection of his own pleasant nature and the fact he worked with Ray.

But for Ray, it was different. It was the first time since his teenage years that he had fostered a friendship. It got so that he would drop in to Peter's house for a beer or a swim in the pool. And when Peter and Margaret had needed a babysitter, they'd called on Susan.

TEN minutes with Susan was enough to convince Peter's wife, Margaret, that the girl was telling the truth about her father. She decided on the spot that Susan would have to come to live with her and Peter. Her resolve hardened when she saw the other inmates. Some, like Susan, were homeless or in need of protection. But most, despite their youth, were obviously prostitutes, thieves and drug addicts; they would be bad company for Susan.

Margaret went home to talk it over with Peter. Next day she came back and took Susan out to live with them. It was a gesture of remarkable kindness; Susan eventually stayed for fifteen months.

Not long after Susan moved in, two policewomen came to interview her. She was reluctant to press charges against her father. The police seemed to Margaret to be interested mainly in checking what sort of a home Susan had found. But Susan's original complaints had found their way into the system. Weeks later, she was asked to appear before a magistrate at Frankston to give evidence about her father's behaviour so that the court could formally appoint Peter and Margaret as her legal guardians.

Colleen attended the hearing. She said later she had been shocked by Susan's evidence of her father's depravity, saying that the girl had 'never told me half of it.'

Despite the magistrate's obvious acceptance of Susan's sworn statement, no steps were taken against Ray except an order that he seek psychiatric help. Later, Colleen made an appointment with a psychiatrist in St Kilda Road and drove Ray there to make sure he kept it. But after she escorted him to the waiting room he bolted – with the car keys in his pocket. Colleen and her son David waited in the street near the car for two hours before Ray turned up and sullenly drove them home.

The courts had ordered Ray to see a psychiatrist, but the courts had done nothing about enforcing it. Police did not interview him either before or after Susan's court hearing. Once more, he had slipped through the system.

SINGLETON, NSW, April 1980. It was the highest paid job Ray had ever had. The farm was run by a company with big ideas and a big budget, and he was in charge of milking 300 cows and growing fodder crops for them. It meant starting long before dawn and working all day, every day, for which he was to be paid $1000 a week – the equivalent then of a senior executive salary.

Despite the lure of the money, Colleen had been reluctant to leave Victoria. She had worked her way into a secure job as a supervisor with the Coles retail chain and didn't want to throw it away just because Ray had an urge to move away from the outskirts of Melbourne. But there was no chance of talking Ray out of it once he'd decided, so Colleen compromised by getting a transfer to the Newcastle branch. It meant a daily round trip of almost 200 kilometres. But that was better, she resolved, than losing her chance of independence.

The long journey to the farm outside Singleton was their third move in less than two years. Ray had finished work at the Australia Seal Company in July, 1978, and a month later they had shifted from the Chelsea Heights farm to another at Nar Nar Goon, just east of Melbourne. Nine months later they had moved down the road to Officer, to the same farm where Ray had milked for Don Miriklis in 1975, but which had since been sold to Vince Vincenzino. Again, they had stayed less than a year, arriving in May, 1979, and leaving the following April. During that time Mrs Vincenzino had received a series of obscene telephone calls which she suspected were made by Raymond junior. When she had complained to the boy's father, he had laughed, she later told police.

Colleen had given up hope of persuading Ray to buy a house and settle in one spot. Even if he agreed, she knew it wouldn't last. Nothing did with him. Eleven months after they had arrived at Singleton, Ray vanished. Colleen was woken at 4.30 one morning by a farmhand knocking on the front door. He asked why Ray wasn't ready for work. Colleen looked around the house; he wasn't there. Then the hand told her that their Fairlane car was missing.

Colleen guessed the truth even before she found the note. It said, in Ray's painful scrawl, that he had left enough money in the bank for Colleen and the five children to get back to Melbourne. Below that, the words: 'I can't stand it.'

SYDNEY, May 1981. In the city where anything goes, Ray went. Easily. Within a few days of arriving he landed a job as a 'private investigator' with an agency that had a cosy relationship with the local police. In reality, the job was little more sophisticated than being a security patrolman, as he had been in Melbourne, and he spent most of his time collecting small debts. But Ray had always gravitated towards positions of authority rather than popularity, and the job impressed him enough that he later boasted about being taken out to lunches with policemen cultivated by his employers, at a restaurant in the policemen's 'patch' where they were not expected to pay. Ahead was his return to Melbourne, a half-hearted reconciliation with Colleen and yet another job, this one with a fencing and security gate contractor in Highett.

212

Behind were the years of dodging from dairy farm to dairy farm. Ray had milked his last cow. There would be no more sour milk soaked into his boots and his clothes, no more warm manure slopped on his arms and legs, no more of the pungent alkaline solution used to wash out the dairy pipes ...

No more of the lingering smell that the mixture of milk, manure and chemical leaves on skin and clothes, even after they are washed.

3. Right Middle Finger | 4. Right Ring Finger

TEN

The moving finger, 1982-1984

EVERY office has its enthusiasts, those who never watch the clock but who, if their eyes happen to catch it, are surprised to see that time has gone so quickly. Tradition has it that the Victoria Police fingerprint bureau, because of the specialised skills and concentration the work demands, attracts the diligent and the self-motivated. And of the 70 or so people working at the bureau in 1982 Sergeant Andrew Wall, in the eyes of both his commanding officer and his peers, was one of the best. Not just dedicated, as many were, but with an extra dimension of talent – a blend of eyesight, memory and instinct – which cannot be taught, though it might well be sharpened by practice.

It was typical of Andy Wall that in late June, 1982, he approached the bureau's commanding officer, Chief Inspector Brian Norton, with an idea which would improve the system. Norton was the sort of boss who encouraged ideas. A year earlier, when he had taken charge of the bureau, he had quietly ordered a review of unidentified fingerprints detected at the most serious unsolved crimes in the previous twenty years; an attempt to prevent important prints from slipping into limbo in the face of the rising tide of work handled by the bureau. Wall's suggestion, an extension of Norton's review, was simple enough: to put together photographs of a hard core of unidentified prints linked with serious unsolved crimes. Norton was enthusiastic, so Wall and other officers started collecting prints they considered the most notorious and stuck them to a large sheet of cardboard. The board was then displayed prominently so that every member of the bureau would memorise the prints by seeing them every day.

Of the five sets, two were especially significant. One, from a case well-known to the public, was a faint print found at the scene of the Easey Street murders, in which two young women were butchered in a Collingwood house in January, 1977. A decade later the print was still unmatched and the crime unsolved.

The second set of prints was to prove a different story. It had been found on a flywire screen at a house in Donvale where a woman had been tied up and assaulted in 1971. But it was not that crime alone that had drawn attention. The prints had been matched with others left at a rape scene in Greensborough in 1975 and a third at Chelsea Heights in 1977. In each case the description of the offender and his methods had convinced detectives that he was responsible for many other rapes reported in those suburbs over several years. Although the public knew little of the offender, he loomed large in the minds of the police because it was likely that the man they called the 'Donvale rapist' would strike repeatedly unless he was caught.

All of which was at the back of Andy Wall's mind when he taped a blown-up photograph of one of the rapist's prints to the centre of his brainchild, the 'top five' board. To his expert eye, the grey smudge in the photograph was instantly recognisable. It was the print of an index finger, selected for the ease with which an expert could pick out its 'small-count loop'. Prints of the rapist's other fingers were not on the board; they were arranged as a composite set and kept on file for comparison against full sets of prints. They were not as clear as the index print, and required study to impress their unique peculiarities in the memories of the bureau staff.

The quiet young policeman was satisfied that the board was worthwhile. But he didn't know that its value would be proved within two weeks. Nor that he would be the one to do it.

IT was not, Andy Wall often said later, anything extra-ordinary. Comparing and matching fingerprints, he would point out patiently, almost apologetically, was what he'd done every working day of his seven years in the bureau. And matching one set of prints was much like matching another. Besides, he'd arrived in Australia in 1969, a skinny thirteen-year-old from Brighton, England, and so he hadn't grown up knowing about the Shepparton murders the way others had.

July 12, 1982, started routinely in the old bureau office at Russell Street. There was the usual backlog of prints taken from crime scenes overnight and from offenders lodged at the city watch house. These had to be processed: checked against known offenders' prints and, if not matched, against unidentified prints from other crime scenes. Despite the classification of fingerprints into groups according to the differences in loops, whorls and arches – automatically eliminating thousands of those on file – each new print still had to be checked against thousands of others stored in the bureau's cabinet full of drawers.

It was to a particular drawer that Andy Wall went in the afternoon of July 12, intent on putting in an hour reviewing old prints. At the front of the drawer, in a tattered envelope, was a collection of developed prints photographed at the scenes of unsolved major crimes. At Chief Inspector Norton's suggestion, he was going to sift through old murder cases for likely future candidates for the 'top five' board.

Wall sat at his desk and shuffled methodically through the pack. An ageing, dog-eared photograph caught his eye. It was of a right hand, of which only two fingerprints were decipherable. They looked like the index and middle fingers, he mused, but it was just possible that they were middle and ring fingers. He sensed something familiar about them.

The feeling grew stronger. Neither of the prints in front of him matched the rapist's index finger print which he had stuck to the 'top five' board a fortnight before … but an instinct told him they came from the same hand. Wall flicked through the file of composite prints, and fished out the Donvale rapist's set, made up from various prints taken from three suburban houses in six years. And there was the answer to the riddle.

The old murder prints in the dog-eared photograph matched two of the fingers in the composite set – not, as seemed likely, the index and middle fingers, but the middle and ring fingers. A tiny fact, but it might have been enough to confuse anybody who had reviewed the murder prints in previous years.

A mental picture of the best example of the Donvale rapist's prints – his index finger – would not have triggered recognition of either of the murder prints. It took something close to intuition, on Wall's part, to do that.

Andy Wall knew he had a perfect match. What he didn't know, until he approached one of the bureau's veterans to ask him to double check the comparison, was the significance of his find.

Senior Sergeant Bob Hadfield, who had worked in the bureau since 1962, knew exactly what he was looking at. He didn't have to check the identification number on the back of the old picture to know the prints were those found on Garry Heywood's FJ Holden, a fact kept secret for the previous sixteen years. Hadfield and his contemporaries had pored over copies of that photograph dozens of times in the years immediately after the murders, and the patterns of the two hazy prints were engraved in his memory.

'Abina Madill and Garry Heywood,' said Hadfield, nodding his head in wonder. It had been one of the biggest cases of his career.

The names meant nothing to Andy Wall. It wasn't until Hadfield explained the history of the case to him that the young policeman realised 'the gravity of the situation,' he said later. He'd discovered that the Donvale rapist was one of the most wanted killers in Australian history ... and he was still active.

Bob Hadfield reached for the telephone.

CHIEF Inspector Norton was in Canberra when he received the news from his men. No matter where he was, whether he was on duty or not, his staff would not divulge anything about a breakthrough without talking to him first. The bureau was like that, its camaraderie strengthened by the suspicion that the public, and even the rest of the force, failed to grasp the part it played in solving crimes.

The Madill-Heywood case brought back memories for Norton, not all of them pleasant. Early in the original investigation the fingerprint men had been dismayed by an unspoken attitude among some homicide detectives that the print found on Heywood's car was useless. The implication was that not all those with a legitimate reason for touching the car had been eliminated by Ken Tyler, who had gone to Shepparton in 1966 to check Heywood's car for prints. Behind this scepticism, Norton knew, was the belief previously held by some detectives that Ian Urquhart had committed the murders. The result was that the bureau staff had always been more confident of the fingerprint belonging to the murderer than anybody else had been.

So confident, in fact, that in late 1969 Norton and another fingerprint expert had requested a senior CIB officer for permission to set up in a hall in Shepparton to check the prints of every adult male in the right age group, on the understanding that any prints recorded would be given voluntarily and be destroyed after inspection. Norton had begun his police career in Manchester before migrating to join the Victoria Police in 1961, and he cited the example of the city of Blackburn in northern England, where in 1948 some 50,000 men were voluntarily printed in the hunt for a child murderer.

Given Shepparton's total population of less than 20,000 in the 1960s, an inspection of around 5000 men, while it might not have produced the killer, would have eliminated almost every local from the inquiry, thereby focusing investigators' attention on a smaller pool of potential suspects. The process, Norton had urged, would require most people only to show their hands as they filed past. Relatively few would have to be actually printed for comparison. If a print were found that matched the one on Heywood's car, it would either identify the killer or it would prove that the print on the car was irrelevant.

It seemed a persuasive argument, but the senior CIB man had been unimpressed. When the frustrated Norton pointed out how effectively the idea had worked in the English case, the officer retorted: 'Well, this is Australia. If you don't like it you'd better piss off back to England.'

Norton had never forgotten the slight to himself and to the bureau. So when, thirteen years later, his men told him they had matched the rape prints with the Madill-Heywood prints, the news was sweet. If the killer wasn't caught through finger prints, he thought to himself, he wouldn't be caught at all.

THE long road that had led Dennis Hanna to Shepparton and the rank of detective senior sergeant, as he was in 1982, began in Ireland in 1949. That year, before Dennis's fifteenth birthday, his father had given him a simple choice: Australia or Canada. Hanna senior, who worked for the British Tax Office, considered the assisted immigration policy of either country an offer too good to refuse. It was a pragmatic attitude, rather than a sentimental one, towards a schoolboy son. Perhaps it was from his father that young Hanna inherited the canniness, a dogged intelligence, that was later to be his trademark as a policeman.

Dennis had chosen Australia. He went to Tasmania, where he worked on a dairy farm at Montage in the island's north-west. His employer was a returned soldier, a man Hanna was to remember affectionately almost 40 years later. It was, he later recalled, a marvellous place for a young man: a slice of pioneer life barely imaginable in Britain. Bullock teams still worked in the bush and plough horses in the paddocks. When he wasn't working Dennis trapped wallabies for skins and caught freshwater crayfish and ate huge baked dinners. It was there that he developed a love of the country that was to lure him back from the city half a lifetime later.

He arrived in Victoria at eighteen, fresh from national service training in Hobart. He went to Heyfield in Gippsland, seeking work, and started felling timber for the mills, sweating on one end of a cross-cut saw. Then to Yarram, where he worked on a farm. It was there that he met a policeman called Clarrie McInnes. 'He was six foot three, straight as a gun barrel,' Hanna was to remember. 'I would say it was his attitude, his completeness as an individual, that convinced me I should put in an application to join the Victoria Police Force.'

Hanna graduated in September, 1955. In the first week of training the squad of 50 appointed a treasurer who collected money from each recruit to pay for a graduation party. But the treasurer vanished after a few weeks, and the money went with him. The lesson wasn't lost on the new constable: trust no-one blindly, even another policeman.

In his first year he was stationed at Port Melbourne, then Richmond. There he learned more lessons: about painters and dockers and the underworld, about how to handle brawls in pubs and at football games. In the courts he saw a diligent young lawyer called John Cain using Matchbox cars and a board to show magistrates how traffic accidents had happened. Cain was not the most flamboyant or aggressive barrister, he noted, but watching him taught an observant young copper respect for the value of a fresh approach. Lateral thinking, as some called it.

Then, in late 1957, Hanna joined the Wireless Patrol. Plain clothes and fast cars – Studebakers, Fords and Ramblers – which were radio-controlled and called first to the biggest jobs. The patrol was a stepping stone to detective work, and some of the force's most ambitious young men went through with Hanna. One of his sergeants – and golf partner – was Paul Delianis, later to head the homicide squad on the way to becoming one of the Victoria's three most senior policemen.

Hanna became a detective in 1961 and started work at Ringwood. When the Shepparton murders were committed five years later he had just been transferred to Russell Street. The case intrigued him, as it did most police, but he had nothing to do with it, apart from one routine inquiry in 1966 when he spoke to the owner of a Mossberg rifle. From Russell Street he returned to Ringwood.

Which is why, in July, 1971, he was called in to investigate the rape of Mrs B and the attempted rape of Mrs Y, both in the Donvale district, and just eleven days apart. A month later a third woman in that suburb was attacked by a man who tried to choke her while she was in bed. After weeks on the cases,

Hanna and his partner were certain of one thing: the three women were attacked by the same man, and he was brazen enough to do it again.

A few months later Hanna was transferred from Ringwood, first to Swan Hill, then back to Russell Street. He was tired of chasing promotion, and discussed with his wife, Del, whether it was time to settle in the country while their three children grew up. They decided it was. After studying the options, he applied for the detective senior sergeant's position at Shepparton. In early 1973 the Hannas found an old farm house a few miles out of town which they rented, then later bought and renovated into a showpiece of Edwardian style.

'The district had everything for a young family,' Hanna was to recall twelve years later, sitting on the manicured lawn he had established beside the sweeping verandas. 'Ballet, scouts, tennis, golf, good schools and good people ... plenty of space and a healthy environment for young Australians to grow up in.' The district the Hannas had fallen in love with in 1973 was Ardmona. Their patch of paradise was just around the corner from Gawnes' farm: the one a sharefarmer called Ray had left suddenly, seven years before.

IN 1982, Dennis Hanna had been head of Shepparton CIB for nine years, time enough to grow familiar with the Madill-Heywood mystery, and a little fascinated by it. The question 'Who killed Garry and Abina?' still gnawed at the people of Shepparton. And although the memory of Ian Urquhart, ten years in the grave, was still slandered by many, there was a constant trickle of information and speculation. Some of which resulted in the sort of inquiries that the police call routine, and mean it. These were variations on familiar themes. A typical 'new lead' would be the return of local holiday makers with a vague story about a conversation with a stranger – often in

Queensland – who had mentioned the Shepparton murders. Others would dredge up belated memories of fruit pickers who had left suddenly 'the day after the murders,' or of conversations overheard in hotels years before and brooded over until they hatched an imaginary significance.

Of the Shepparton police who handled inquiries stemming from this desultory flow of information, Ken Mansell was one who took a sharp interest. He had returned to the town as a detective in late 1971, not long after the wet July night that he had been first on the scene at the house of the Donvale rapist's second victim. The big, red-headed Mansell had grown up around Shepparton, had known Garry Heywood, and had a brother who had driven a hot FJ Holden almost identical with Heywood's. The murders held a special poignancy for Mansell, as for other locals; at the back of his mind was the unspoken thought that the tragedy could as easily have struck his own family.

In 1970, a Dandenong couple called Lucas had taken over the Railway Hotel at Murchison East. Their son, Denis, who had joined the police force a couple of years earlier, transferred to Kyabram in 1971 and started playing football for Murchison – which, remarkably, he was still doing sixteen seasons later. The murders hung over Murchison East, where the bodies had been found, and provided a recurring topic of conversation in the hotel. The quiet young policeman couldn't help but grow interested in the case. He was transferred to Melbourne, but returned to his adopted district in 1976, as a detective at Shepparton. In the next six years Denis Lucas, like Mansell and Hanna, was often to delve into the Heywood-Madill file, which had been lying around the station since the inquest, the yellowing pages taunting their readers with the riddle of the killer's identity … until early August, 1982, when the news of the fingerprint breakthrough reached Shepparton.

SECURITY was tight. The head of the homicide squad, the taciturn Ted Page, drove to Shepparton with Brian Norton and Andrew Wall to explain in detail the cryptic outline Hanna had received on the telephone. The fingerprint bureau had searched half a million prints in vain, looking for a match. The prints had been circulated world-wide, and two experts had flown to Sydney for a week to comb the NSW records. Meanwhile the homicide squad had looked over some potential suspects, and a confidential circular outlining the link between the rapes and the murders had been drawn up to send to every station. Now, somewhat as an afterthought, it was Shepparton CIB's turn to be told what was happening. And not happening.

The meeting took place over lunch. The meal, Dennis Hanna remarked later, was more like 'a council of war' than a social event. It seemed to the Shepparton detectives that because the new evidence had not brought instant and easy results in the previous few weeks, the case was in danger of being put back on the shelf in the vague hope that the killer would eventually blunder into a situation where he would be routinely finger-printed.

It was Denis Lucas, ('I'm a rude bastard, see' he was to say later, unrepentant) who voiced the misgivings of the country detectives. If no-one else was going to follow up the new information it was up to the Shepparton CIB to take it on, he said. His argument was simple. Why should the local police have carried out murder inquiries for years – then fail to take advantage of the first strong lead in the case's long history?

Every face at the table was turned towards the tall, slow-talking detective as he said his piece. If only detectives could get a decent description, he finished bluntly, there was a big chance of catching the killer.

Hanna nodded in quiet agreement, his bushy ginger eyebrows knitted in thought. There is a type of personality that revels as much in preparation as it does in execution. In his spare time Hanna was a fly fisherman, the sort that takes as much pleasure in the precise discipline of tying the tiny flies as in catching trout. Plans were already taking shape in that methodical mind.

Suddenly the restaurant door swung open, and a well-dressed blonde woman strode in. The Melbourne detectives knew her well. She was a television reporter renowned for her police contacts. She had got wind of new developments in the Madill-Heywood story, and had been tipped off to follow the Melbourne contingent north. One of the detectives asked her how she'd found the lunch meeting. 'I'm not just a pair of pretty legs,' she retorted.

But this time she had to wait for her story. For the moment, the talking was finished, and the fingerprint match was still under wraps, as it would be for another three months.

Which meant that although Ian Urquhart had been proved innocent at last, no-one in his hometown knew it.

WITHIN a week of the lunch meeting Hanna and Lucas went to Benalla to put their case to Detective Chief Inspector Dallas McDonald, the officer in command of their CIB region. Without McDonald's approval, their ripening ambition to mount a fresh investigation would be thwarted. They need not have worried. McDonald, like the two detectives, had not been in the district in 1966, but the murders fascinated him. If Hanna and Lucas thought they had a chance of cracking the mystery, he would support them. The first step, he agreed, was to go to Melbourne to interview the rape victims and establish a clear picture of the man they were hunting.

Later, back at the station in Shepparton, Hanna rolled a sheet of quarto into the big office typewriter and carefully pecked out the date: 23.8.82. Then the words, 'It has been established by the Finger Print Bureau that the prints found on Heywood's FJ Holden after his death in 1966 are identical with ...'

The new inquiry had begun.

T HE detectives' first task was to study the original statements of women attacked by the rapist. Straight away this presented a puzzle.

The rapist's first two victims had suggested that the man had either a Scottish or North England accent. But none of the ten other victims known at that time had reported an accent. This put the odds four to one against the accent; but that didn't satisfy. When they re-interviewed each victim, they asked about the accent; the answers they got made the picture hazier than ever. Although they hadn't noticed a British accent, few of the ten would dismiss the possibility outright. The uncertainty was deepened because the women agreed that the man had spoken softly and fairly well, that he didn't swear, and even when he threatened he rarely lapsed into crude language or tone. All this, combined with the rapist's fair complexion and soft hands, and despite the fact that he sometimes wore the shorts and singlet of the manual labourer, built an impression that he was probably a middle-class British migrant with a white-collar job. The seeds of this conviction were planted in the investigators' minds even before they started interviewing the women. Detectives are hungry for clues, and the accent seemed the strongest of a weak collection of clues. It was natural that much weight was attached to it.

The rapid adoption of the supposed accent as a firm lead was demonstrated in the meticulous records the detectives kept. On August 23 Hanna had noted carefully the aims of the inquiry: 'To establish whether or not the offender had a Scottish or North England accent ... ' and 'To obtain all evidence relating to the identity of the offender, thus laying a foundation upon which a thorough inquiry may be successfully conducted.' It was a copybook example of correct procedure and keeping an open mind.

But within two days the practical reality of having to narrow the field asserted itself. On the running sheet of August 25 the detectives noted: 'That due to mention of Scottish accent ... re rapes at Donvale commencing 15.7.71 it can be assumed that offender was of Scottish origin.'

It was a brave assumption. The original statement made by the first victim, Mrs B, had been lost, and so Hanna and Lucas had to rely on her memory of events eleven years before. She was adamant that the man had an odour, but was unsure about the accent. The statement of the second victim, Mrs Y, was found, but she could not be re-interviewed. She had died in 1976, of a tumour which her husband attributed to the shock of the attack.

Hanna and Lucas were moved by the reactions to their round of interviews. At first, some of the victims were reluctant to talk about their scarifying experiences. But once the women's confidence was won they seemed relieved to talk frankly to someone who understood the extent of their distress, who did not want to blame them for the attacks or to trivialise the crimes against them. This pattern, apparent with six women interviewed in the first few days, was to impress the detectives deeply over the following months, as many more women were added to the list of rape victims. In almost every case, their visit was the first chance the women had to pour out feelings which had been bottled for years. The terror they had suffered left psychological scars, but the worst thing, the more articulate women said, was the reaction of relatives and friends after the rapes. Of the few marriages that had survived until 1982, none was stable.

Detective Chief Inspector McDonald had given Hanna and

Lucas a roving commission. They could work from any police station that was convenient, stay in motels during the week and drive back to Shepparton at weekends or when they were needed. During these long trips they 'threw ideas around,' as Lucas put it. By the end of the first week, after a hectic round of interviews, they were forming a vague picture of the man they sought – and it didn't tally well with different police artists' impressions done in the 1970s following three of the attacks. Given the chance to study the old sketches, none of the women had been impressed with them; one even suggested that it might 'do more harm than good' to publish them. It seemed a prudent warning, because police artists would have to rely on descriptions from witnesses who had seen the rapist briefly between five and eleven years before. But Hanna and Lucas decided that the risk was worth taking, providing they could pool the knowledge of the victims to come up with a composite picture everyone was happy with.

On August 28 they noted in the running sheets the names of three victims who 'should be invited to each do another identikit. Then, if willing, all three should be put together for discussion on description with view to firmer knowledge being obtained.'

But within a week the long talks on the two-hour trip to and from Shepparton gave birth to something more ambitious than mere identikits or sketches … Hanna and Lucas decided they wanted a three-dimensional likeness. A bust.

It was, in its way, as ingenious as the young John Cain, later to become Premier of Victoria, using Matchbox cars in court. Unfortunately, it was not to prove as successful.

INVESTIGATION of the Scottish connection theory gathered pace. Hanna, himself a product of the Big Brother scheme, found that the Dhurringile prison farm, between

Murchison and Tatura, had previously been a Presbyterian hostel where British boys had once been housed. A series of telephone calls led to a former hostel official who had records showing that Scottish orphans brought to Australia had stayed at the hostel between 1959 and 1965 before making their way into the community, mostly around the Shepparton district.

It fell into place so neatly ... a reservoir of Scottish youths, many of them hardened and some probably disturbed as a result of their fractured lives, all familiar with the district where the bodies were found, all the right age to attend a rock concert in 1966.

The easy part was to find out who they were. The hostel records gave the names and dates of birth of 93 Dhurringile 'old boys,' and their last known addresses. Then came the time-consuming part: tracking them down and fingerprinting them. It was to take months.

DESPITE the publicity it attracted later, the idea that the attacker had a distinctive odour was based on evidence only slightly stronger than that suggesting that he had a Scottish accent. Of the twelve victims known early in the investigation, only four reported that the attacker had an odour. Of these, one thought it was like cigar smoke, another that it was possibly bitumen or diesel, one that it was body odour, and another simply that it was a 'strong smell' which she couldn't identify or describe. Months later, one other victim was located who recalled that the attacker had a smell, which she likened to stale cigarette smoke.

So much for the odour. Hanna and Lucas identified traits which were less unusual but were ultimately to prove more accurate. Eight women reported that the man was barefoot, and it could be guessed that the other four would not have been sure if he were wearing shoes or not. Nine were menaced with a knife – all but one with a long-bladed butcher's knife. Ten were young, married women whose husbands were out that night. And, the most chilling statistic of all, eleven of the women had small children in the house ... usually in bed with them.

'What he did, in effect' Dennis Hanna was often to say, eyes narrowed with contempt, 'was to take the children hostage.' There had been the implicit threat that the man would harm the children if he met any resistance. Women who, alone, might scream for help or try to fight off an attacker, would submit to anything to protect their children.

THE problem of finding someone to sculpt a bust was solved by the police surgeon, Dr Peter Bush. After talking over the idea with Hanna and Lucas, Dr Bush approached a Melbourne sculptor he knew, who agreed to do the work on the understanding that he remain anonymous.

The first session was on September 16, at the sculptor's studio in Kew. The sculptor started work with the four women who had agreed to help, a hair dressing expert and a cosmetician. Dr Bush and several police who had become involved in the inquiry came along to watch the new idea unfold, and to discuss progress with Hanna and Lucas.

Several hours and many adjustments later, the modelling-clay bust was still not close to its final form. The women sat in a semi-circle around the sculptor, who fielded their suggestions patiently as he tried to incorporate each woman's impression into his creation. Of the four, two had studied the attacker closely in good light, and their recollections dominated the session.

For the women, there was more to the gathering than making the bust. It was the first time they had spoken to other victims, and the meeting was the start of a friendship between them that was bonded by their shared experience. The sad thing, one of them said, was that they would not have met each other but for the investigation.

The bust took 45 hours to complete in sessions scattered over several weeks. The victims and the detectives who gathered to watch the sculptor and a make-up artist apply the finishing touches were pleased with the result. But that didn't alter the fact that what they saw was the sculptor's interpretation of fleeting impressions of a man seen years before. Those impressions could not allow for the effects of advancing age, changing weight, or a different hairstyle. Realistically, all it could be was a guide to the physical type of the killer: that is, pot-bellied, thickset, with a fair complexion and sandy to auburn hair. What it wasn't – and could not hope to be – was a photographic likeness of a particular man the way a bust modelled from a live subject could be. The police knew this, but would the public?

WE were looking, Dennis Hanna was to muse later, for a total overview – a pattern. It meant drawing together the fragmented knowledge gained from the old homicide inquiry and from the scattered rapes, which had been investigated separately in the various police divisions.

One way to achieve an overview was to plot the twelve attacks then attributed to the 'Donvale rapist' on a map of suburban Melbourne. On the map the symbols representing attacks extended in an arc from Greensborough in the north-east to Chelsea Heights on the Bay in the south-east. They were grouped in four clusters which had occurred in a rough chronological sequence.

The first three, at Donvale, were within a few blocks and thirteen months of each other: two in July, 1971, and the third in August the following year. The second cluster, also of three, was in Greensborough; the first in late 1973, the second in January, 1975, and the third five months later, just 200 metres away.

Three months later, in October, 1975, the first of five similar attacks was committed in Wheelers Hill. The second was almost exactly a year later, the third was in March, 1977, and the fourth less than six weeks after that. The fifth attack, in July, 1977, showed the offender's propensity for murderous violence. Two schoolgirls had been home alone in Homestead Drive, Wheelers Hill, while their parents were out to dinner. After watching television until 11.15pm, the girls had gone to bed in separate rooms. Soon afterwards the younger child, aged eleven, had heard her fourteen-year-old sister screaming. She ran to the other girl's room, where she saw her sister lying on the floor with a man standing over her. She saw him strike her with something in his hand. She screamed and the man brushed past her and left the house. Behind him the teenager was bleeding from severe injuries to her face which received emergency surgery in hospital. Police later found that the girl had been struck with an iron jemmy bar which the man had picked up inside the house.

The fourth district was Chelsea Heights. In late 1982 only one rape – that of Mrs D in February, 1977 – had been attributed to the offender in that area. But as the investigation gathered momentum many more attacks in that area were to be added to the list. Until, if they'd been asked to play a hunch, the detectives working on the case would have guessed the killer lived somewhere in the bayside suburbs.

IN the time he didn't spend talking, which was a lot, Denis Lucas thought a lot. He was intrigued by the conundrum of a man who had soft hands and yet was often seen in the sort of clothes usually worn by manual workers. And the more Lucas wondered the more he had reservations about the theory, based solely on the offender's speech, that he was a white collar worker. Lucas had never forgotten a point made by the finger-print bureau about the prints found on Heywood's car. From the way they were formed, the experts said, they belonged to someone with soft hands. To Lucas this meant that the man they were hunting had, both at Shepparton in 1966 and around Melbourne's eastern suburbs in the 1970s, followed a trade that softened his hands. If you discarded the notion that he was an office worker who dressed down for sex attacks, it suggested someone who worked with food or with animals: occupations which might also explain the elusive odour.

Lucas worked out the rough possibilities: a cook or kitchen hand, an abattoir or saleyard worker, even a dairy farmer. The abattoir angle seemed most promising; there were plenty of meatworks in and around Melbourne in the 1970s. The chance of the rapist being a dairy farmer seemed slighter, but Lucas didn't dismiss it. He had milked cows himself, and knew how the constant washing and contact with greasy udders made a man's hands soft as butter.

The most recent rapes had been in the outer bayside suburbs, so abattoirs anywhere near that district would be top of the list of places to start looking, he thought. Then commercial kitchens. Then farms.

But before these logical lines of investigation could be followed through to the big man's satisfaction, events overtook the inquiry.

STEVE O'Baugh was a crime reporter, a seasoned tabloid newspaper man who moved sure footedly in the no-man's land between law enforcers and law breakers. The job was never easy, and working for a weekly newspaper, the *Sunday Press*, made it harder: any exclusive he landed usually had to be hidden from radio, television and the daily papers for days. Most galling of all to a reporter of O'Baugh's competitive instincts was the cosy understanding he sensed between a handful of influential police and some branches of the media. There was, strictly speaking, nothing improper about it, nothing more than a few free lunches and Christmas gifts to oil the working parts of an arrangement that benefited both parties.

But that was no help to the *Sunday Press*. O'Baugh could do nothing about it but try harder for the stories he suspected were being saved for others. This was why, when he heard just one discreet word passed from a senior policeman to another reporter at a function in early November, 1982, it pricked his interest. The word was 'Shepparton,' and although O'Baugh was American-born, he had read and written enough about the Madill-Heywood murders in his ten years in Australia to make the connection. But what was new about the case that had the favoured few at Russell Street swapping knowing looks?

The question gnawed at O'Baugh. He tried to bluff it out of the genial, cigar-smoking CIB officer everyone called 'Fat Harry'. But the CIB man, who could usually be relied on to confirm a story if a reporter had ferreted it from somewhere else, wasn't buying any of O'Baugh's nonchalant queries. He had plans of his own, and they didn't include handing over one of the best crime stories in twenty years to one weekly paper that had never done him any favours. When he let the story go it would run in all the dailies and every television and radio station.

O'Baugh knew this was the reality of the public relations game, but it was cold comfort. He cast around for an answer – and found it. He decided to try the New South Wales police in case the story had travelled north. If it worked it wouldn't be the first time that one state force had betrayed another's secrets. O'Baugh had once worked on the Sydney *Sun*, and he remembered a homicide detective in the harbour city with the reputation of knowing most things. He rang him. Two minutes later he started to smile ...

His contact's story was that a few months earlier two Victorian fingerprint men had flown to Sydney at short notice and spent a week searching the records. They were trying to match prints which had something to do with the Shepparton murders. Not long afterwards Victorian homicide detectives had arrived to print a rape suspect they thought might be the Shepparton killer.

The details were scanty, but O'Baugh was satisfied. He knew he had enough cards in his hand to bluff with. He spent most of the day on the telephone, and by afternoon had the story stitched up. He wrote it next day ready to go to press that night. It was Saturday, November 13. Lucky for him. Unlucky for Hanna and Lucas.

THE headlines screamed from posters outside every milk bar and newsagent in Victoria: 'KILLER PRINT CLUE'. And on the front page of the paper the story unfolded in the racy prose of the tabloid press. The first paragraph said that police were 'on the brink of solving a gruesome double murder'. The second said police believed they had linked a rapist with the Shepparton killings. Nothing in either to make Hanna, Lucas or the finger print men wince. But the next paragraph did.

'The dramatic breakthrough came as the rapist's fingerprints were matched with those taken from the scene of the grisly murder that shocked the nation,' it read.

O'Baugh had a bigger story than he realised. Unwittingly, he had blown a secret that had been kept for sixteen years ... the fact that fingerprints had been found on Heywood's car. It was a secret that a previous generation of police had entrusted to a previous generation of reporters, and one which O'Baugh would have kept without harming his exclusive – if someone had told him.

The public relations strategy had been too clever by half. But it was too late for recriminations. The killer, if he read the *Sunday Press*, now knew as much as the police.

H ANNA and Lucas were unhappy because they feared that that the story demolished their one possible advantage over the killer: the chance that he would continue to be careless with his fingerprints. But there were others, higher in the police hierarchy, who were peeved with the *Sunday Press* scoop for a different reason: that was, it stole the thunder of the official Press release they had planned. Left to themselves the Shepparton detectives would have been happier to dampen publicity until they had exhausted their existing 'lines of inquiry', and needed the public's help to generate more. But the decision was out of their hands. Two days after the *Sunday Press* exclusive a formal Press conference was called to unveil the bust.

The tiny conference room filled to overflowing. Before the microphones was turned on ground rules were spelt out: there would be no mention of finger prints – only 'forensic links.' Then the cameras and tapes rolled, and ballpoints hovered over notebooks. Denis Lucas, reluctantly the focus of attention, sweated in the glare of the television lights and stolidly began to recite the things the media had come to hear.

The man they were hunting was 'the most vicious criminal in Australia,' he said. Police were sure he was responsible for two attempted murders, eight rapes and two attempted rapes between 1971 and 1979. They believed he was probably still in Melbourne and could commit more crimes. It was possible, even likely, that he could have committed twice as many sex offences either not reported or not linked with him.

Then came the aspects of the case that were gradually to dominate the media coverage of the inquiry over the following months.

First, the bust. It was so realistic, said the detective, that a teenage girl who had seen the rapist attack her sister, had burst into tears when she saw the bust. This was accepted by the gathered reporters as proof positive of the bust's accuracy rather than a natural reaction by an overwrought child.

Second, the odour. 'Several' victims had reported a 'strong odour' but could not identify it. This was true, and yet the ambiguity of the words led reporters to place too much emphasis on the odour.

Third, the accent. 'The man's speech was soft and slow and had a cultured Scottish or Northern English accent,' was the way *The Age* reported the official line next morning.

Because of their novelty value, the bust, the accent, and the odour were starting to overshadow the firmest clues, the fact the man was almost always barefoot and carried a long butcher's knife. Through no fault of the investigators, the subtle process of transforming unchallenged assumptions into unquestioned 'facts' had begun.

THE floodgates opened. The police telephone numbers tagged to the bottom of newspaper stories were besieged with calls. In the three months from the time Hanna and Lucas had started the inquiry until the Press conference on November 16, they had logged 116 pages of running sheets. Yet in just 48 hours after the Press conference more than 800 calls filled 60 pages. Although the torrent eased after the first wave of public interest, the publicity was to attract hundreds more calls over the following weeks. Many were fatuous, a few sounded promising; all had to be taken seriously, which meant investigating and eliminating. It took six months slogging to clear the backlog, Hanna calculated later. It would have been a cheap enough price to pay, had just one lead been the right one. But as it turned out, the Shepparton detectives' private doubts about the risks of publicity were vindicated.

Public curiosity fuelled more stories about the inquiry, but because there were few new angles to report, the media eagerly picked over the same ground. The *Sunday Press*, keen to follow its scoop, led the way in keeping the story alive. For the November 21 edition Steve O'Baugh made the most of an offer by the Outdoor Advertising Association to give free use of 100 billboards to display photographs of the bust. As a story it was a pot-boiler, shrewdly seized on as an excuse to remind readers that the paper had broken the story three days before the rest of the media had it handed to them. But the billboard story spawned a name that was to label the unknown killer and the case for years, an example of the tongue-in-cheek inventiveness that explains why newspapers have coined a rogues' gallery of nicknames for criminals.

Lyall Corless was chief sub-editor of the *Sunday Press* when O'Baugh filed his story on November 20. It was hard to write a snappy headline in a few words because the offender did not have a name. The answer, he knew, was to invent one. He tossed the problem around the desk. It had to be short, immediately identifiable with the case, and have a sinister ring.

One sub-editor suggested 'Pongo' but Corless rejected it. O'Baugh came closer with 'Mr Smelly'. Corless thought for a moment, then doodled on his blotter: 'MR STINKY GETS TOP BILLING.' He counted the letters. It fitted the space beautifully.

Two days later *The Australian* used 'Mr Stinky' in a headline; other papers soon followed suit. The name stuck. The more that people read about 'Mr Stinky' the more it reinforced one of three basic ideas implanted in the public mind: that the wanted man had a 'foul odour', as one newspaper had put it, that he looked exactly like the photographs of the bust, and that he had an accent.

Repetition gave these impressions the resonance of absolute truth.

T HE publicity had been distracting for the detectives. They were swamped with hundreds of calls about men who looked like the photograph (one woman reported that the bust resembled a man she had glimpsed in her rear vision mirror), men who had accents, men with body odour, and men who had once lived in or visited Shepparton. But between recording the calls and the eye-glazing task of checking them, Hanna and Lucas plotted other ways to hunt their man.

Earlier in November they had briefed a government psychiatrist with what little was known about the killer, asking for a character profile of a likely suspect. The psychiatrist wrote, in part: 'It is likely he comes from a family with more than one child. He would be the youngest or perhaps have a younger sister. His parents are country people, his father a red-headed Scots or English immigrant, a violent, maybe alcoholic man. His mother Australian born, a passive but attractive and possessive woman. He has at least one elder brother but since there is little evidence of heterosexual social skills it is unlikely he had any elder sisters. The family has a farm and property.

'As a child he was shy, immature, fearful. He suffered nightmares, perhaps school refusals and when his parents were in conflict, enuresis (bedwetting) ...

'He shows no signs of a formal psychiatric disease, that is he had normal thought processes, no evidence of delusionary or strongly held beliefs and no emotional incongruity ... He obviously has a good IQ, but a late achiever. He left school at fifteen but eventually gained trade qualifications.

'He has limited social activities, collects coins and stamps, does hobby joinery and likes cricket. He has been to the opera, but by himself.'

Months later, Hanna was to seek another professional opinion, this time from a well-known consulting psychologist. His assessment was pithy:

'May have been born in Britain and spent childhood there, but possibly grew up in Shepparton area at least as a teenager; then most likely quiet, withdrawn, and shy (especially with girls), and timid, so probably not very noticed, except perhaps as a 'good boy'. Yet probably already sexually deviant, most likely a voyeur, perhaps around homes and lover's lane areas; may have made clumsy uninvited approaches to girls, but almost certainly no girlfriends.

'Now, likely to be a shy and withdrawn adult, especially with women; probably no close friends; probably lives alone, possibly with parents; probably not married but, if he is, the marriage will be in trouble, especially in the sexual area; probably no successful love or sexual relationships.

'Possibly immature and childish in some mannerisms. Probably still a voyeur, and may be involved in other antisocial or delinquent behaviours, but most likely in secretive ways …

'We doubt that he is a high performer (i.e. professional work), but he may be known for a methodical approach to work; may have a history of changing jobs as a result of not getting on with workmates or accepting criticism. Could be given to outbursts when pushed or under pressure.

'Overall, he probably does give other people clues that he is "odd" or "strange", but mostly in a direction of being shy, quiet and timid, rather than potentially violent; may have a reputation for exaggerating about girlfriends and sexual conquests;

but still probably gives impression of being a "good boy". People who know him well will probably be surprised when he is identified.'

Hanna wondered how much faith could be put in such speculation. He was mindful of the warning the psychologist included in a covering letter:

'The profile's limitation: it is made up of our predictions combining what is known about your offender individually with what we know about sex offenders in general. So almost certainly some of our predictions will be correct, and some wrong. But which it is we sadly can't say … '

A T Benalla, 180 kilometres north-east of Melbourne, an oddly-assorted trio of police was following the investigation. One was Detective Chief Inspector Dallas McDonald, who had approved Hanna and Lucas going to Melbourne, and was officially in charge of the inquiry. The second was his driver, Frank Eyre, the constable who had been on night shift in Shepparton the night that Garry Heywood and Abina Madill had disappeared. The third was Senior Detective Norm Gillespie, who as a teenager in 1966 had attended the concert at the civic centre, and in 1982 was stationed at Wangaratta, near Benalla.

Eyre had been fascinated by the mystery from the moment he had found Garry's FJ Holden abandoned by the lake the morning after the murders. Gillespie, whose family had attended the same church as the Madills, had an even deeper personal interest. He sometimes wondered if the murders were the underlying reason for his decision to join the force in 1969. In his second year in uniform he had been posted to Footscray, where one of the detectives was a former homicide man who had worked on the 1966 inquiry. Gillespie had often tried to talk to the senior man about the case, but had never won more than a brusque reply that 'it was Ian Urquhart.' Despite the widespread condemnation of Urquhart, Gillespie had always doubted his guilt. At every opportunity he would wangle his way into the homicide squad office at Russell Street and study the Heywood-Madill file. 'I was always real keen to relieve both families,' he said later.

Twelve years since then hadn't dulled Gillespie's hunger for the truth. After Hanna and Lucas had gone to Melbourne, Gillespie made sure that if Dallas McDonald wanted anything checked in Shepparton, he got the job. 'I was breaking my neck to interview the rape victims,' he was to recall, 'because I thought I might know the bastard that did it.'

His first big task was to trace the 93 Scottish-born men who had spent time at the Dhurringile hostel. Gillespie had gone to Shepparton Technical School with some of them. Several, he knew, were still living in the district. Many had scattered all over Australia, and a few had gone back to Britain.

Before the Dhurringile group was accounted for, another 35 British-born suspects were added to the checklist. These were former residents of an Anglican boys' home, Burton Hall, which had operated in the Shepparton district until 1960. One of those eliminated through fingerprint records already held by the police was a Graham Sweatland, whose whereabouts was unknown. The Graham Sweatland who had fought with a farmer's son at Yarroweyah twenty years before, over the killing of a dog.

A $10,000 reward had stood for almost seventeen years. After the burst of publicity in November the Minister for Police, recommended raising it to $50,000. The new reward was approved two days before Christmas and made public on January 4, 1983, in the first Government Gazette of the new year. It was a tacit admission that the police needed all the help they could get. It prompted a new wave of calls, but no breakthroughs. Of all the useless information gathered in the following weeks the most interesting was a report from Hampton CIB that Bob Hawke's house in Royal Avenue, Sandringham, had been entered in late February by someone who drilled holes in the window to release the screws holding the latch, a rare burglary method in Australia ... and the same method used by 'Mr Stinky' at Greensborough in 1975. No prints were found at the Hawke house and, strangely, nothing was reported stolen.

The house breaking provided a brief diversion for the detectives before being dismissed as a coincidence.

By April, 1983, Denis Lucas, frustrated with the hundreds of dead-ends created by the public response to the publicity, returned to Shepparton to work because of a family illness. Ken Mansell came from Shepparton to take his place. The first task Hanna set Mansell was to copy every page of the thousands in the Madill-Heywood homicide file, and to study them. On April 26 the two went to police headquarters at William Street to pick up every scrap of material that could be found on the murders, and to talk to Assistant Commissioner Reg Baker. It was Baker, as a young homicide detective, who had interviewed several suspects in 1966, and had kept the Mossberg file. Hanna and Mansell were keen to plumb his attitudes about the murders.

A chance meeting at William Street that day altered the course of the investigation. Hanna ran into Deputy Commissioner Rod Hall in a corridor. They knew each other from the Wireless Patrol days of the early 1960s. Hall asked what brought Hanna to the tenth floor at headquarters. Hanna showed him some pictures. Hall was interested. He asked more questions, then ushered his old squad mate into an office to see another deputy commissioner: Paul Delianis, Hanna's former golf partner and wedding guest. Afterwards Hanna and Mansell went to Russell Street to find and copy more material. Soon after arriving there they were given a message to return to William Street at 2pm that day.

When they got back they were shown into a conference room. Waiting for them was a gathering of commissioners and the heads of the CIB and the homicide squad. Half an hour later Hanna had permission for a taskforce. Someone up there liked him.

T HE taskforce was born on May 6, 1983. The birth notice, clattered out on the police telex network, was a circular summarising most of what Hanna and Lucas had learned about the killer in eight months of intensive investigation.

Under the heading NOT FOR PRESS, it read: 'A group of detectives under Detective Senior Sergeant Hanna are located at the Police Academy, Glen Waverley. Their role is to investigate a series of rape offences which took place at Donvale, Greensborough, Wheelers Hill and Chelsea Heights between 1971 and 1979 ...

'The description of the man sought is as follows: native of either Australia, Scotland, or England, now aged between 34 and 44 years, 163 to 178cm, flabby build with pot belly, thick set, sandy brown reddish blond long bushy hair, pasty fair complexion, soft hands, well spoken. In 1971 he spoke with a slight Scottish or North English accent. On a number of occasions the victims noticed a strong smell (unidentified) coming from him.

'His *modus operandi* is to enter superior quality homes between 8.30pm and 4am either by unlocked door or removing the fly screen from unlocked window. Knows husbands are not home. Very attractive victim with small children. Carries large knife and does not wear shoes. On occasions wore stocking mask. Leaves house carrying trousers and knife. Has obviously spent time looking at victim prior to attack. It is significant that he gained entry to a locked house at Greensborough by drilling a three quarter inch (2cm) hole with a brace and bit through lower timber frame of laundry window, then inserting a metal rod or similar to engage and dislodge inside metal spring-loaded window catch. This is a very rare method of entry. On another occasion he neatly cut a fixed flywire screen around bottom and sides and neatly rolled it to the top of the kitchen window ... '

The *modus operandi* reflected a calculating mind, that of a man who studied ways of entering each house and equipped himself, if necessary, with specific tools to carry out an attack. There were other things that Hanna and Lucas had worked out. By comparing the statements of each victim, they found the rapist nearly always used the same approach. The first 40 words used by the man in each attack were almost identical. From this they had drawn up a list of signature words and phrases, most of them reassurances that the victim and her children would not be hurt ... providing she submitted. After producing his knife he would usually say: 'Keep quiet. Don't scream, I don't want to hurt you.' Sometimes he would add that he had been watching the victim, and that he knew when her husband was due to return. Often he used the words: 'I just want someone to love me', or 'I want to make love to you.'

To a psychiatrist, Hanna was to say later, 'this would be a symptom of something. But to detectives it is just a clue to the puzzle – an identifying thing like a tattoo or a scar.'

Despite the conciliatory words the rapist used, his overtures did not blunt the menace felt by the women. One victim was to recall how the man had been completely unmoved when she screamed at the top of her voice. The scream (heard, ironically, by neighbours who ignored it) could easily have brought a rescuer, but the man had not flinched. He had calmly forced her to strip, thrown a blanket over the head of her four-year-old son on the bed next to her, then raped her.

The man's calmness had only heightened the woman's fears for herself and her children. A man of such unnatural coolness, she told police, seemed capable of anything. Hanna agreed. Their quarry, he guessed, would not be rattled if routinely stopped and questioned near a rape scene at night. It seemed likely that the killer who wanted to be loved would be a nerveless liar as well. Some opponent.

FROM their newly-allocated office on the second floor of the police academy at Mount Waverley Hanna and Mansell and the four suburban detectives seconded to the taskforce commanded a sweeping view of the south-eastern suburbs. 'From here,' Hanna often muttered, 'we can probably see the house where this bloke lives.'

It was a tantalising thought. Within a fortnight it became a taunt. That was when they studied details of a rape which had happened a few weeks earlier … only 800 metres from the academy. The attack had all the hallmarks of the Shepparton killer. After interviewing the victim, a seventeen-year-old girl, Hanna was sure of it; he listed the girl as the thirteenth victim.

The striking thing about the crime was that it was the first rape to be credited to 'Mr Stinky' after 1979. It proved that the killer was still active, and buried the nagging doubt that he might have died or fled overseas. The knowledge spurred the detectives. Any time they looked out the window they could see the house where the teenager had been raped. It was as if, after much casting about, the hounds had found a fresh scent to follow.

There were two things about the latest attack which stood out. One was that the attacker was obviously trying to avoid leaving fingerprints. The girl saw him cover his hands with the end of his sleeve when he touched something, and he had ordered her to turn on a bedside lamp rather than touch the switch himself. The implication was that the publicity about fingerprints had made him wary.

The second aspect was less predictable. After terrifying the girl for half an hour, forcing her to endure gross sex acts, the man had made a bizarre show of concern for her welfare. He advised her to see a psychiatrist.

To Hanna and Mansell, this seemed to suggest that the rapist had himself seen a psychiatrist. If so, and if he revealed that he had committed serious offences, a responsible practitioner should notify the law, they hoped.

THE pressure was on the taskforce from without and within. Such groups are a luxury in a busy police force, and plenty of police thought a seventeen-year-old murder didn't warrant six full-time detectives, as well as various others 'borrowed' by Hanna when he could get them.

The self-imposed pressure came from the knowledge that unless the killer was caught, there would be more rapes, perhaps more murders. And there was something else: the knowledge that the people of Shepparton were watching and waiting. There was an obligation to them beyond the call of duty. Hanna recalled the mayor of the town, Bill Hunter, trying to explain how deeply the murders had affected people, telling him that it 'was a blot on the character of Shepparton.' The memory of the murders still haunted the town. Only catching the killer would exorcise it.

The taskforce members knew roughly what the killer looked like, his approximate age, that he might once have lived in the Shepparton district, and that he now probably lived in Melbourne's eastern suburbs. The information was teasingly vague. Barring the possibility that the killer might allow himself to be finger-printed after chancing into police hands, or nominated by a public-spirited psychiatrist, the odds against finding him were long. There were two ways to tackle the problem, and Hanna – with Dallas McDonald's blessing – decided to try both.

The first was conventional: to wear out boot leather working through the pool of possible suspects arising from the rapes and, to a lesser extent, those not properly eliminated by the original murder inquiry in 1966. This approach would be based on selecting the most likely areas of investigation and following them. It meant starting with the victims and moving outwards. Who would be in a position to know each woman's movements? Who would be familiar with particular houses? Streets? Suburbs? It meant a relentless search for patterns, for a common denominator. What occupation would give a man the chance to observe each victim without being noticed?

The lists of possibilities were long, and were to grow longer as the months passed. The victims all lived in modern houses, so the names of building firms, employees, tradesmen and sub-contractors were checked. Then the service workers: electricity, gas and Telecom meter-readers and technicians. Then it was noticed that six of the women used the Commonwealth bank, several others the ANZ. Could it be a teller who had changed jobs? Garage employee? Shopkeeper? Milkman? A schoolteacher who had been transferred from suburb to suburb after teaching or living at or near Shepparton.

Then there was Denis Lucas's original idea of abattoir workers. At the Shepparton end, Norm Gillespie regularly drove to his home town from Wangaratta to fill the gaps in the old murder investigation. After eliminating the Dhurringile and Burton Hall old boys, he turned to the attendance rolls from every school in the district, noting any male who was old enough to have committed murder in 1966. Each possibility raised many others, and they all had to be followed up. It was classic police work.

Hanna's other option was not classic police work. It was, to stretch a fishing simile, to use a net rather than a rod. Instead of dangling lines for one man they could try to gather everybody who fitted the criteria and then set about sorting out the catch. Fingerprinting would make the sorting easy, if tedious. The challenge was to find a way of identifying and listing all the men who met the criteria.

The solution Hanna and McDonald worked out was to use a computer. The premise was simple enough: feed in the names of everybody who had lived at Shepparton in the 1960s and in Melbourne's eastern suburbs in the 1970s and programme the machine to look for those who had been in both places. Then start sorting by sex, age, and appearance to get a pool of likely suspects. Then start knocking on doors ...

DALLAS McDonald had become engrossed in the case, his distance from the taskforce's headquarters seeming to sharpen his appetite for the battle, like a chess master playing a match by telephone. He asked for copies of everything that the taskforce detectives gathered, and monitored their progress daily by telex from Benalla. As the months passed without a breakthrough, his wife grew concerned at how the case consumed him. He had always been conscientious, but now he began to stay up late at night poring over folders full of material gathered by the taskforce, chain-smoking and frowning as he willed the jigsaw pieces to fall into place. He would sometimes say distractedly to his wife: 'We're missing something, it must be here.' And he would read to her and ask her what she thought, hoping that a fresh view, an oblique angle, would miraculously crack the code. 'We are policemen,' he would say. 'We might be overlooking something because of the way we think ... ' It was to get that way, later, that he would light a cigarette even before answering the telephone. It was the beginning of the illness that was to kill him.

McDonald had another confidant in Frank Eyre, his driver. The chief inspector was not one to stand on rank, but he had an unconscious grace which transcended police station politics, and won him the warm respect of his staff. Eyre, a hard bitten veteran of the force not much younger than his boss, was entrusted with collating details of the investigation for McDonald as the taskforce sent them. He provided a sounding board for McDonald's ideas, which were unfettered by the dogmatic adherence to the conventional that hobbles some police minds. McDonald considered many theories, and his willingness to research small details was endless. One exercise that stayed in Eyre's mind was his boss's study of astrological tables to see if the rapes formed a pattern with the phases of the moon. Another was to calculate on which days of the week the crimes fell – an exercise which revealed that the attacker had not set out to commit any rapes on Sundays. Coincidences also fascinated McDonald; in particular the fact that the first known rape victim at Donvale, Mrs B, had been living in Shepparton in 1966, within walking distance of the place Garry Heywood's car was found. Another rape victim, at Chelsea Heights, was related to a famous VFL football coach who had coached in Shepparton in the early 1960s. 'There must be a Shepparton connection,' he would say to Eyre.

When Hanna broached the subject of using a computer, McDonald was delighted. He championed new ideas, and would back anything he thought might get a result, orthodox or not. One of the first people he discussed the idea with was Eyre. Whose niece, it turned out, was a computer programmer with a leading accountancy firm, Arthur Andersen & Co., in

Melbourne. Through her Eyre arranged an introduction for Hanna and Mansell.

After much discussion about computers' capabilities and the type of data that could be fed into them, the firm agreed to donate an expert programmer and computer time one day a week, when it was needed. Hanna was pleased with the coup, but bemused by the technical side of the deal. As the two detectives left the Andersen offices in Collins Street Hanna asked his companion if he'd understood any of it. Mansell knew little about computers, but he had been a telephone technician for four years before joining the force, and he was confident that he could get by. 'Yeah, I think so,' he answered.

'Well, you've got it,' Hanna said dryly.

T HE computer needed information. To get it, Mansell had to find help for the huge task of gathering names and addresses from every possible source. The nearest pool of available labour was one floor below the taskforce office at the police academy. As each intake of recruits finished basic training and entered the Independent Patrol Group stage, Mansell swooped. He addressed each group about the inquiry, then called for volunteers to spend a month doing the rounds of estate agents in the eastern suburbs. Their job was to record on cards the names and addresses of every person who had rented a house or flat in the previous twenty years.

Meanwhile, Mansell scoured every other source he could think of for lists of names. The obvious ones were electoral rolls for Shepparton and the eastern suburbs, and the school rolls Norm Gillespie had already obtained. Next were records of house sales kept at the Titles Office. Beyond that, it was up to his powers of persuasion: some large organisations considered that the public interest outweighed the normal considerations of individual privacy; others didn't. One of the notable refusals was from the Costigan Royal Commission on organised crime, which declined to supply names culled from the taxation records it was studying. Nor would the commission staff use their computer to pinpoint the people who met the taskforce's criteria. Neither refusal worried Mansell; he had so many names, from such a variety of sources, that he was confident that if the wanted man did live in the eastern suburbs he would be listed when the computer sorted the data according to the criteria.

And Mansell had no doubts about where the killer lived. He often ran his finger down the map that had the rape scenes marked on it, sketching an invisible line parallel with Springvale Road, the traffic artery running north-south from the hills of East Doncaster to the Bay at Chelsea. Apart from the Greensborough offences, the rape scenes were close to the road. 'He lives in Springvale Road or close to it,' Mansell would say. So often that it became a standing joke among the detectives. Mansell laughed along with them, but he believed it.

IT was Melbourne Cup Day, 1983, but Hanna, Mansell and another detective, Mike Edwards, weren't going to Flemington. As the first of the public holiday crowd headed to the track that sunny November morning the three policemen gathered at the crime statistics office at Russell Street, rolled up their sleeves and started pulling files from the crowded shelves.

Behind them were thousands of hours of investigation which had turned up alarming evidence that 'Mr Stinky' had raped many more women than originally thought. The list of possible victims ran to at least 50, and even when reduced by stringent checking of *modus operandi* and description it was more than twenty, an extraordinary catalogue of misery inflicted by one man. The purpose of the detectives' visit to the statistics office was to study the crime reports for every rape and aggravated burglary in the previous decade. It was tedious, but they couldn't afford to be lax; that could lead to overlooking some small detail in a statement which might provide the key to the case. Ninety per cent of the rapes they were to look at that day had been solved. Therefore, if the statement of any of those victims revealed a pattern of words or phrases similar to the ones 'Mr Stinky' always used, they would have their man.

The detectives started with an armful of files from 1973, sat down and started reading. By the time they paused that afternoon to listen to Kiwi charge into racing history each man was surrounded by files. By the end of the week they had studied more than 2000. But not one revealed anything that sounded like the wanted man.

THE fourth biennial meeting of the Association of Australasian and Pacific Area Police Medical Officers was to run over two days in February, 1984, at Melbourne University. At the request of the Victoria Police surgeon, Dr Bush, Dallas McDonald had agreed to open a session devoted to the Madill-Heywood inquiry, after which Dennis Hanna and other detectives would present the history of the case and the methods used to tackle it. From the taskforce's point of view it was worth devoting time to preparing the presentation thoroughly in the hope that a lecture theatre full of police surgeons playing detective might produce a new idea.

McDonald grabbed the opportunity to put the case before such an audience. If nothing else, it was recognition of the gravity of the crimes and the depth of the investigation. At other seminars held by the association, notorious and complex cases – notably the Yorkshire Ripper inquiry – had been dissected. McDonald knew from his voracious reading of criminology that his taskforce had mounted one of the most sophisticated murder investigations in the world. He was determined to demonstrate the breadth of the inquiry, and worked hard on his opening address.

Too hard.

On the morning of February 14, an hour before he was due to make his address, McDonald vomited in his motel room. He told his wife it was only because of the orange juice he'd had with his breakfast. Mrs McDonald was not convinced. When he stood in front of the lectern half an hour later she knew there was something wrong. She was partially blind, and couldn't see, as others could, that her husband was ashen. But when he started to speak she couldn't understand a word. He stopped, knuckles whitening as he gripped the lectern, breathed deeply, and with a supreme effort of will delivered his speech. The strange thing, Mrs McDonald was to remember, was that in an audience of eminent doctors she seemed the only one to realise how ill her husband was.

Next morning, McDonald vomited again. Travelling home to Benalla he drove erratically, his judgement of speed and distance clouded by some malign force that made his wife uneasy. He vomited next morning, and the morning after that. The doctor at Benalla thought it might be a middle ear infection, and admitted him to hospital for observation. After a week of watching him decline, Mrs McDonald could stand it no longer. She insisted he be transferred to the police hospital in Melbourne …

The brain scan revealed two shadows. It took the physician an hour and thousands of words to tell Mrs McDonald the news she dreaded: it was a tumour. Her Dallas was going to die.

ONLY the result was certain; the time it would take for McDonald to die could be 'days, weeks or months', according to the doctor. The news hit the taskforce hard. The diagnosis meant that if 'Mr Mack' was to realise his last ambition, the arrest of the murderer, they had to get somewhere fast. It was frustrating that the painstaking process of eliminating suspects could not be hurried. Any more, Hanna knew, than you could hurry the catching of a trout. If the fish were there and the lure was equal to the task, then it would be landed eventually.

Even the gathering of tenant records from estate agents to run the computer program depended on the availability of each batch of recruits; the rest of the taskforce was busy keeping abreast of the dozens of leads which had to be followed. Each detective tried desperately to come up with something fresh before going to see McDonald in hospital, and any lead that was remotely promising was polished until it glowed for the sick man's benefit. It was heartbreaking for the detectives, going to the police hospital time after time, knowing inside that only the news of a breakthrough would please the dying man. Heartbreaking to be acting out a cheerful and optimistic part, knowing all the while that the pain-wracked figure in bed was staunchly pretending he didn't know they were faking it for him.

It reminded Hanna of a time, years before, when another policeman he knew had been dying of cancer in the same ward. The stricken man had been young, married with small children and much to live for, and he had taken it hard. Hanna had never forgotten how, every few days, a different member of the dying man's squad had admitted himself to hospital with a virus, or influenza, or a cold ... they were not going to let their mate face death alone.

But sentiment, loyalty, mateship, 'seeing the job through' – none of it counted for much when the accountants did their sums. The taskforce had been going for a year, and Hanna and Lucas had been absent from their normal duties eight months before that. The taskforce could not last much longer. With Dallas McDonald too ill to defend it the rumblings of discontent about its length and expense and apparent lack of results were growing louder. Until the day came, just before Christmas, 1984, when Hanna and Mansell were ordered back to Shepparton, and the tail end of the taskforce was handed over to another officer.

The new man made it clear he thought the computer exercise a waste of time. But after coming so far, Ken Mansell was not going to be thwarted. He quietly arranged for everything that had been collected to be put into the system and processed. When it was finished the computer had printed some 2000 pages containing about 100,000 names in alphabetical order, of which more than half could be automatically eliminated because they were the names of companies, businesses or women.

The computer operators divided the pile of print-outs into a dozen folders. Mansell took them to Shepparton and stacked them on a shelf in Dennis Hanna's office. He and Hanna were determined that one day every man on the list who was in the right age group would be seen, and any who matched the description would be politely asked for his finger prints. They weren't going to let almost two years' work go to waste.

DALLAS McDonald died on October 11, 1984, a week after being flown back to Benalla by air ambulance. He was 56. The funeral was held at the Baptist Church in Kew, with full police honours. Dennis Hanna gave the eulogy, and spoke bluntly of McDonald's dedication to the investigation, of the fact that he had believed in it to the end. It was a pointed reference to the decision to wind up the taskforce and the lack of interest in following through the computer exercise.

Frank Eyre was close to tears. 'It was the saddest day of my life,' he was to say, 'because he died without the murders being solved.' He remembered something 'Mr Mack' had often spoken of in their long talks about the Madill-Heywood investigation. It was a notorious murder case in England where the only clue had been an unidentified fingerprint at the scene. It had gone unsolved for years until an alert policeman matched the print with one found on a stolen car. The police picked up the thief, and he confessed to the murder.

'That's the way we'll get him, Frank,' McDonald had told him. And Frank had always believed it.

ELEVEN

Endplay, 1985

ALBURY, NSW. Saturday, March 16, 1985. It was almost lunchtime and Pat Halpin's attention was wandering. The cash register from which she ran the electrical department of Walton's department store was next to the big display windows, and watching passers-by went with the territory. The manager had often joked that he should hang curtains in the windows, but such jibes didn't bother Mrs Halpin, grandmother of three and a fixture in the shop.

She had worked 'on and off' at the store for 30 years, outlasting two proprietors and more managers than she could remember.

Mrs Halpin could recall the faces of most people who had shopped there regularly. And this day, when she glanced at the driver of a Ford station wagon parked outside in Kiewa Street, she thought his face was vaguely familiar. He was a beefy man with sandy hair, his thick forearms and pot belly easily seen beneath the blue workman's singlet and shorts. She had a clear view; the car was parked parallel to the kerb. He must have been a customer once, she thought idly, and turned back to her cash register.

A few minutes later Mrs Halpin glanced out the window again. The station wagon was still there. This time, she noticed, the driver had his seat laid back at the comfortable angle most people use when resting. But this man wasn't resting. His face looked agitated, she thought. And he was drumming on the steering wheel with his hand, or at least …

Mrs Halpin looked harder. Suddenly, her expression changed: first to disbelief, then a sort of shocked amusement. It wasn't the steering wheel the man was tapping. He was, as Mrs Halpin later stated euphemistically to police, 'giving himself a real going over.' She looked across the aisle at John Arnott, who was in charge of menswear. He caught her eye. 'What are you grinning at, Halpin?' he asked flippantly.

She motioned him closer and whispered conspiratorially: 'Come and have a look at this. There's a man out there playing with himself.' Arnott darted to the window, where he was well-hidden by a display of microwave ovens. He peered at the man in the car. 'You're right,' he said. 'He's up to no good.' As he spoke two young women parked their car behind the station wagon, got out and walked past it. They couldn't miss seeing the man in the Ford leering at them … or what he was doing. They clasped their arms around their breasts in an instinctive defensive gesture, and hurried off. The man had made no effort to conceal himself. But whenever a male walked past the car he covered his lap with a handkerchief.

Meanwhile, other shop assistants had gathered round. One of them told the acting store manager, Brian Huxley, who was just about to finish for the day to play tennis. The manager, Alan Chapman, arrived to take over from Huxley for the afternoon. When he heard what was happening Chapman came over to the window and had a look. It was not the sort of scene he wanted outside the front door of his store. He went to his office and rang the police.

IT was a quiet day for crime in Albury. When the call came through from Waltons two police cars were sent. Both parked at the rear of the store out of sight of the station wagon. Three uniformed constables came through the back door of the store and watched the man through the window. Then Constable Glenn Taylor slipped outside and approached the station wagon from behind. When the man in the driver's seat saw the blue uniform he looked shocked. At first he tried to deny doing anything wrong. Then, realising the futility, he fell silent. Taylor signalled to the other policemen. One of them, Kevin Savage, fetched one of the cars and parked it near the Ford. While Taylor went back into the store to share the tedious business of taking details from the staff with the other constable, Peter Chemings, Savage drove the flasher back to the station, just around the corner in Olive Street.

The man was crestfallen, almost meek. He sat in the front of the police car. Savage didn't bother to handcuff him: 'He didn't seem the type.' At the station they went into the muster room and sat down. Savage asked the usual questions and got the usual answers. Yeah, it was a pretty silly thing to do. Childish. Stupid. No, he hadn't done anything else like that before. Savage stifled a yawn and started to fill in the charge book: '… in view of a public place did wilfully and obscenely expose his person.' It was just another street offence.

When Chemings and Taylor arrived Savage artfully dodged the dirty work. Being a constable, first class, he could pull just enough rank to get Chemings to take the offender's fingerprints. It was tedious, it got ink on your hands, and you had to do the paperwork. If the Victorian blokes had picked him up just across the river in Wodonga, he knew, they wouldn't have to bother printing micky mouse offenders like this. But in NSW it was compulsory.

Chemings grimaced, and told the flasher to wash his hands. Then he got out the fingerprint board and started rolling black ink on it.

S YDNEY, Thursday, March 21, 1985. Ray Butterfield, a senior detective in the Central Fingerprint Bureau, was working late. Every fingerprint in Australia had to be assessed and filed by the bureau, which was shorthanded, and overtime was a fact of life for the staff. Butterfield had started at 7am and was theoretically due to finish at 3.30pm. It was now almost 5pm, and there was still a pile of fingerprint forms in the in-tray.

Butterfield walked over to the central table, took a form from the pile and returned to his desk to study it. In the few seconds it took to stroll back he had scanned the back of the form, which held the offender's name and address. A Melbourne address, he noted, then turned the form over and glanced at the print. And caught his breath.

Two things leapt at Butterfield's expert eye. One was the strongly-defined index fingers. The other a scar on one little finger, cutting across the tiny ridges as clearly as a brand on a bullock's hide. Once seen, distinguishing marks like that were not forgotten by a professional. And Butterfield had seen them just eight months before, when two Victorian fingerprint men had come up for a week to search the Sydney files to match the print he had in his hand.

He shook his head, amazed. 'This has got to be the bloke they're looking for in Melbourne,' he said to the detective next to him. 'What bloke?' asked the other man, blankly. Butterfield hardly heard him. He had no doubts, but the discipline of the bureau's credo – check and double check – asserted itself. Outwardly calm, he searched the folder devoted to serious unsolved crimes, which he knew contained the details of the Madill-Heywood investigation. He took out the composite set of developed prints sent up by the Victorians. It matched. He knew it would.

A sergeant walked past. 'Hey, check this out!' Butterfield called exultantly. The sergeant looked at the composite photographs and then at the form sent from Albury. 'Well, I'll be buggered,' he said slowly. Here, in the mundane way of the real world, was law enforcement history. After nineteen years, a double murderer and multiple rapist had wandered into the net. It was then they realised they didn't know the name the Victorians had wanted since 1966. Butterfield turned over the form and read it.

Raymond Edmunds.

MELBOURNE, Thursday, March 21, 1985. Brian Norton, head of the Victorian fingerprint bureau, was at his daughter's place in Williamstown when the news came. It was his day off, and he and his wife had spent the afternoon there. Just before 5.30pm Norton took his three-year-old grandson for a walk to the local greengrocer's, to save his daughter the effort of shopping.

She was eight months pregnant and the weather was hot, so he was surprised when she 'came waddling up' to the shops after him. The office had rung to say there was an urgent message, she said, and he was to ring back straight away. Norton handed his grandson to his daughter and walked back to the house.

A woman at the bureau answered his call. She was excited. 'You'll never guess what's happened,' she blurted. 'We've got some great news … '

Norton interrupted. 'Oh, I suppose you've got Mr Stinky,' he joked, then waited for her to finish the message. But all he heard was a sharp intake of breath.

'How do you know?' she asked, incredulous.

It was Norton's turn to be surprised. 'You can't be serious,' he said weakly.

Norton telephoned Sydney. The sergeant at the finger print bureau told him the name of the wanted man, that he had been picked up in Albury the previous Saturday and fined $400 in the local magistrates court for indecent exposure. Despite the Melbourne address, given as Victoria Street, Mordialloc, Edmunds was thought to be working near Albury. Norton asked for a set of the Albury fingerprints to be sent by facsimile. Then he rang the duty CIB officer for the day, Brendan Cole, who had heard something big was on and had left a message at the office for Norton to ring him. Everyone wanted to be in at the kill, Norton thought wryly. He decided to ring the detectives who were the most entitled to know about the breakthrough. Meticulous as ever, he noted each call in his police diary.

It was 6.45pm when he got through to the Shepparton CIB office. Ken Mansell 'was over the moon' at the news. Norton asked him to tell Dennis Hanna. Next, Norton rang the duty commissioner, Kelvin Glare, later to be Victoria's chief commissioner, and went through the formality of informing the chain of command of the facts.

At 8.30pm the telephone rang. It was Hanna. The two men, of similar age, experience, and with the same phlegmatic approach, knew they should be delighted. But, somehow, a sense of anti-climax was already nibbling at them. 'We were both deflated,' Norton was to remember. The thrill of the hunt had drained away. It was time to face the demanding task of putting a case together and making it stick.

Norton made his last call of the night at 9pm, to Noel Jubb, the chief superintendent in the CIB operations section. They made tentative arrangements for Norton to fly to Albury early next day. Until somebody said differently, it had to be assumed that the killer was still there.

K EN Mansell couldn't resist it. He went into Hanna's office and surveyed the folders of computer print-outs he'd stacked on a shelf a few months before. He picked up the folder labelled 'E-F', and flicked the pages. He stopped at page fifteen, and ran a broad finger down the names listed alphabetically in the left-hand column. There, halfway down the page, was the entry that proved the computer exercise had worked … 'EDMUNDS, Raymond; Victoria Street, Mordialloc.'

Mansell smiled. It was good to be right. But what a pity, he thought, that they hadn't been allowed to prove it.

F RIDAY, March 22. Norton was up at 6am ready to go to Albury, but before 7am he took a call from the crime intelligence bureau to say they had found Edmunds and had undercover surveillance police tailing him. The revised plan was that he and Andrew Wall should go to Mordialloc police station as soon as possible because Hanna, Mansell and the other Shepparton CIB members would be picking up Edmunds early.

Norton drove straight to the fingerprint bureau at Russell Street to collect Wall and the gear they would need. They left at 7.30am – and drove straight into a traffic jam in King Street. A truck had hit a bridge, and the peak-hour traffic was banked up for blocks. In an unmarked car with no emergency lights or siren, they were trapped. By the time they extricated themselves they were running half-an-hour late. Because of the rule limiting questioning of a suspect to six hours, it was vital that not a minute be wasted once Edmunds was arrested. Six hours wouldn't be enough time to question him properly about the murders, let alone the confirmed total of 32 sex attacks and the possibility of other serious crimes. He called D-24 on the radio and explained the dilemma, hoping that headquarters could postpone the arrest to give them time to get to Mordialloc. Headquarters had a better idea: divert to St Kilda police station, a few minutes away. Hanna and the Shepparton crew would meet them there instead. Norton heaved a sigh of relief.

When they reached St Kilda there was no sign of the Shepparton detectives and their prisoner. Norton and Wall went into the station mess room, made a cup of coffee, and sat down to wait. It was 8.30am.

THE previous night had been a long one for the Shepparton crew. After Norton had broken the news over the telephone Hanna rang Albury police to ask them to find Edmunds and watch him, with strict warnings against telling anybody or scaring him off. Unbeknown to Hanna, a senior CIB officer from Russell Street had also rung Albury with an identical order, to the bemusement of the young constable who had taken both calls. Office politics was flourishing. Mansell did some digging, found which motel Edmunds had used in Albury and rang to see if he was still booked in. He wasn't, but that didn't mean he wasn't elsewhere in Albury. By this time Denis Lucas and Norm Gillespie were in the office and chafing to go. But for the moment, it was a dead-end. After talking to Norton at 8.30pm Hanna decided that they would take a chance and head for Albury.

The car had barely cleared Shepparton's outskirts when the radio crackled to life. The surveillance people had located a car registered in Edmunds' name at the Mordialloc address he had given Albury police the previous Saturday, and they had the house under watch.

This was it. Norm Gillespie spun the car around and cut back through Shepparton to the Melbourne road. The atmosphere was tense, replacing the mood of expectation earlier in the evening. The six-hour rule suddenly loomed over events like a black cloud. Six hours to establish the facts about a double murder that happened half a lifetime before, leaving aside the rapes. It was depressing. As depressing as the accommodation they scrounged when they got to Russell Street just before midnight. Mattresses on the floor of the old barracks, two to a room.

They were up at 6am, ready for the call from criminal intelligence that would steer them to the confrontation that Mansell and Gillespie, the hometown boys, had thought about for half their lives. They had dealt with murderers and rapists before, but this was personal.

Mansell rang two of the Melbourne-based detectives who had been in the taskforce, so that they would have the chance of sharing the moment of triumph. Security dictated that he couldn't explain, over the telephone, why it was important that they rendezvous at Mordialloc. One of the two took the hint, and said he would be there. The other was puzzled by Mansell's ambiguous invitation, and said he had a previous engagement, a decision he was to regret later.

They drove to Mordialloc and met the other taskforce man, Mike Edwards. Gillespie joined him in another car, ready to 'turn over' Edmunds' house when the time was ripe. A message came from the 'dogs' who were tailing Edmunds. He had left the house and driven to a factory in Teton Court in Highett, a nearby suburb.

Hanna, Mansell and Lucas set off. They met one of the surveillance cars at a pre-arranged spot in Highett. The sergeant of the surveillance crew said he had a clear look at the man they'd followed and he matched the descriptions. The detectives looked at each other. Lucas eased the CIB car around the block and into a parking spot in the court in front of the factory. They left the car and walked towards the factory door, hearts thumping.

Inside, there was an office partitioned off from the factory. Through the frosted glass door they could make out someone talking to a man seated behind a desk. The door opened, and a factory hand walked out. He wasn't the man they wanted. But the man behind the desk was.

If there had been ten men in the room, Mansell was to say later, they would still have known which was Edmunds. He was round-shouldered and pot-bellied but powerful looking, and dressed in a blue work singlet, shorts, and work boots. His greying hair had an auburn tinge. His light hazel eyes were small and unfriendly, and the long, slightly curved nose gave his face a predatory look not softened by the confident, businesslike smile.

'Come in, gentlemen,' he said quietly. 'What can I do for you?'

It was 7.50am.

THE record of interview started from that moment. With the law limiting questioning to six hours every second counted: if the man was unco-operative and the police couldn't elicit enough to charge him with in that time, they would have to let him walk. The detectives were tense. Hanna asked the man if he was Raymond Edmunds, then produced his identification badge and introduced himself and the other two. Mansell scratched furiously in a notebook, noting the conversation.

The first thing was to get Edmunds outside the office and into the car, away from any weapons he might have stashed against a day of reckoning. Edmunds looked around warily, then agreed to go to the car. He sat in the back, wedged between Mansell and Hanna. Lucas took the wheel. Hanna went straight to the point. 'I want to speak to you regarding the murder of a young couple at or near Shepparton in 1966,' he said. 'You are in custody and you are not obliged to say anything further unless you wish, whatever you say or do will be taken down in writing and may be given in evidence.'

Edmunds said he understood.

He was eerily calm. Not a flicker of emotion strayed across his face when Hanna asked if he had killed the teenagers at Shepparton. Nor when he was told his fingerprints had been found at the scene of the crime. Nor when he was told they were going to Mordialloc police station to fingerprint him for comparison. 'Fair enough,' he said, and shrugged. A guilty man's inner fears should surely have seeped to the surface some way: beads of sweat, a twitching jaw muscle, white knuckles, faster breathing? An innocent man would surely have been protesting in rage and disbelief. Edmunds did neither. Here was a man marooned from birth on an emotional island, and who had grown up totally amoral, grotesquely self-centred.

O N the way to Mordialloc police station Edmunds politely answered questions about his two marriages. While Lucas went inside to see if Norton and Wall had arrived to take the fingerprints, Hanna and Mansell continued questioning and writing. Edmunds told them he had been boarding at a house in Springvale Road, but that he was hoping to get back together with his second wife, Colleen, who had divorced him the year before. Mansell felt a glow of satisfaction at the mention of the Springvale Road address. And again a few moments later when Edmunds said he had share-farmed a property in Wells Road,

Chelsea Heights. It was just off Springvale Road – and right in the centre of a cluster of unsolved rapes.

The detectives didn't know it then, but for all his apparent frankness Edmunds was making neat omissions from the answers he gave about his past. Before working for Danwire in Highett, he said, he had share-farmed at Singleton – an answer which conveniently overlooked his time in Sydney, working as a 'private investigator,' collecting debts.

Hanna went back to the beginning, from Edmunds' first marriage in 1961. He described living at Yarroweyah, then working on the two properties owned by the same person ('I can't remember his name') at 'Girgarre' (meaning Stanhope) and Tongala. The next step in the interview was significant. From Tongala, he lied smoothly, he had moved to Finley. Which meant, he said, that he had worked at Girgarre and Tongala 'altogether for about three years.'

He was a plausible liar but not a wise one. He denied ever owning a .22 rifle, a statement which could easily be disproved. While merely having owned a rifle would not necessarily add to the case against him, lying about it certainly would, once the truth was established. Impervious to the scepticism creeping into Hanna's questions, Edmunds emphatically denied having fired a rifle in his life, despite having grown up on farms in the back country. Similarly, he said that before going to Shepparton to meet Colleen in 1971 he had 'never' been there.

He was, Hanna and Mansell sensed, protesting his ignorance of Shepparton too much: a sign of feeling the pressure. Lucas returned to say that Norton had gone to St Kilda. Hanna kept talking. Polite, insistent, insinuating. For the first time Edmunds volunteered something he wasn't asked.

'I know how this come about,' he said in a now-I'll-come-clean tone, 'it's from that Albury episode.'

Hanna struck. 'Not only Albury.'

'No,' said Edmunds, and fell silent.

Hanna pursued his tiny advantage. 'We have been working on this investigation for a couple of years and we believe your fingerprints were found at the scene of the murders.'

'I can assure you they're not mine.' The confidence was starting to sound a little forced.

'We will be able to establish that very soon after we get to St Kilda,' said Hanna evenly, giving the words time to sink in. The fly fisherman was confident of his tackle. It was a matter of time ... but that was what they didn't have much of.

Edmunds reverted to the Albury incident, as if to imply that he was being accused of murder merely because he had been caught exposing himself. Hanna stepped out of the car and gave Norm Gillespie the Springvale Road address where Edmunds said he was boarding. Gillespie and Edwards drove off to search it and the house in Mordialloc.

Hanna got back in the car. They drove off. Hanna asked Edmunds where he had been living in 1971, then where his children were, then about the cars he had owned. Working backwards, Edmunds obligingly listed his new Ford, a 1974 Fairlane, a 1973 Ford station wagon, a Holden station wagon and the red 1960 EK Holden. No mention of the red Falcon bought from Smith's Motors, Shepparton, in 1965.

By the time Mansell had scribbled another page of questions and answers about the places Edmunds had lived and worked they were at St Kilda. They parked near the police station, and entered it through a backdoor opening into the CIB mess room. Sitting at the table, each nursing a cup of coffee, were Norton and Wall. Mansell looked at his watch. It was 8.58am.

AFTER the introductions Hanna and Lucas left Edmunds to Norton and Wall, with Mansell recording the interview. Norton was obliged to give Edmunds the opportunity of refusing to be fingerprinted. Edmunds agreed that Wall take both his fingerprints and footprints. He seemed more at ease, to have gained a second wind after surviving Hanna's constant questioning. Norton cautioned him and briefly outlined thee circumstances of the crime. Then he produced the fingerprints taken by Wall and compared them with the photograph of the prints taken from Heywood's car. Edmunds watched, impassive.

'I say that the fingerprints found on the motor car are your light middle and right ring fingers,' Norton said. 'Can you give me any reason as to why your fingerprints were found on this car?'

'I can't give you any reason whatsoever.' Edmunds was still confident, but hairline cracks were appearing in his story. When Norton asked him if he had been in Shepparton in 1966 he replied warily: 'I might and might not have been.' It was a significant departure from the cavalier denials made to Hanna earlier, but hardly represented an admission.

Suddenly, Norton switched tack. One by one he put the provable sex offences to Edmunds. First, the attempted rape of Mrs Y in Donvale on July 26, 1971. Edmunds denied it. Norton, watching him closely, recited the damning evidence against him: the fact that his index fingerprint was found on a flyscreen.

Edmunds replied evenly: 'I can't explain how it got there.' Norton produced a photograph of the fingerprint. No reaction.

Norton, poker-faced, played his next card: the rape of Mrs M at Greensborough on January 31, 1975. Again, he parried each question Norton put to him about the crime: Can you tell me anything about the offence? Do you know Mrs M? Have you ever been to or visited the address?

The answers were no, no and no. But with each denial his chin dropped a little towards his chest and he spoke even more quietly, an unconscious sign that his confidence was crumbling under the weight of evidence. Norton played his last strong card: the rape of Mrs D at Chelsea Heights on February 15, 1977. The cumulative effect had eroded Edmunds' defences. 'His head went down to his chest,' the policeman was to recall. 'He wouldn't look me in the face and his answers were half-hearted.' Norton, veteran of countless such interrogations, sensed that the moment was near.

A few more seconds pressure and he would crack. Again, he presented Edmunds with the photographs of prints from the crime scene and the sample prints taken from him that morning. The accused man hung his head and said nothing. Norton left the room to fetch Hanna. 'I think he's had the gong,' he told him quietly. 'He knows the game's up and he'll confess the lot.'

It was 10.33am when Hanna entered the interview room. Almost half the allowable time was gone and he knew that even if Edmunds was willing to confess there would not be enough time to question him properly.

'I believe that Chief Inspector Norton has put to you in detail the location where we believe your fingerprints were found in 1966,' he said.

'Yes, he did,' Edmunds mumbled distractedly. He put his head in his hands.

The fisherman knew the fish had struck the bait. It was time to jag the hook deep into the flesh. 'I understand you were not able to offer any explanations as to how your fingerprints were found on the deceased Garry Heywood's car,' he said with relentless formality.

It was enough.

'That's right. Stupid, bloody stupid,' Edmunds rambled. 'This will ruin Colleen. I've asked myself why, many times. I don't want to hurt anyone any more.'

Hanna suddenly became encouraging, sympathetic. A role he played well. 'What do you mean?' he said soothingly. 'Look, I'm not religious but would you contact a priest and ask him to come and see me.' The words came in a rush. 'I want to talk to him. I want him to look after Colleen. You can talk to him after I do. He can tell you what I tell him. I have some money here for Colleen. After I talk to him I'll tell you what you have been asking me.'

Hanna sighed. More wasted time, he thought … and a faint chance that Edmunds could be deliberately trying to waste it. But it was a chance that had to be taken. He left the room and asked one of the St Kilda police where the closest priest would be. It was 10.45am.

Mansell put down his pen. While they waited, Norton came back in and started chatting to Edmunds off the record. 'Surely you must have known we had your prints,' he said.

The other man shook his head. 'No. I don't read the papers or watch TV,' he said.

Hanna returned at 11.15am. He'd found a priest, he said. A Catholic. Father Ernie Smith.

The priest arrived ten minutes later. After quarter of an hour with Edmunds he came out and asked Hanna into the interview room. Edmunds blurted: 'I don't want to hurt anyone any more,' and started to sob.

He had confessed.

Father Smith said he had told Edmunds that, if he wished, anything he confessed could remain confidential, bound by the seal of confession. But Edmunds had agreed that the priest could relay everything to the police.

Hanna grabbed the chance to get Edmund's confession on the record while he was willing to talk. He sat at a typewriter and started asking questions, typing each one and then Edmunds' answer as they talked. Edmunds was co-operative, the picture of a remorseful man baring his soul. But he was also rather vague. First he said he had met a 'mob of eight or nine people' in the street in Shepparton and had gone 'for a drive' with Garry and Abina and had shot them after 'a bit of an argument.'

Hanna pressed for details. Edmunds elaborated, but seemed oddly reluctant for one so overcome with remorse. He said that after going into the bush paddock at Murchison he and Garry had gone for a walk, leaving the girl in the car. Edmunds said that he had carried 'the rifle'. There was no reference to who owned the weapon or who had produced it. He had then shot Garry, he said, and returned to the car where the girl was waiting. 'I told her what happened and she got out of the car and started to run over to where I came from. I run after her and hit her with the rifle several times.

'She fell to the ground and I threw the rifle beside her or wherever ... I hopped in the car and drove back to Shepparton.'

The story was too smooth, too simple. Hanna knew how improbable it was that Edmunds had met a group of people who had seen him get in Heywood's car on the night of the murders. If the 1966 inquiry had done nothing else it had made sure every teenager who had been in the town that night was thoroughly questioned.

In which case the man, regardless of confessing his guilt, was lying. And his tears were false.

FATHER Smith left after promising Edmunds he would break the news to his wife, Colleen, and ask a priest near Chiltern to tell his father, Harold Edmunds. He also took a wad of cash from the accused to give to Colleen.

It was after midday. There was little more than an hour left to get an extension of time from a magistrate ... if Edmunds was willing.

Hanna approached the subject gently. He had to. It was

galling, he was to say later, that to get enough time to question a suspect thoroughly enough to make a case stand up in court, a policeman was forced by the law to soft-soap a man who had just confessed to a double murder, attempted murder and dozens of rapes.

He explained to Edmunds that to continue the interview they would have to go before a magistrate to ask for a further six hours questioning time. Then he handed him a copy of the written application which had to be made in accordance with the Crimes Act. The wisest course, he thought, was to treat the whole thing as if it was a mere formality, rather than the escape hatch it was for those who knew how to twist the rule to their own advantage.

There was no way that Edmunds could avoid being charged with the murders – though there was still the task of properly proving the case against him, regardless of his confession. The most frustrating thing about the six-hour rule in this case was that unless Edmunds agreed to several extensions there would be no chance of clearing up the rape charges. The victims deserved better than that, thought Hanna.

This time, luck was on the police's side. Edmunds read the application. Asked if he understood it, he said: 'Fair enough, yes.'

They left St Kilda and drove to the City Court, arriving at 12.44pm. As Edmunds and his escorts went into the court they brushed past a detective there on other business. His name was Peter Jacobi. The same Peter Jacobi who, as a teenager nineteen years before, had discovered Abina Madill's corpse.

The extension was granted until 7pm. They'd need every minute of it, and more, thought Hanna. Confessions weren't worth much unless they were backed up with provable facts. Fingerprints apart, they still didn't have much for a court. After a hurried lunch of sandwiches, questioning resumed at 1.20pm, this time at Russell Street. Edmunds was calm, polite, seemingly anxious to help. No, he said, he had never met Garry or Abina before the night of the murders, nor did he know why he went to Shepparton that night. His car? 'I think it was a red '62 Holden I had at that time.' Stroke by stroke, he painted details into the rough outline sketched at St Kilda before lunch. Straining, apparently with the effort of recall rather than invention, he spoke of meeting 'about four boys my age' in the hotel 'on the corner nearest to the police station.'

Outside the hotel, he alleged, the group started talking to 'a boy and a girl' in a car parked near his own. Then the group left to go to the concert at the civic centre, leaving him talking to Garry and Abina.

To this point, ignoring the fact that several witnesses had testified that Garry and Abina had not been near the hotel at the time Edmunds said they were, the story sounded plausible. It didn't stay that way. Next, Edmunds claimed, Garry had invited him to get into the rear seat of his car to go for a drive. After circling a couple of blocks, he alleged, Garry had headed for Murchison.

'We were all talking about sex,' he said, 'then she hopped over the back seat with me and we had sex as Garry drove.'

Hanna, expressionless, motioned him to go on. Edmunds was committed. He continued with a story which, taken at face value, cast himself as a hot-tempered lover drawn into a tragic confrontation with a supposedly jealous and armed Heywood. It was a story which slurred the characters of Abina Madill and Garry Heywood, casting both in an improbably bad light. He alleged that the girl had taunted Heywood by saying that he, Edmunds, was a better lover.

Without prompting, Edmunds volunteered the sort of detail that he evidently calculated would add to the credibility of his version of the events of February 10, 1966. 'Garry produced a rifle,' he said, 'It was a sawn-off rifle. It had a little grip, what you call the stock, and a short barrel, there wasn't much barrel at all. Garry was shooting out the driver's side window as he was going along.' The rifle was a .22 calibre 'automatic', he added. He said he didn't know what make it was. Edmunds remembered the weapon well, considering he had supposedly handled it only briefly, at night, nineteen years before.

Next, he said, Heywood drove the car down a side road 'and then down in toward the river at Murchison … '

Hanna halted the interview. A police photographer had arrived with a copy of the film shot in 1966 which traced the movements of Heywood's car on the night of the murders. Edmunds agreed to watch it.

He readily identified the dark-coloured FJ Holden in the film as Heywood's, and recognised the Shepparton civic centre and the public gardens opposite it. Such apparently trivial detail was all part of the burden of proof that the police had to establish to show that Edmunds was not confessing to a crime he had not committed.

The interview resumed. Edmunds said that he and Garry had argued about the girl and then 'Garry and I went for a walk. I had the gun. Something was said. I know we walked for a long way. We had more words about Abina then I shot him.'

Hanna asked where he had got the rifle. Edmunds hesitated slightly before answering. He had been 'firing out the window' earlier, he said, as Heywood had driven the car into the bush paddock. It was an oblique admission that he had been in possession of the weapon as Heywood drove.

'Why did you first fire at Garry?' Hanna asked.

'I can't answer that. I have asked myself many a time that question,' Edmunds said.

Hanna pursued it. Edmunds repeated his earlier statement that Abina had been in the car. 'I said to her that I had shot

Garry and all she said was she heard the shot. She got out of the car and started to run over to where I had come from. I run after her and hit her with the rifle … She dropped down, or stumbled. I hit her again … '

More questions about detail. Then, slipped among them, a loaded punch. 'Did you tie up anyone that night?'

It got under Edmunds' guard. 'I don't remember,' he mumbled. 'I can't say I didn't tie Garry or Abina – if I did I don't recall it.' Of the many questions that were to follow, none produced a more damaging concession.

A little later, before seeking a third extension of time to take Edmunds to Murchison to see if he could reconstruct the crime accurately, Hanna formally charged him with the murders.

Just before handing Edmunds his statement to read and sign Hanna asked if he had any disability. The answer was unexpectedly frank.

'I'm fit and healthy,' he said, 'but I must be sick in the head. I think I need destroying.'

A VICTORIAN country town, Friday, March 22, 1985. When the telephone rang late in the afternoon Lesley felt a stab of apprehension. She had been depressed all day, weighed down with a premonition that something was wrong, the way she had felt 21 years earlier when she first saw the old house at Ardmona with Ray. She picked up the handpiece. It was Colleen.

Lesley was shocked to hear the voice of the woman she had blamed for the loss of her three eldest children. When she heard the message, she felt faint. 'My ex-husband Raymond Edmunds has been arrested for a double murder – ' Colleen began, her voice edged with hysteria. Lesley interrupted. 'Oh God,' she gasped. 'Garry Heywood and Abina Madill.'

She stopped, shocked by her own words. How had she

known? Numbly, she listened to the rest of what Colleen had to say. She hung up, frightened that, if asked, she could not explain how she had known which murders Ray had been arrested for. Who would believe that a suspicion had been locked deep in her subconscious for two decades? Who would believe that she hadn't been hiding something? Maybe it was lucky, she thought, that it wasn't the police who had broken the news to her.

When a detective telephoned later that night Lesley had regained her composure. He was surprised and obviously annoyed that she already knew. In the rush of the arrest no-one had any reason to guess that Colleen might ring Ray's first wife, and ruin the element of surprise.

Lesley agreed to be interviewed as soon as possible. She was wary of police since Ray's faked drowning in 1970, when she had suspected a local constable of delaying her while Harold and Colleen hid her children. But, she thought, she must do whatever she could to help clear up such a terrible crime. For the sake of the two families at Shepparton.

SHEPPARTON, Friday, March 22. Heather Halsall was serving in Fairley's store when she heard the news. The woman who owned the hairdresser's across the street ran into the shop and asked to see Heather and her sister Ivy. The hairdresser, Robyn, was a friend of Lorraine Sinclair's. Heather and Ivy were Ian Urquhart's older sisters; Lorraine was Garry Heywood's.

Despite vicious speculation that Ian had murdered Garry, Lorraine had always got on well with the Urquhart women. They had been touched by the same random evil, and understood each other's grief. Lorraine had worked at the same shop, and the three had endured years of being public property, of being pointed out and stared at each time the murders cropped up in the media. They often talked together. This time, Heather could tell, something big had happened. Lorraine's friend was excited. She blurted out the news, Lorraine had just rung from home to say the police had called her with news that a man had been arrested that morning and had confessed to the murders.

'Ivy and I just broke down and cried,' Heather said later. 'We'd never done that before.'

MRS Hazelman was in the kitchen of her neat Victorian weatherboard house in Archer Street, Shepparton, when Ken Mansell rang her. He asked her where her son Peter was. In Darwin, she replied. 'I just wanted to tell Peter we have got somebody for the murders,' the detective said gently.

It was the moment that Mrs Hazelman had always believed would come, even in the darkest days when her own in-laws and people she thought were friends had accused her son of helping Ian Urquhart commit the murders.

Yes, she thought, their names had been properly cleared this time. But it had come too late for her husband. He'd had 'a lot of heartbreak over it,' and he had died. And it had come too late for her eldest boy, Kel. He had died in tragic circumstances, wandering away from the local hospital, collapsing in the grounds out of sight and perishing of exposure before he was found.

Mrs Hazelman had never let herself be bitter, but she couldn't help thinking that her husband and two sons would be alive and living in Shepparton if it hadn't been for Ian Urquhart and Peter being wrongly blamed for the murders all that time.

As it was, Peter had been in the far north for years and seemed likely to stay there. It was heartbreaking for an old woman who wanted no more in the evening of her life than to see her surviving son and her grandson.

THE telephone jangled at 1am, waking Ernie Maw and his wife. Maw, who as a tough young mate of Ian Urquhart's nineteen years before had shrugged off a hiding from a rogue detective, grumbled when he saw what time it was. He picked up the handpiece.

It was a long distance call. There was a long pause. Then the man on the other end of the line started sobbing, a strange sound from thousands of kilometres away, after midnight. They were sobs of relief, sorrow, frustration and anger, precipitated by beer but no less genuine for that.

So it was over, Ernie Maw thought. But that didn't make up for Ian Urquhart or Garry Heywood or Abina Madill losing their lives. Or for Peter Hazelman, the man on the other end of the line, losing the best years of his.

ARDMONA, Saturday, March 23, 1985. Stewart Gawne stepped into the dairy to start the morning milking just in time to hear the early news on the radio. The newsreader said a man had been arrested for the Shepparton murders, three counts of rape and two counts of assault with intent to rape. He had been questioned by police for eighteen hours the previous day and charged at an out-of-sessions court in Shepparton soon after midnight.

Gawne stopped working and listened, fascinated. When he heard the name of the accused man he 'went cold with shock,' he was to recall. He knew it had to be the same Raymond Edmunds that had worked for them. Edmunds was not a common name, and the age given on the news – 41 years – would be just right.

Ray Edmunds had been on the farm at the time of the murders, and Gawne clearly remembered him turning 21 some time in 1965. He turned to his teenage nephew, who was helping him, and stuttered in amazement:

'That bloke worked here. Right here in this dairy.' The boy stared blankly. He was fifteen, born four years after Edmunds had left the farm.

The farmer finished milking, then hurried back to the house and told his wife. They marvelled at how close the family had been to a double murderer without suspecting anything. But something was nagging Gawne. He remembered that back in 1966 a detective had visited the farm, looking for Edmunds. At the time he had assumed that it was because Ray owned a Mossberg, and that he had been checked out like the hundreds of others who had been questioned around the district. Since then he had never thought about it.

Then Gawne remembered something else. Nine years before, after he and his wife moved temporarily to the old weather-board sharefarmers' house that Ray and Lesley Edmunds had lived in a decade earlier, he had found part of a gun stock in the shed where Ray had kept his car. It was the length of wood that runs underneath a rifle barrel in front of the trigger. It had obviously been sawn off a weapon: a weapon Gawne had automatically dismissed as an air rifle. This was because of a long groove rebated into the stock identical with the design used for air rifles to house the pull-down action. Being 'a bit of a bower bird,' Gawne had tossed the piece into an old billy and put it in a cupboard under the stairs. And when they had moved to the new house later, he had moved the billy to the barn with a lot of other odds and ends. Which is where, in March, 1985, it still was.

He went out to the barn, fetched the gun stock and brought it inside. 'I always thought there was someone, somewhere who knew something they weren't telling,' he mused later. 'I didn't realise it was me.' Gawne had some urgent cattle work, and he went off to do it, wondering if he should ring Norm Gillespie when he got back. He had gone to school with Norm, and thought he might be interested in his find. Gillespie was. By the time Gawne returned from the paddock the detective had rung and left a message to ring him back at the police station. They talked about Edmunds for a while, then Gawne mentioned the piece of sawn-off rifle stock. Gillespie was excited. 'That's it,' he said. 'That's the second time in 24 hours I've heard the mention of a sawn-off rifle. Edmunds said Heywood had one.'

As the significance of what Gillespie was saying about the rifle stock struck Gawne, he grew confused.

'Hang on,' he said. 'You've already got Edmunds on your file as owning a Mossberg, haven't you?' It was a statement rather than a question.

'No,' said Gillespie, puzzled.

The farmer shook his head in shock and disbelief. Someone had made a terrible mistake. They should have caught the killer in 1966.

T HE Shepparton CIB had no time to worry about the blunders of 1966. Privately, there was speculation about who might have gone to Gawnes looking for Edmunds not long after the murders, and later there was to be some quiet checking of old diaries in the hope of uncovering a clue to the mystery. But in the last week of March, 1985, with Edmunds being held in remand, it was vital to build a case against him in case he decided to plead not guilty.

The first step was to get hard evidence – and that meant linking Edmunds with the weapon used to kill Garry Heywood. On Sunday, March 24, Norm Gillespie drove to the farm at Ardmona to talk to Stewart Gawne about Edmunds' Mossberg rifle. Gawne described watching Edmunds stand at the garden gate and shoot at a target set up on a fence post. Gillespie took the piece of sawn-off rifle stock. 'If it is only off an air rifle and no use to you,' Stewart Gawne joked, 'I want it back so I can get it mounted as a talking-point.'

Edmunds had been transferred to the city watch house in Melbourne the previous day, and when Hanna and Mansell drove down to see him appear in the City Court the next morning they took the sawn-off rifle stock with them. Edmunds was remanded in custody to appear again a fortnight later. After the brief court appearance, he refused to be formally interviewed about the sex attacks he had readily admitted to in conversation the previous Friday. 'He said he would like to help us further, but his lawyer's advice was not to agree to any more questioning,' Hanna said later. So ended any chance of justice for 27 of an estimated 32 victims. Edmunds would never be charged with more than the five sex offences Lucas and Gillespie had questioned him about briefly before driving him to Murchison three days earlier.

Afterwards, Hanna drove to the old forensic laboratories in Spring Street to discuss the ballistics evidence with Brian Thompson, the expert who had identified the cartridge cases and broken plastic 'beetle' found at the murder scene in 1966, and the slug found in Garry Heywood's skull. Gawne's revelation that Edmunds had owned and used a Mossberg .22 rifle at Ardmona fascinated Hanna. He wanted to quiz the expert on the possibility of digging up evidence ... such as empty cartridge cases buried for two decades in the farmyard at Ardmona. If found, would such bullet shells be sufficiently identifiable to be used in court? Thompson was cautious, as always. First, it would be looking for the proverbial needle in a haystack, he said. Second, even if shells were found there was no guarantee they would be well-preserved enough to compare accurately with the two recovered from the murder scene. Hanna was undaunted, and outlined his plan to dig over the farmyard. He was about to leave when he remembered the 'piece of an air-rifle' that Gillespie had retrieved from Gawne's. Thompson's ears pricked. 'We'd better have a look at that,' he said, and followed Hanna outside to the CIB car. Hanna pulled the piece of wood out of a plastic bag and proffered.

'That's no air-rifle,' said Thompson intently. 'That's from a 352 K Mossberg.'

S TEWART Gawne had thought of something else. He walked over to the packing shed where the fruit was stored and fished around until he found what he was looking for. It was a rusted telescopic sight which had been lying around for years. The cross-hairs on the lens were long-since broken, but occasionally the sight was handy to look at some distant spot on the farm. Until now, Gawne had never spared a thought for its origins. On a place that employed up to twenty pickers each summer a lot of odds and ends were left behind. But now he wondered if Ray's Mossberg had been fitted with a telescopic sight. He decided to take it into the police station.

The detectives were interested. One of them put the sight in a plastic bag and labelled it. 'You won't be getting your talking piece back,' Norm Gillespie told Gawne. 'It's off a Mossberg.'

Two days later – Thursday, March 28 – Brian Thompson and two other ballistics men arrived at Gawnes with Hanna and the other Shepparton detectives. Thompson had identified the sight as a common variety that would fit the Mossberg 352 K – and any other rifle with standard narrow mountings. After he arrived, he opened the boot of his car and produced a 352 K Mossberg selected from the police firearms library. Gawne was standing on the other side of the yard, but as soon as he saw the rifle he recognised it. 'That black plastic thing at the front folds down into a handle,' he called. 'It's the same as the one Ray had.'

Hanna, ever ready to press outsiders into service when the occasion demanded, had persuaded a local quarry owner to send a truck to carry a load of filling back to the quarry to put through its mechanical sifter. Gawne used his tractor, fitted with a front-end loader, to scrape the top fifteen centimetres of dirt from an area between the shed and the back gate where Edmunds had stood when he was shooting. The result was half a truckload of gravelly soil.

The mechanical sifter removed the biggest lumps and the dust from the pile, but it took Thompson and his two helpers all day to sieve the rest of the material by hand. By sundown they had found eleven empty shells, but even before cleaning and studying them under the microscope, Thompson knew they weren't from the Mossberg that had killed Garry Heywood.

Hanna wasn't deterred. He started making plans for a more ambitious search. What he wanted was more dirt, more men and more sieves. That way, he calculated, they might find more empty shells.

'Once he gets an idea,' Norm Gillespie was to say later, 'Dennis is like a dog with a bone.'

EDMUNDS appeared again in the City Court on April 8, was remanded to appear on May 6 and taken back to Pentridge while evidence was gathered. Two days later, Brian Thompson returned to Gawnes' with ten helpers. This time, the entire farmyard was scraped bare to a depth of fifteen centimetres, resulting in three truckloads of dirt. The mechanical sifter was fitted with screens which sifted out coarse stones and fine sand, reducing the amount of material to be sieved by hand. As it was being sifted, Thompson dropped six marked bullet shells in the hopper to go through the system. Unless all six were found, the system wasn't thorough enough. By the end of the first day a truckload – some nine cubic metres – of machine-sifted gravel was taken to the backyard of the Shepparton police station for hand-sieving. Another truckload was brought in at 3pm. After three days of painstaking work Thompson had collected 65 .22 calibre shells from his men, as well as the six he had planted. He drove home to Melbourne on Saturday, April 13, tired but satisfied that nothing had been missed.

On the Monday morning Thompson gently rubbed the caked dirt from the rims of the shells so that he could see the marks left by the firing pin. To him each mark was the signature of a particular weapon.

He was looking for shells with a rectangular mark; the sort of mark he remembered clearly from studying the two shells found at the murder scene. He didn't have the original shells to compare them with; Hanna had taken them to Shepparton on the day of Edmunds' arrest. But that didn't matter. 'I had a picture of it in my mind from years before,' he was to say. He cleaned the shells he had chosen, slipped one under the microscope, and peered in.

Bingo.

The ballistics man almost smiled as he dialled the Shepparton area code. 'Can I speak to Dennis Hanna, please?' he said.

Two hours later Frank Eyre arrived from Shepparton and handed over the original shells so Thompson could make a positive comparison for the court. There was a sense of deja vu. It was Eyre who had brought the same shells from Shepparton in 1966, two days after the bodies were found.

'As a result of that comparison I say that nine of those 65 cartridge cases were fired in the same weapon as the two received on the 28th of February, 1966,' Thompson later wrote in his statement.

The case against Edmunds was made.

FOR the public, the arrest and its aftermath was an anti-climax after the lurid publicity surrounding the murders and the 'Mr Stinky' investigation. The only glimpse of Edmunds – and likewise the case – was when he appeared briefly for the third time in the Magistrates Court on May 6 and was remanded to appear again on August 5.

But the Shepparton detectives were still working feverishly.

Despite Edmunds' confession, he had not entered a plea, and they were determined to polish the already strong prosecution case until it dazzled.

It was a matter of working outwards from the people who knew Edmunds best: his two ex-wives, and his father. From lengthy interviews, particularly with Lesley, the detectives compiled a biographical outline steadily filled in as they traced his relatives, former employers, workmates and – in two cases – his lovers. The picture that emerged was of a man who was valued by employers for his ability to work hard, though disliked by other men because of his moodiness and offhand behaviour. Women, on the other hand, seemed either attracted to him or frightened of him. Until his arrest at Albury, Edmunds had been able to maintain a facade of normality. Only those closest to him knew his propensity for sexual deviation, violence and lying, all of which had gravely disrupted the lives of the six children belonging to his two wives.

Step by step, the investigation traced the path which had led Edmunds to Shepparton on the night of February 10, 1966. It showed how, after that night, the path had zigzagged all over Victoria, as if he were trying to cover his tracks. And how, almost everywhere he went, there were unsolved sex crimes.

It took six months for a date to be set for Edmunds' committal hearing. In that time Hanna, Mansell, Lucas and Gillespie interviewed hundreds of people from all over Australia. They winnowed the number of witnesses down to 66, whose statements took up 260 pages of the brief being compiled for the court. There was ample evidence to have Edmunds committed for trial. And, if he contested the case, for a jury to find him guilty. But the detectives wanted more than that, especially Gillespie and Mansell, who had grown up in Shepparton and felt how deeply it had been scared and scarred by the murders. They were determined that the Madills, the Heywoods and the Urquharts deserved to have the complete truth brought out. To settle forever the twisted speculation which had made their family tragedies public property for nineteen years.

With painstaking care, they wove a web of evidence that – had it been made public – would have destroyed Edmunds' version of the circumstances surrounding the murders. His confession was riddled with lies told in an attempt to show himself in a better light. They set out to prove the truth beyond doubt.

First, Edmunds had alleged he had never owned a rifle. But his father told Gillespie and Lucas that he had bought him one in Myrtleford when he was a teenager. Neville Varcoe, son of Edmunds' first employer at Tongala in 1963, said Edmunds had often taken him shooting, and that he had a self-loading .22 rifle. Keith Trezise, who worked with Edmunds at Tongala, also remembered the rifle. Edmunds' first wife, Lesley, said she remembered that he had the rifle when they moved to Ardmona in 1964. And Stewart Gawne, who used the rifle himself, remembered that it was a self-loading .22 calibre Mossberg with a fold-down pistol grip.

Edmunds alleged that Heywood had produced a sawn-off rifle from under the seat of his car. But Heywood's family and friends stated that he had never owned or carried a weapon, sawn-off or otherwise. Edmunds was the first and only person to mention that a sawn-off weapon had been used. Significantly, the piece of sawn-off Mossberg rifle stock was found in the shed Edmunds used in 1966.

Edmunds alleged that early on the night of the murders he had met four youths in a Shepparton hotel who had introduced him to Garry and Abina as they sat in Heywood's car parked in the main street. Exhaustive interviews of the last people to see Garry and Abina alive that night proved that Heywood's car was not parked in the main street as Edmunds said, and that no-one had seen or met Edmunds.

Edmunds alleged that he threw the murder weapon near Abina Madill's body. No weapon was ever found, despite extensive searches in 1966 and in 1985, leaving a strong suggestion that Edmunds had, in fact, carefully disposed of it. Edmunds alleged he did not know the Murchison area and that Heywood had turned down the River Road at random. But the detectives traced a man in Western Australia called Trevor Sinclair who, in 1965, had done relief milking for Edmunds ... and whom Edmunds had driven home to the Sinclair family home in River Road, Murchison East. A house a few hundred yards from the bush paddock where the bodies were found.

Diligent checking of Edmunds' employment history produced his application to be a tram conductor in February, 1968, in which he had falsified the details to indicate that he had never lived at Ardmona.

A writing expert confirmed that it was Edmunds' handwriting, and the fingerprint bureau found his prints on the form, miraculously preserved after seventeen years filed somewhere in the bowels of a Melbourne building.

It was damning evidence. Later, sweating over a typewriter in the red-brick police station, Norm Gillespie was to put it into words. What started as a routine summary became a 5000-word essay on every aspect of the case, written with a passion rarely seen in police correspondence. Towards the end of his piece the detective wrote of Edmunds:

'I believe he had his sawn-off rifle with him and that he kidnapped them as they were together down the back of Lake Victoria, in a popular parking area near the Goulburn river. I believe he forced Heywood to drive at gun point to East Murchison where he tied him up with a pair of stockings that he, Edmunds, had with him. I believe he then raped Abina, that Heywood got free and he then shot him through the head and then clubbed Abina to death …

'I believe that Edmunds fabricated his version and then pleaded guilty to avoid being proved a liar in that he didn't want to be proved to the cold, calculating, vicious sex killer he is.

'I am quite confident that if the police were able to spend any length of time with Edmunds that he would answer many unanswered questions.'

The committal hearing was set for October 21, 1985, at the Melbourne Magistrates Court.

Benalla, October 21, 1985

THE day Allen Heywood had waited on for almost twenty years had dawned. From where he sat in his car he could see the morning sun running down the hills and spilling across the lake stretched below his house. It was an idyllic setting, soothing for a man so tormented by memories that he had left his hometown to try to escape them. But the scenery held no peace for him this day. For Heywood had to make the biggest decision of his life, balancing freedom and prosperity and the love of a woman against pride and revenge and a promise he had made on his murdered brother's grave.

In three hours his brother's killer would be led from a prison van and up the stairs into the Melbourne Magistrates Court. He had confessed to the murders and the evidence against him was flawless. He would be standing or sitting by himself in court. It would be so easy …

Heywood was a crack shot. He could hit a fox on the run at 200 metres. Every winter he shot dozens. And often when he squeezed the trigger he thought about shooting the bastard that had tied Garry up and killed him like a dog. Now, after all this time, when it seemed that no-one would ever be caught, he had the chance he dreamed of. Inside, he had a weapon chosen for the task, one of his collection of firearms.

Heywood had not been conscripted for Vietnam, but there was about him the nervy restlessness of a man who had lost on some distant battlefield the peace of mind that most people take for granted. A vein of controlled aggression ran close to the surface, the legacy of his private war. The one inside his head.

It had begun the day they'd found Garry's body rotting under a tree. He had sworn to avenge him, and through two decades and a broken marriage he had lived with the promise day and night. It was like an amputation: even after the wound healed, the sense of loss remained, and he nursed the hatred born on that far-off summer Saturday in 1966.

He had been fourteen, young enough to hero-worship his big brother with the uncritical love of a child; old enough to understand every terrible detail of the way he died, and the experience had seared his soul, and his pride. He had been angry, frightened, so grievously shocked that it had crippled his education. He forgot much of what was already learned and was incapable of concentrating on anything but fantasies of revenge, leaving him barely able to read and write despite a keen intelligence that had later made him a skilled tradesman with his own flourishing business.

He had been frightened because he thought that his brother's killer or killers might try to get him next. It was not logical, but then Garry's murder had not been logical. For a time Allen had carried a cut-down rifle in his schoolbag, ready to use it if the unknown assailant who haunted his fevered imagination appeared. That had been the first sign of the attachment to firearms that had resulted in a private armoury ranging from high-powered sporting rifles to collectors' items.

It was one of these, a handgun, that was occupying his mind now. It was waiting for him. All he had to do was go inside, load it, put it in his jacket pocket and drive to Melbourne.

An eye for an eye. Life for a life.

He opened the car door. The dark-haired young woman in the passenger seat looked at him pleadingly. She knew what he was thinking. He went inside the house. When he came back he had the gun. But the woman sensed he was still undecided. She spoke gently, careful not to stir the emotions inside him. She reminded him what he would be giving up. His business. His big house by the lake. His children from his first marriage. Her.

It was natural that he wanted to hurt the man who'd killed his brother, she said. But what was the use of it if it only hurt himself – and his father. The old man had lost his eldest son and then had watched his wife die of grief. Surely he had suffered enough, she said.

Allen stared at her for a long time. His hand slackened its grip on the wheel. The tension drained from his face.

'You're right,' he said. 'It's not worth it.'

He got out of the car, slowly walked inside and locked revenge away forever.

APPENDIX

RAYMOND Edmunds, 41, was committed for trial on October 28, 1985, after a five-day hearing at the Melbourne Magistrates Court during which he pleaded not guilty to two counts of murder, three counts of rape and two counts of attempted rape. He appeared before Mr Justice Nicholson at the Supreme Court, Melbourne, on April 3, 1986, and pleaded guilty to all charges against him. He was sentenced to two terms of life imprisonment for the murders. Sentencing for the sexual assaults was adjourned to a date to be fixed, and was eventually carried out on October 28, 1986.

ON Thursday, January 3, 1980, Elaine Jones, 40, went missing from the Murray Valley township of Tocumwal. Her husband found her body snagged in the Murray River next day, and died of a heart attack while attempting to pull the dead woman into his boat. Her throat had been cut. The case is unsolved.

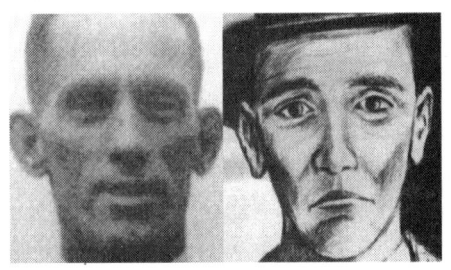

An awful neatness

THE man who found the bodies is 70 now, the oldest drinker in the public bar of the Plaza Hotel in Townsville. He's seen and done a lot of things since he left South Otago, New Zealand, back in 1952. But nothing sticks in his memory like the day he played a walk-on part in a cruel story that haunts all who know it.

He tells it his way. A knockabout carpenter, he'd been building houses for the nickel mines out past Kalgoorlie, then got a bankroll and itchy feet and headed east across the Nullarbor in his new Falcon, camping on the way.

He'd meant to go home to New Zealand to see his family, but good intentions slipped away as easily as last week's wages. After a little work at Woomera Rocket Range building a 'secret' satellite-spotting post, he turned north.

First to Coober Pedy, then further into the desert to the 'Three Ways', where a traveller has to make a lonely choice. The Adelaide road was behind, narrowing the choice ahead to

Darwin and Townsville. He tossed a coin. Townsville it was, via Mount Isa. He arrived late on August 27, a Thursday, to find the sleepy coastal city in a frenzy, shocked out of its tropical torpor by the worst tragedy since the war. Two sisters had vanished on their way to school the previous morning. Their mother was under sedation, their father half-mad with unspeakable fear.

The old man puts his glass on the bar, fishes in his coat pocket for two pieces of paper – worn, grimy, folded small – that he's kept almost half his life.

It's the carbon copy of a statement he made to police the day it happened. This is what it says: 'I am a married man, 40 years of age, at the present time of no fixed place of abode in Townsville, having only arrived from Boulder, Western Australia, on the night of 27th August, 1970.

'About 8.45am on Friday 28th August 1970 I joined a number of other persons in a taxi cab … In company with two other men I was engaged in a search party for two missing girls who had disappeared whilst on their way to school.

'We travelled along the Townsville to Charters Towers Highway and made a search in various places along this road prior to going to a spot near Antill Creek. We parked the car and set off in various directions. I traversed the creek bank and dry creek bed.

'Whilst searching in the creek I saw what appeared to be child's footprints in the sand. I continued to walk along the creek bed and, about ten yards further on, I then saw the body of a child … in a small hollow and the child was in a more or less sitting, reclining position. I saw that the child was wearing a pair of panties. At this stage I was a distance of approximately ten feet from the body. The child appeared to be dead. I now know that the body which I located was the body of Susan Debra Mackay.'

S USAN was five, the baby of the family. Judith was seven. They were 'late lambs', as they say in the bush, born well after two boys and two older girls. They were dark-eyed, olive-skinned and pretty, like many children of the far north, where indigenous, islander and Italian influences have tempered the anglo-celtic majority.

Bill Mackay kissed his babies goodbye as they slept, when he left for the meatworks before dawn. He never saw them again.

The Mackays lived in Albert Street, Aitkenvale, a suburb sprawled along the Ross River road, a highway that leads inland from Townsville to Charters Towers and beyond.

Susan and Judith left home about 8.10am, after their mother, Thelma, got them ready for school. They walked to the corner, turned left into Alice Street and vanished.

The girls would have crossed the road to wait at their usual bus stop. But when their brother, Alan, rode past on his bike about ten minutes later, they weren't there. They weren't at school, either, but it wasn't until they didn't come home that afternoon that the alarm was raised.

When Bill Mackay got home from work his wife was distraught. He grabbed photographs of the girls and went to the police. By nightfall, police and friends gathered to search back-yards in the district.

Next day hundreds more joined in. The meatworks offered its entire workforce, and police doorknocked every house in the area. By Friday, the search had spread, which is how a wandering Kiwi carpenter, called Richard Tough, and two men he didn't know, were sent to Antill Creek, a sluggish watercourse meandering across an ugly plain, 25 kilometres south-west of Townsville. It is an empty place where scrawny cattle poke through stunted scrub and feral pigs tear up the barren ground.

Tough waited by the little girl's body for an hour until the police arrived. They followed foot prints in a sandbank running along the creek bed, which was almost dry. About 70 metres away, near the opposite bank, they found Judith's naked body.

The only mercy was that the pigs hadn't got to them first. Both girls had been raped and stabbed in the chest. Susan had been strangled, Judith choked from having her face rammed into the sand. It looked as if she had fled while her little sister was being killed, and was then run down.

Beside the bodies, their school uniforms: folded inside out and placed with an awful neatness. Their shoes, socks, hats and school bags were nearby.

A senior sergeant cried when he saw it. Another policeman said he wouldn't go home until they caught the killer. He was as good as his word, staying at Townsville police station day and night, with his worried wife bringing in food and clean clothes. Until he died of a heart attack two weeks later.

Had he lived, he could hardly have guessed that the case would see his generation out of the force.

IN the days before drugs multiplied crime, homicides were mostly simple domestic murders, or brawls gone wrong, as easily solved as the average burglary.

But the motiveless and random killing of two innocent children produced a huge outcry and no obvious culprit. There was intense pressure from the top for a quick arrest, when a slow, painstaking investigation was the best chance of cracking the case.

From the start, the police's problem was not that there were too few leads, but too many.

Townsville was, and is, an army town, and the meatworks had its own blood-spattered corps of itinerant slaughtermen, butchers and boners, not all model citizens. Add meatworkers to a barracks full of soldiers and there were thousands of potential suspects. It was inevitable that the sheer weight of numbers – and of public expectation – would affect the investigation. Local knowledge, sometimes a police officer's best tool, didn't help the tedious elimination of hundreds of suspects. Ironically, it might have been a handicap, because it would encourage assumptions about who should be put on – or left off – the long list of people to check. The temptation was to take shortcuts. The risk was that they would miss their man.

Meanwhile, there was the mammoth job of piecing together witnesses' accounts – often contradictory, or apparently so.

A teacher, Judith Drysdale, saw a man driving slowly near the Mackay sisters and staring intently at them. Much later she was able to pick a photograph of the man she saw from a series of pictures.

Nola Archie, in the grounds of the Aboriginal hostel behind the bus stop, saw two small girls talking to a man in a car. She wasn't sure of make or model, but agreed it might have been a Holden.

Bill Hankin was driving a road-roller on Ross River Road that morning. About 8.15 he pulled over near the Aitkenvale school for a smoke and a cup of tea. He noticed a man in a car with two girls in school uniforms; while everyone else was driving children towards the school 'like ants to a nest', this man was taking children away from it.

Hankin had been a driving instructor in the army, and he noted automatically that the driver was thin-featured, swarthy, not tall, and drove badly. He looked middle-aged, with a tanned complexion and dark, wavy hair, cut short. A face like the character 'Beau' in the television series *Days Of Our Lives*, but older, he was to tell police later.

Around the same time, Neil Lunney was running late for work at the army barracks. Just back from Vietnam, he had a short fuse, and was incensed when a car in front of him sped up and veered to block him when he tried to overtake. 'He tried to put me over the embankment,' Lunney was to recall. 'I did my cool. I was going to bumper roll him but, when I got up level with him, I saw the kids in the car.'

The older girl, on the passenger side, had shoulder-length hair, as Judith Mackay did. The younger one, sitting in the middle, had shorter hair, like Susan Mackay. Both wore green Aitkenvale school uniforms.

Lunney yelled at the driver, and looked at him hard in case he saw him in the street. He'd been taught recognition in the army; it could mean life and death in jungle warfare. This enemy had high cheekbones, short hair, and 'Mickey Mouse' ears stuck out from a narrow skull. Lunney wasn't so observant about the car, except that it was blue-grey 'like a battleship'; it wasn't a Ford but might have been a Holden, and had an odd-coloured driver's door. He did notice two 'STP' oil stickers on the rear mudguards, and venetian blinds in the back window.

J EAN Thwaite was cleaning a car in the Shell service station she and her husband ran at Ayr, more than an hour's drive south-west of Townsville, when a car pulled up. It was covered in dust and her memory is that it was 'dirty white' or beige colour, and arrived between 11.30 and noon.

The driver was thin, dark-haired, looked to be in his 40s, and wore a faded, fawn or off-white shirt. He seemed preoccupied, and ignored her request to cut the motor while she pumped the $3 worth of petrol he ordered.

The petrol inlet was on the left side, and she had to open a flap to get at the screw-on cap, similar to her own 1965 EH Holden. This ruled out the car being a 1950s Holden but, unknown to her, was a design feature shared with the Vauxhall Victor, uncommon in country Queensland.

Thwaite, mother of a five-year-old, took notice of two

children in the car. In the back seat, a small girl who looked as if she had been crying asked: 'Are we there yet?' In the front seat was an older girl, who said to the driver: 'When are you taking us to mummy? You promised to take us to mummy.' Both wore green school uniforms.

The driver silently handed Thwaite exact change. By the time she looked up from the till, the car had gone. When she heard next day about the abduction in Townsville, Jean Thwaite was sure she had seen the Mackay sisters, but found it hard to get the local police to take her seriously.

There was so much information – some obviously contra-dictory and some apparently so – that the police felt pressured to make choices: to play hunches that one lead was better than another. Unfortunately, they got it wrong about the car.

Although the descriptions of the car given by Hankin, Lunney and Thwaite varied in details, between them they had enough key information about it to find a driver whom they all described the same way.

But the police, punting on a description of a car seen near where the bodies were found, concentrated on looking for an early model Holden. Their enthusiasm to find the 'right' car rather than to build a picture of the driver caused confusion. As one legal insider was to remark dryly 30 years later, witnesses who first thought they'd seen a Vauxhall ended up signing statements they'd seen a Holden – and an FJ Holden, at that.

Worse, despite the matching descriptions of the driver – apart from his age – there was no sketch or photofit picture of him published. Instead, the newspapers and television ran pictures of FJ Holdens.

It put the investigation so far off course it never recovered. For the wanted man, it was an unbelievably lucky break. For others, it was a tragedy, because sex killers almost always kill again.

304

JOHN White was only 19, but he'd worked alongside men for years, and knew his way around. He'd been a carpenter, bridge builder and meatworker. Now he was a trainee psychiatric nurse, working shifts at the mental hospital in Charters Towers. Which is why, late on a weekday afternoon – probably the first Tuesday of September, 1970, he was to say later – he was sitting in the deserted bar of the White Horse Tavern in the main street, when a stranger walked in.

White guessed the man was old enough to be his father, perhaps in his 50s, but wiry and fit. He put his height at 'five seven or five eight' (about 172 centimetres) and his weight at no more than '11 stone' (about 70 kilograms). He was wearing clean work clothes – a checked flannelette shirt, long brown trousers, brown hat.

The man sat at the bar a couple of metres away, produced a tin of tobacco and rolled a cigarette. He was out of matches, and he asked the younger man for a light. White didn't smoke, so the stranger bought matches from the barmaid and started talking.

He asked White if he'd been following the murder of the Mackay sisters a few days before. White nodded, and the man stated that the police, were 'looking for the wrong sort of car'.

Before White could ask how he knew that, the man kept talking quickly. 'You know,' he said, 'I killed those two girls.' White wanted to think it was a tasteless joke, but it didn't quite sound like it. So he kept talking, trying to draw out more information. The stranger said he was staying at the Crown Hotel down the street, that he was a carpenter who did a bit of maintenance work for the publican, and that he sometimes did some prospecting in local creeks.

It was as if the older man had 'a monkey on his back, and happened to choose me to get it off,' White was to muse later.

The stranger got up to leave, and White tentatively arranged to meet him next day for another drink. And, as casually as he could, he asked him his name.

As soon as the carpenter left, White borrowed a pencil from the barmaid and wrote the name on the back of the empty matchbox the man had left on the bar. Then went looking for police.

He found two, locking the station to do their afternoon patrol. He knew one of them, a Constable John Cooper, and told him what the carpenter had said and where he was. He gave them the matchbox with the name on it.

The policemen went to the Crown Hotel. Next day, the carpenter turned up at the tavern, as arranged. He told White the police had spoken to him, but didn't seem worried. If anything, he was a little cocky. He showed White a photograph of his house, which was small and low to the ground, with sawn timber stacked neatly in the yard. Then he had a beer, and left.

White never saw him again. He ran into Constable Cooper a few days later. 'He just said he'd been to see him (the carpenter) and there was nothing in it.'

And that, as far as John White was concerned, was that. He rarely thought about the strange encounter again, though he never forgot the name he wrote on the matchbox.

Arty Brown.

IN late March, 1972, two children in north Queensland disappeared, feared murdered. One was a two-year-old, Shay Maree Kitchen, at Mount Isa. The other was a cane farmer's teenage daughter, Marilyn Joy Wallman, at Eimeo on the coast near Mackay.

It was before the state's homicide squad was formed, and local police investigated murders. Charles Bopf, prominent Townsville detective and future homicide chief, did the

Kitchen case. He quickly arrested the de facto husband of the child's mother – another sordid domestic tragedy to add to his big tally of cases solved. The Wallman mystery, outside Townsville's police district, wasn't so easy. It was as brazen as Judith and Susan Mackay's abduction 20 months before, but with no clues. No cars. No suspects. No leads. Not even a body.

On Tuesday, March 21, the three oldest Wallman children were going to school. Marilyn, 14, had to catch the high school bus on the main road, a few hundred metres away along the small road that led to the farm. She left, riding her bike, a few minutes before her brothers – David, 10, and Rex, 8 – who went to the local primary school.

Wallman's road went over a hill that hid most of its length from the house. When David and Rex rode over the crest they found their sister's bike lying on its side.

The puzzled boys looked around, thinking Marilyn had fallen, bumped her head and wandered off in a daze. David went home for his mother while Rex stayed, sitting near the bike. He heard voices on the other side of the canefield next to him, but couldn't tell if one was his sister's.

Their mother came with the car. They drove around the blocks of cane, searching and calling, fear rising as the minutes passed.

The boys' father was out fishing, and someone went to get him. Friends and neighbours gathered and began a search that has never really ended for the Wallmans.

As the days became weeks, hopes of a miracle ebbed. It seemed clear Marilyn was almost certainly dead and her body well-hidden. If buried, it was deep. If put in water, it had not floated or washed ashore.

At least the Mackays had bodies to grieve over. The Wallmans prayed for even that bitter-sweet mercy. Thirty years on, they still do.

EVERY day is a private hell for the broken hearted, but anniversaries torment most. The Mackays had moved from Townsville to Toowoomba to get away from the stares and whispers, the crank calls and the well-meaning solicitudes of their hometown, but they took their grief with them. And nothing could ease that, only mask it.

On the morning of August 26, 1973, the third anniversary of their girls' murder, they woke to nightmare news. Lightning had struck someone else. In Adelaide, where the Beaumont children had disappeared seven years before, two girls had been abducted from a football game. In a public place, in daylight, like the Beaumonts and their own girls and Marilyn Wallman.

Joanne Ratcliffe was 11; Kirste Gordon was four. At three-quarter time in the preliminary final between Norwood and North Adelaide at Adelaide Oval, Joanne had taken Kirste to the women's lavatory, about 300 metres from the stand where her parents were sitting with Kirste's grandmother. Neither was seen again.

A teenager selling lollies, Anthony Kilmartin, saw a man watching the girls in the stand and, later, hurry after them near the southern gate. He lifted the young girl under his right arm and started walking fast. The older girl, whom he later identified from photographs as Joanne Ratcliffe, had looked frightened and tried to stop the man.

Kilmartin was vague about the man's age – 'about 40' – but gave a detailed description of his clothes and appearance. He was thin, narrow-shouldered, wearing a brown broad-brimmed hat, grey checked jacket and dark trousers.

And there was one other thing, Kilmartin was to tell police in 1973, and an inquest six years later. The older girl had kicked the man in the knee, causing him to bend down. As he did, a pair of black, horn-rimmed glasses fell from his pocket, which he snatched up. A small thing, but it signified a man too vain to wear glasses all the time, or who needed them only for reading.

Kilmartin wasn't the only witness. An assistant curator at the oval had earlier seen a man and two girls apparently attempting to entice some kittens from under a car near a shed. The man was thin, about 172 centimetres tall, and dressed in a grey-checked sports coat, brown trousers and brown, wide-brimmed hat.

Sue Lawrie, her father and little sister heard the football siren as they left the zoo, about a kilometre from the oval on the other side of the Torrens. Sue's father guessed it was the start of the final quarter of the big game. They followed the river bank towards the new Festival Theatre, opposite the oval. Minutes later Sue, then 14, saw a middle-aged man hurrying towards them, carrying a small girl. Behind him was a girl about 11, running to keep up, punching him in the back and yelling at him, 'We want to go back!'.

Sue was surprised the man would let his 'grand daughter' hit him without chastising her. She stared long enough to be able to describe details years later that tallied with other witnesses, but the hat and the man's face caught her eye most.

In 1970s Adelaide, the most English of Australian cities, if a middle-aged man wore a hat at all in winter it was usually a tweed, peaked cap or a natty, narrow-brimmed felt. Wide-brimmed hats were not yet a fashion affected by city people – big hats were for practical protection, and worn in summer in the country. And there were regional differences even then. The only time Sue had seen a wide-brimmed hat with a low, flat crown like this one, was when visiting relatives in Queensland, where a lot of men wore them. It was, as she was to say later, 'very Queensland country'.

Next day, Sue went for a country trip for a week, and missed most of the furore over the missing girls. When she returned, police were concentrating on events around the oval, so she dismissed what she had seen near the zoo. It wasn't until some time later, while discussing lack of discipline in some families, that Sue commented on the young girl she'd noticed thumping her 'grandfather' in public.

'When was that?' her father asked.

'The day we went to the zoo,' she replied. As she spoke she remembered it was the day the girls had been abducted, and she realised the sinister significance of what she'd seen. But she was young, her father thought she had the timing wrong, and he didn't take it further.

For years, it played on her mind. In late 1980, married with a baby of her own, she told her husband about it. He urged her to go to the police. She told detectives about a man in his 50s with a wide hat and a thin, hollow-cheeked face she couldn't forget.

IT was the darkest secret she knew, and she'd spent half her life wanting to tell it. But it took a move to the other side of Australia and a crisis of conscience for Merle Martin Moss to make the call she'd rehearsed so many times in her head.

She was sitting alone in a flat in suburban Perth in October, 1998, looking through her family 'birthday book' when a wave of revulsion hardened her resolve. On the page under May was the name of an old man who, she knew, had molested at least five female relatives among her extended family. She despised him.

It was a family secret, shared between cousins, aunts and husbands. But an inner circle – Merle Moss, her sister Christine Millier and two of their cousins' wives – suspected something more sinister was linked to the old man's predatory ways.

Moss had bowed to family pressure not to embarrass or

distress the victims by forcing them to reveal things they'd learned to live with. The problem was, if such delicacy masked the fact that the old man was a deviate, it would be hard to accuse him of murder. She had no hard evidence he was a killer. Her suspicions relied on a web of circumstance, detail and intuition spun around the knowledge that he had covered up decades of sexual offences against children. Without knowing that background, she feared, any police officer bothering to check out a telephone tip would find nothing but a couple of harmless, old-age pensioners in a neat house in a sleepy Townsville street.

But, this night, Moss decided she had to act. The Crime-stoppers number flashed on her television. She reached for the telephone. It took three days for the message to filter through to the Queensland homicide squad in Brisbane. Sergeant David Hickey, who had just finished investigating a baby's death, was about to open an old file allocated for a routine review when he got a note to call the woman in Perth.

As he spoke to her, the coincidence hit him … the old file on his desk was the Mackay sisters' murder in Townsville. Hickey, a methodical investigator, isn't superstitious – but when he told the woman on the line which file he was review-ing, she took it as a sign. She poured out her heart about an old man in Townsville called Arthur Brown.

For Hickey and another detective, Brendan Rook, it was the beginning of an exhaustive investigation.

Starting with a circle of the woman's relatives in north Queensland, their inquiries rippled outwards, interstate and, in one case, to New Zealand.

Some people they spoke to were shocked at the allegations of sexual abuse, others guardedly confirmed them. But Merle Moss's younger sister Christine Millier and two cousins-by-marriage filled the gaps in a Gothic horror story, played out among three generations of slow-talking, hard-working, apparently respectable folk.

It seemed that, until 1982, most family members had not suspected Arthur Brown of anything except being a 'big noter' who fancied himself as 'a ladies' man'. But, that year, a tearful teenager told her parents he had molested her as a small girl, and Brown's carefully constructed cover was blown. Four other girls – sisters and cousins – had quickly admitted similar secrets. To all but a few who refused to believe the girls, he was a pariah. And some suspected worse.

A RTHUR Stanley Brown was born at Merinda, near Bowen, on May 20, 1912, one of three children whose parents separated when he was young. His mother went to Melbourne and Arthur was to spend several years there. He told people later he had been a paperboy and had got a Victorian driver's licence before returning to Queensland.

He attached himself to the Anderson family, who also came from Bowen and had six daughters and two sons, most of them younger than Brown. Their mother and some of the girls ran 'the galley', cooking for workers at the Ross River meatworks, where Brown worked during and after the war, apart from a spell doing wartime construction work.

A beach photograph of Brown in the 1940s, bare chested, shows a wiry man with the lean muscles and dapper toughness of a lightweight boxer or a heavyweight jockey. The high cheekbones, long jaw, and prominent ears below a short-back-and-sides haircut were distinguishing features that age was not to soften.

Active, fit, and a light drinker, Brown didn't gain weight or lose his hair as he got older. He was delighted when a shop assistant once mistook his first wife as his mother; a stranger could easily have mistaken him for fifteen years younger than his real age. Even in his 50s, he would show off by gripping a table edge and balancing his body in the air above the table, lifting himself up and down.

If this showed a dash of the exhibitionist, there was also an obsessive neatness. He would line up his perfectly shone shoes, fold a piece of paper before putting it in the bin, and iron knife-edge creases into work clothes when others wore rumpled shorts and singlets.

Brown was to marry two of the six Anderson sisters, and was close to two others. He was first married in June, 1944 – to Hester, then freshly divorced, with three small children, but whom he'd known before her first marriage. They were to live an outwardly normal life for 34 years, but Hester's oldest sister Milly, now dead, was convinced she made the best of a dreadful mistake.

Milly disliked Brown, said he couldn't be trusted. She told relations that Hester feared him, and had once confided to her about his well-known womanising: 'He doesn't just like big girls – he likes little girls too.' Hester had caught him interfering with a child and tried to prevent him from being alone with them. But she was stricken with crippling arthritis in early middle age, and was no match for the man she increasingly relied on to care for her.

Hester's younger sister, Charlotte, had also been married before and also had three children. One son bore a strong resemblance to Brown, as did another sister's boy. As Hester grew more infirm, Charlotte visited the Browns often and even went on interstate holidays with them.

Hester kept up appearances but, once, called aside a young female relative and gave her prized lacework she'd inherited from her mother, saying bitterly: 'I don't want his next lady love to get it.' Asked who she meant, she blurted: 'Charlotte, of course.' Hester, in constant pain, became confined between a walking frame and bed, a virtual prisoner in the fibro and timber house Brown had built long before in Lowth Street, Rosslea, an old suburb of Townsville. Her torment ended late at night on May 15, 1978, when Brown told the family doctor by telephone she had fallen while trying to get on the commode next to her bed, hitting her head and killing herself.

As far as the police could ascertain twenty years later, the doctor had written out a death certificate at home without viewing the body, which Brown took to an undertaker's himself. Hester Brown was cremated, which meant the injuries to her skull could never be examined.

At the time Brown pointedly told family members he'd paid for a post mortem to be done. Detectives told them years later it wasn't true, although at least one insisted she'd been there when police spoke of an 'autopsy'. Hester's big sister, Milly, didn't believe the death was an accident.

'The day Hester was found dead,' another relative was to recall, 'Arthur was shaking with fright. He wasn't grieving, because he never showed emotion. He was worried.'

Suspicion didn't appear to worry Charlotte who, family gossip had it, had been sent packing by Hester not long before her death. She moved in with Brown and married him the following year.

She was a small woman and, even in her 60s, had the odd custom of wearing little girl's pyjamas, much to the bemusement of her female relatives. When one of her cousin's grandchildren asked her once why she wore such childish clothes to bed, Arthur Brown interrupted, saying: 'Because she's my little girl.'

MERLE and Christine's mother was a cousin of Hester and Charlotte, and the girls often visited the Browns while they were growing up.

As youngsters, they accepted Brown as a jovial, talkative man who liked to be the centre of attention. But as they matured and he aged, they tired of his boasts that he knew everybody of importance in Townsville. And they didn't like his fascination with sex crimes. He kept a collection of lurid 'true crime' magazines and showed the graphic photographs to children. He went on about how dangerous it was for young girls to be alone, and told them to 'trust nobody'. He spoke of 'silly mothers' dropping their children too early at school.

There was another side to his 'concern'. He would say he felt sorry for male teachers because girl students were 'prick teasers' and that it was too easy for girls to 'scream rape' on a whim. 'The kids of today will set you up,' he would say. 'They'll get you hung.'

It seemed to the sisters, even then, that Brown protested too much. They recalled that their grandfather had detested Brown, and refused to be in the same house with him. 'Pop always said Arthur was a bad man,' Merle was to recall. 'He would say to me "See after yourself, love, and don't be on your own with him." I often wonder what he knew.'

Apart from one minor incident, Merle was old enough to be out of Brown's reach. And he didn't try to molest Christine 'probably because I had a mouth and would have fought to the death'. But, looking back on it, she thinks she was lucky. Twice.

The week that John F. Kennedy was shot in 1963 Christine, then thirteen, was staying at Brown's. One day, when Hester was out, Brown proposed taking her 'for a swim'. She refused because she couldn't swim, and there were no other children to play with.

Three years later, on another visit, Brown came home early from work while Hester was at bingo and Christine was home alone. He suggested driving her to a mountain outside

Townsville, to take some pictures with her new camera. She refused because she didn't like the steep, winding road. Much later, she realised it was such a slow trip, it would have been too dark to take photographs by the time they arrived.

At sixteen, she was too articulate to be molested and scared into keeping quiet, as younger girls had been. So what was his plan? If she had disappeared, no-one would have known where she'd gone. Brown was supposedly at work, and she would have been just another teenage runaway. But that thought didn't strike her until after 1970.

THE day the Mackay sisters were murdered, Christine was staying at Brown's. She was twenty, with a year-old baby, on her way north to rejoin her husband at Weipa after visiting family in Bowen.

That morning, Brown got up about 7am, cut his lunch, and went to work. Christine remembers nothing unusual about his return that afternoon, except that the radio that was usually on was switched off that night and next morning – which meant she didn't hear news of the abduction until she got to Cairns the following evening.

Another relative, who trusted Brown with her children until 1982, when his sexual abuse was exposed, was puzzled at something he said a few weeks after the Mackay girls' murder.

'I could've done that,' he told her. The woman didn't go to the police, she was to explain years later, 'because I didn't think he'd be the type'. She was to change her mind in 1982, but stayed silent rather than involve his sex abuse victims.

When police were looking for a car with an odd-coloured driver's door after the murders, Brown took the dark-blue door off his Vauxhall and buried it, according to another relative. He told her at the time 'he didn't want anyone interviewing him or annoying him'. Because they thought police were looking for an FJ Holden, they accepted his explanation. Later still, he told Christine he knew the Mackay sisters' father, and that he had worked at the girls' school. He offered to drive Christine and Merle to look at the spot where the bodies had been found. They refused, and wondered at his weird tastes.

T HE detectives came for Arthur Brown after breakfast on December 3, 1998. Car after car pulled up outside the neat fibro-cement house in the neat street. There were fourteen detectives – and photographers, forensic experts and army sappers with metal detectors used for mine sweeping.

While the soldiers swept the big backyard for any remnant of a buried car door, the detectives painstakingly searched the house. They were especially keen on a spare room they'd been told about, which had a door fitted with a bolt on the inside. It was where Brown kept, among other things, his personal papers. Yet there was no record of registration or insurance or mechanical work to indicate he'd ever owned a blue-grey Vauxhall Victor sedan – a car he tried to deny having owned, until they produced a photograph supplied by a relative.

There was no warning of the raid, but even when the officer in charge read the warrants, detailing allegations of murder and sexual abuse, the old man did not seem shocked. 'Didn't raise an eyebrow,' one detective was to recall. When the officer reading the warrant used the married name of one of the sex abuse victims, Brown instantly queried it, nodding when the officer corrected the surname to one he knew.

Before they left to go to the police station for questioning, Brown said to an increasingly agitated Charlotte that he'd done some terrible things she didn't know about, and it was time to pay for them. It seemed an odd comment, given that she must have known about the sex abuse allegations. At the watchhouse, Brown reportedly said another strange thing, later denied. 'Those Mackay sisters have me stumped,' he declared. 'I've lived in Townsville for 30 years and I haven't heard of the Mackay sisters.' This, a prosecutor was to tell a hushed court months later, was a clumsy lie that pointed to guilt of a crime the judge himself called 'one of the most notable events in the city's post-war history', of which 'no-one in Townsville at the time would not be aware'.

At the start, detectives thought they were talking to 'a silly old bloke,' as one was to put it. But when questions swung from the general to the particular, Brown's attitude hardened.

Asked if he would go to Antill Creek with police, he retorted 'No way I am going out there with you,' then demanded to see a lawyer. Arthur Brown had never had a conviction in his life, but he'd worked at the meatworks and around courts and police stations, and he knew the drill. He got a telephone book and looked up a law clerk, who called a solicitor who made another call. Mark Donnelly, a policeman's son and one of north Queensland's toughest criminal barristers, soon turned up to represent his new client.

From then on, Brown was silent. And his wife refused to repeat in a formal interview what she had already told police informally.

The police were left pondering what had come from the arrest. One thing they'd found in the bolted room was a bottle of port, which tallied with claims by some of Brown's alleged victims that he'd given them liquor before molesting them.

And something else had been locked away for years – a set of worn work clothes, musty and yellowed with age. It included a singlet with a large, faint stain that washing had not removed.

'Arthur would never wear a stained singlet,' one relative was to say. 'I reckon it was the clothes he wore the day the girls were killed in 1970. He's kept them like a trophy.'

318

JOHN White, late of Charters Towers, was in Brisbane when he heard a man had been charged for the Mackay sisters' murder. 'I bet his name is Arty Brown,' White blurted to his astonished partner, then told the story of his conversation with a thin stranger in his hometown 28 years earlier. He couldn't sleep for several nights, and wrote down details as they came back to him: Brown's name, the name of the tavern, the time he spoke to the police, and the policeman's name, John Cooper. Then he called Brisbane CIB.

Sue Lawrie was living in Melbourne when she saw fleeting footage of an old man in Townsville on the television news. Something about him pricked her memory. 'Where do I know you?' she said to herself uneasily. Next morning she took a call from an old friend in Adelaide, who asked her reaction to the news. Before the friend could explain that there was media speculation in Adelaide about a connection between the old man arrested in Queensland and unsolved Adelaide abductions, Sue interrupted.

'My God! It's him,' she screamed into the telephone. The man she'd seen on television was older, more gaunt, but – in her mind – the same one she'd seen on the banks of the Torrens, 25 years before.

John Hill had been apprenticed to the Public Works Department in Townsville as a teenager in 1974, and worked with Brown intermittently for eighteen months. The first radio bulletins about the arrest brought back a memory of a 'capable tradesman' who'd once said something so strange the younger man remembered it, word for word.

They'd been driving past Townsville police station in 1975 in Brown's Vauxhall when Hill, then sixteen, had remarked that the police hadn't solved the Mackay sisters' murder. Brown, a 'big-noter' whose habit in conversation was one-upmanship, had said immediately: 'I know all about that – I did it.'

This had troubled Hill. 'It chilled me because of the way his face looked when he said it. But I didn't believe it because it was so out of character for the person I had worked with.'

Hill had a restless night, but Brown seemed at ease next day and the boy didn't ask questions. 'Being a kid, when it wasn't reinforced, I put it to the back of my mind.' But he didn't forget it, either. When Brown was arrested 23 years later, his former apprentice called the police.

He told them about an obsessively neat tradesman who sometimes wore black, horn-rimmed glasses and who had been right under their noses for years. So close, in fact, that no-one had seen him.

FROM the day Brown was arrested, he was described as a roving school maintenance carpenter. This was correct as far as it went, and it was understandable that it was emphasised: the fact Brown had worked at schools, supplies one of the planks of a copybook prosecution case – opportunity and, perhaps, motive.

Brown, after all, had worked at Aitkenvale State School, which the Mackay sisters attended. He was known to eat lunch with the children, who called him 'uncle'. None of which, unfortunately, seemed to strike anyone in 1970, despite the seemingly obvious need to interview any men who had contact with the victims, such as teachers, cleaners, or gardeners.

Such an apparently glaring oversight isn't the only reason several retired or veteran Queensland police might have been secretly embarrassed when Brown was arrested. Schools, in fact, had been a minor part of Brown's rounds. As a Public Works employee, he regularly did jobs in every state public building around Townsville … he was a familiar face at the police station, the prison, the courthouse and the orphanage.

Brown carried some tools in his car boot, but stored other

gear in an outbuilding of the old courthouse to which he had the key. He regularly parked in spots reserved for police next to the police station, and was friendly with the court registrar, the bailiff, the matron at the orphanage and many local police.

Hill recalls that when working at the old police station Brown usually had 'smoko' with ex-police who worked in the police garage. Hill, in fact, bought his first car from one of them. If working at the courthouse, Brown would have coffee with the bailiff and discuss seized goods due to be auctioned. He was on first name terms with court staff and police, who called him 'Arty' or 'Browny'.

When police houses needed work, Brown did it. When one policeman needed dining chairs mended, Brown arranged for Hill to do it. Brown was a notoriously bad driver and parked wherever he liked, but he boasted that he never got a ticket. He also boasted he knew the most senior police in town, notably Charles Bopf, the man whose brilliant career had only one blot – not finding the Mackay girls' killer.

In a state that had rewarded some senior police with knighthoods, an Order of Australia was the least a grateful Queensland could do for Bopf. Townsville's best-known detective for years, and head of the state's new homicide squad in the 1970s, in retirement he is still a noted citizen in what is an overgrown country town.

Unlike Arthur Brown, whose mind has ostensibly been eroded by age, Bopf is still alert. He lectures in law at a local tertiary college, follows current and legal affairs, and easily summons details of his career after joining the force from the railways in 1946. But no-one's perfect: the sleuth who made a living for almost 40 years with his memory for names and faces has trouble recalling a man who claims to know him well, and he swiftly ends conversations that raise the question.

As a youngster in the 1960s, Christine Millier was walking

in the street with Brown when he stopped to chat to Bopf, and made a great show of introducing her to him. Afterwards, he claimed 'Bopfy' as 'a mate' and boasted that he was chief of police in all of Townsville. This overstated Bopf's rank, and probably the relationship, if indeed there was anything more to it than Brown scraping acquaintance with an authority figure.

But the fact remains that in 1970s Townsville, Brown knew the police well enough that he blended into the scenery, and police knew his car so well nobody even noticed that it once had an odd-coloured door. They were looking for a Holden driven by a crazed killer, not a Vauxhall driven by someone they knew.

Familiarity breeds contempt. Like the postman who appears at the same time every day, Arthur Brown had become invisible.

John Hill marvels at how trusted Brown was around the police station. Brown worked any hours he liked, and Hill thinks that if he'd wanted to he could have got access to records and files. Speculation, perhaps. And yet …

When police spoke to Neil Lunney in 1998 he said he'd made a statement in 1970, but was told it was missing. They had found his name with others on an old file note, and had a record of him taking part in an identification parade in 1971, but nothing else.

It wasn't the only evidence to disappear. Samples taken from the murder scene were, apparently, lost when the police forensic section in Brisbane was flooded in 1974.

The floods of 1974 – which struck vast areas of Queensland – might also explain why there are no Public Works records of Brown's work history. There is no record of when he joined the department, no pay records and, crucially, no record of when he took leave, when he was absent, or for what periods he was not sighted by a supervisor.

With Brown, at almost 90, unwilling or unable to answer detailed questions, his working life is a mystery. He didn't have to report to work except to draw his pay and pick up maintenance requests. He was trusted to work unsupervised. The state couldn't have employed a more careful man.

J UST as southerners go north in winter, seeking the sun, northerners head south in summer to avoid it. One of the perks of working for the Queensland Government north of Rockhampton is getting five weeks annual leave instead of four – a legacy of when it took a week to travel to and from Brisbane by train or steamer.

But, by the 1960s and 1970s, with better roads and cars, a traveller could go a long way in a week – and five weeks was enough time to visit Sydney, Melbourne or Adelaide. Relatives know that the Browns visited the youngest of his wife's sisters and her husband in Victoria more than once. No-one willing to talk about it now knows if Brown ever went on to South Australia.

But Christine Millier has her suspicions. She believes the man she's known all her life killed the Mackay sisters, and that the fact a jury did not reach a verdict in a murder trial proves only that its members could not be told everything the family and the police know. There are coincidences that intrigue investigators, though they would never be put before a jury. Judith and Susan Mackay's bodies were found at Antill Creek at the spot where Brown had taken little girls to molest them. That place was only 500 metres from where the body of a murdered teenager was found in 1975.

Her name was Catherine Graham, and she was last seen selling encyclopaedia door to door, near Brown's house. The last night of her life she had made a call to her mother in Brisbane from a public telephone box. The last thing Graham told her mother was that a man was standing near the telephone box, staring at her, and that she didn't like the look of him.

Other things unsettle Millier and her sister, Merle Moss. They believe that around the time of Marilyn Wallman's disappearance in 1972, the Browns were visiting Hester's relatives nearby, in Mackay. His car broke down, causing them to come home by train. Brown returned alone to get the car, the story goes, and didn't come back to Townsville for some time. All the police can confirm is that a 'chalky blue' Vauxhall was seen in the district around the time of Marilyn Wallman's disappearance.

In early 1991, Christine was working as a carer with teenage wards of the state, at what had been the local orphanage, where Brown had once been a regular visitor as maintenance man. On Wednesday, January 23, she wrote in her diary: 'Kids (state wards) and I went for walk to Strand. Arthur Brown drove by and the kids called him "rock spider", shouting it out. Eventually they told me what a rock spider was.'

'Rock spider' is prison slang, never used jokingly, for a child molester. Somehow, at 79, Brown had a reputation outside the family as a sex offender.

Some instincts die hard. In Brown, the reflex to boast about what he'd seen and done was stronger, at times, than his sense of self-preservation.

Buildings were a favourite topic. He had a carpenter's eye for the way they were made and where they were, and once he saw a building he didn't forget it. Talk about other cities, and he'd talk about something he'd seen there. Mention Sydney and it was Martin Place. Brisbane and it was The Valley. Melbourne he knew backwards, of course, having lived there. Perth he'd never seen.

And Adelaide? It seemed to Christine that he'd been there, too. When the city's name came up one day, he mentioned seeing the Festival Theatre when it was almost finished. He agreed when she said what a beautiful building it was, with the steps down to it, looking over the river to the oval …

Work on the Adelaide Festival Theatre, commissioned in the 1960s, started in 1970, and the first stage was completed in June 1973, when a symphony orchestra performed in it for the first time.

Joanne Ratcliffe and Kirste Gordon were abducted from the Adelaide Oval on August 25, 1973. It was Australia's worst child abduction case since Grant, Arnna and Jane Beaumont were abducted from Glenelg Beach on Australia Day, 1966. Their bodies were never found.

In a corner of the prosecutor's office in Townsville is a board with half-a-dozen photographs on it of Arthur Stanley Brown at different stages of his life, in different clothes, bareheaded and wearing hats. In the middle of the collection is a computer-generated sketch of a man's face, based on the recollection of the schoolteacher who saw a driver staring at the Mackay girls before they were abducted. The similarity between the sketch and the photographs is striking. So is the resemblance to the police sketch of the man seen taking two girls from the Adelaide Oval in 1973.

In July 2001, 28 years after Kirste Gordon and Joanne Ratcliffe disappeared, South Australian Police had still not taken a signed statement from Sue Lawrie about the thin-faced man she saw.

Arthur Brown's secrets died with him on July 6, 2002. He was 90.

The suicide that wasn't

FOR anyone callous enough to pull the trigger, shooting Jennifer Tanner wasn't the problem. Making it look like suicide was, and that's where her killer got it wrong.

Faking suicide meant using the only firearm available to the victim: her husband's bolt-action .22 rifle. When the first shot didn't kill the terrified woman instantly, the self-appointed executioner had to fire another shot into her forehead as her body twitched and thrashed.

In fact, the killer might have fired even more shots on that Wednesday night in November, 1984. If he did, they missed. At least, they missed her head. When Laurie Tanner came home and found his wife's body he didn't notice the bullet holes through both hands, but they were there: the sort experts call 'classic defence wounds'.

All of which, you'd think, would make it likely that someone might consider foul play …

Even if the pair of country policemen first called to the

Tanners' house at Bonnie Doon were fooled by the fact Jennifer's body was slumped on a couch with the rifle between her knees, the muzzle pointing towards her still-bleeding head.

Even if a local doctor dragged from a dinner party agreed it looked like suicide, pronounced life extinct and went home without a clue how many bullet wounds there were, let alone where. As he pointed out later, it was his job to verify death, not to investigate its causes.

And even if the detective sergeant on call that night ignored alarm signals when the uneasy constables telephoned him again after finding a second bullet shell near the body. Detective Sergeant Ian Welch, known locally as 'Columbo', stuck to his original decision not to make the long drive to attend, nor to bother with fingerprinting or forensic tests.

Even photographs were ruled out, which was lucky for the accredited police photographer on duty that night, a Sergeant Neil Phipps. Despite being rostered on, Phipps had allegedly left Mansfield police station to attend to a private affair – a practice later described by a fellow officer in court as 'working a phantom'.

And so the die was cast. The word 'suicide' – repeated to each new person introduced to the case – settled over the tragedy like a shroud.

Bill Kerr, older of the two uniformed policemen at the scene, knew more about traffic fines than shootings. But some things niggled him. Such as the half-drunk cup of coffee and plate of biscuits near Jennifer Tanner's body. And the fact she had asked her husband to bring home a local paper, milk, bread and a 'surprise' – a chocolate bar. It hardly seemed the behaviour of a suicidal woman.

There was, too, the fact her 21-month-old son was alone in the house. What mother, if not actually deranged, would suicide without making sure her baby was taken care of first?

There was no evidence Jenny was even unhappy, let alone deranged. And she hadn't left a suicide note. It didn't jell.

Past midnight, after the ambulance had taken the body to the local hospital, Kerr and his partner, Don Frazer, drove through the lonely countryside. It was time to face the job for which no constable's salary is enough – breaking the news every parent dreads.

Along the way, they heard a radio message that Footscray police had gone to Denis Tanner's house in Melbourne, three hours drive away, but that he wasn't home.

Kerr knew Denis Tanner was the dead woman's brother-in-law, younger brother of Laurie, the shy farmer and shearer who'd married Jenny a few years before, after his first wife had left him. Denis was a seasoned detective who'd worked much of his time in Melbourne's inner suburbs. He would soon loom large in Kerr's mind.

But as they turned into the neatly-kept property where Jenny had grown up, the policemen decided to keep any twinges of doubt to themselves. In a few hours, a fatal shooting had become just another sad domestic incident, to be settled as tactfully as possible.

JEN had never given us a moment's worry, Kath Blake was to say often of the eldest of her four daughters. She and her husband Les lost more than their first-born the night the police brought the news; they lost peace of mind.

For years, hardly a day would pass that they didn't think about their 'Jen' … and wonder how she really died. Often Les and Kath Blake were to sit at the same timber table as the grim-faced policemen did when they brought the news that night, and relive the worst minute of their lives.

'They said,' Les was to recall softly, 'They said "Jennifer's shot herself'." The Blakes didn't believe it then, and never have. It would have made life easier to accept suicide as an explanation, and let it rest, but time didn't erode the belief they don't put into words. Their girl was murdered.

Nothing the Blakes were told about Jennifer's death rang true to them. She had no reason to kill herself, they insisted. And, if she had, she wouldn't use a gun, because she hated guns.

None of Jennifer's behaviour seemed to indicate she was dangerously depressed. A year later, a coroner would accept sketchy evidence from her doctor and her husband about her emotional state and difficulties with her child. But the doctor readily conceded later that his evidence would have been different had anyone questioned the apparently firm police view it was suicide.

The Saturday before her death, Jennifer had gone to a clearing sale with her mother and had been delighted to buy an antique jug for herself, and two small tables for her son's room. Two days before she was killed, she'd gone to Melbourne to do Christmas shopping, ordered more furniture for the baby's room, and invited her grandmother home for Christmas dinner. She saved $100 on the furniture, and said she'd put it towards a family holiday at the beach.

To the Blakes, it was all evidence of her commitment to family and future – as was an earlier visit to a specialist to discuss if she could become pregnant again.

All of which contrasted with her husband's halting recollections. He was to claim Jennifer had suffered from 'post-natal depression' but that her own parents, sisters and friends didn't realise because 'she covered it up pretty well.'

On the day she died, Jennifer hosted a playgroup of mothers and their children, and was normal and happy. She spoke to a friend, Angela McCormack, on the telephone, for about twenty minutes from 9pm, and seemed cheerful.

There were other telephone calls to the Tanner house that

Wednesday. One, at around 5pm, was from Laurie's policeman brother, Denis. Much later, in a statement, he asserted he'd spoken to Laurie about getting a horse broken in. No-one else knows if anything else was discussed.

THREE weeks before her best friend was killed, Rosslyn Smith took a call she never forgot, and was to give unfaltering evidence about at two inquests twelve years apart.

Her story goes like this. About 11 am on 23 October, 1984, Jenny Tanner rang her home on Queensland's Gold Coast. The two had been friends since schooldays, and often called each other, but this was no idle chat. Jennifer sounded disturbed by an incident that had happened the previous night.

She said she'd been surprised to find her brother-in-law, Denis Tanner, on the back step when she went out for some firewood. She asked what he was doing in Bonnie Doon. He said he'd had a fight with his wife, and had told her (his wife) he was going to the races. He told Jennifer he wanted to 'go shooting'. Then, according to Rosslyn Smith, he asked for Laurie's .22 rifle, which Jennifer fetched.

He loaded the weapon, Jennifer told Rosslyn, then followed her around the house, and asked her if she was going to leave Laurie. She protested that she wasn't.

Denis warned her not to tell Laurie of the conversation, then left. But, Jennifer told Rosslyn, she had immediately complained about Denis's threatening visit to her husband when he'd returned from a meeting.

Curiously, when Laurie was asked in a coroner's court a year later about that peculiar conversation, he claimed to have been told only that Denis had walked across from the property he owned next door for a cup of coffee and a chat after delivering some building materials.

Not in the witness box, nor in his original statement to police, did Laurie say Jennifer had told him about Denis handling the rifle and asking her about marriage splits. He was not, and never has been, vigorously cross-examined about the stark difference between his story and Rosslyn Smith's.

WHEN Bill Kerr typed what police cryptically call an '83', the formal notice of death to the coroner, he stopped at the space where the phrase 'no suspicious circumstances' is usually inserted. He left it blank.

Kerr's instincts were soon proved right, though not soon enough to open a murder inquiry. An autopsy wasn't done for two days, which meant that by the time the pathologist found two bullets in Jenny Tanner's brain the death scene had already been cleaned up (read destroyed) and a funeral organised by her husband's highly efficient family.

Suddenly, the police had an embarrassing problem: a body, but no body of evidence. It was the killer's lucky break. And, for a long time, his luck held.

Of course, it would still have been possible to mount a proper murder investigation. But, by then, too many policemen stood to get into too much trouble. If there's one thing police learn faster than where to get half-price hamburgers, it's to keep themselves, and other police, out of trouble. The instinct for self-preservation goes with the territory in a tough and often thankless job.

This might explain why the pathologist, a shy and obliging man called Dr Peter Dyte, hit a wall of polite scepticism when he halted the autopsy to telephone Mansfield police from Shepparton to ask if they were absolutely sure Jennifer Tanner had shot herself, because he'd found two bullet wounds, not one.

When Dyte called again to say he'd found two bullets in the brain, he sounded like someone who thought he had important news. But, after a few minutes on the telephone to Sergeant Phipps, an old homicide squad hand gone bush for a quiet life, the doctor must have wondered why he'd been so eager.

Phipps turned it around – herding Dyte towards an elaborate scenario that had Jenny Tanner shooting herself twice while holding her hands over the end of the barrel and pushing the trigger with her toe. The doctor was led into halfheartedly agreeing it was 'possible' that with one bullet to the brain she would still be able to reverse the rifle, work the bolt with four separate hand actions, and shoot herself again. But he sounded dubious.

Dyte wasn't the only one with private doubts. By this, Kerr was already on the way to being the only police officer in Victoria (as it later seemed to him) to take any official interest in the possibility Jenny Tanner had been murdered.

From the time he'd found the second bullet shell at the scene, Kerr had been suspicious. Suspicious enough that he used a new toy, a micro-cassette recorder, to tape interesting conversations about the case. One of these (taped with Phipps's knowledge, ironically) had been the telephone conversations between Phipps and Dyte.

It was the start of the worst year of Bill Kerr's career. He kept the tape, along with others, and his notes, in what became one man's attempt to investigate a death other police ignored. Worse, he was ostracised for it by the police 'brotherhood', an experience that was eventually to make him leave the district, then the force.

Meanwhile, Kerr did what he could – and far more than he was ordered – to prepare a brief for Jennifer Tanner's inquest.

As far as Kerr's superiors were concerned, the investigation was to be based on what the pathologist called the 'possibility' of suicide. Five months later, on 30 April, 1985, Detective Sergeant Welch took the trouble to drive for more than an hour from Alexandra to Shepparton to get Dyte to 'clarify' his opinion that suicide was possible – and to make additions to his autopsy report to that effect. Another lucky break for the killer.

Dyte, suffering a terminal illness which was to prevent him attending the inquest, gave in to Welch's peculiar request. But he seemed to mistrust the way his report was being used. When Jennifer Tanner's youngest sister, Miriam Blake, spoke to him before the first inquest opened, he told her there was a strong case that Jennifer had been murdered.

Which was exactly what Kerr was trying to prove – without fingerprints, photographs or a body. Jennifer had been buried just 60 hours after her death. All he had was the rifle – but each time he requested the weapon be tested, he was ignored. 'They kept saying it wasn't warranted,' he was to recall bitterly. He was told to use 'proper channels', but they were easily blocked.

He asked for various people, but especially Denis Tanner, to be interviewed by the homicide squad and asked particular questions. But when they were interviewed, key questions weren't asked. To Kerr's frustration, Tanner was allowed merely to write out his own statement, avoiding vital points – such as proving where he was on the night of the shooting.

The day after Jenny Tanner's funeral, Laurie Tanner had gone to Mansfield police station to make a formal statement. Denis went with him.

Kerr secretly taped a conversation with them, in which he casually asked Denis where he'd been on the night Jennifer died. He replied that he'd been to 'the trots'.

It wasn't until ten months later, just before the first inquest into Jennifer Tanner's death was to open, that Kerr saw a deposition made by a Melbourne bookmaker, the late John Francis O'Hanlon – an associate of Tanner and several other police, including Sergeant Paul Higgins, later to serve a long jail sentence on serious corruption charges.

Kerr was startled, because the deposition gave Tanner a different alibi for Wednesday, November 14, 1984 – stating, albeit unconvincingly, that he was 'minding' a bingo night in the inner suburb of Middle Park.

The deposition was vague about days and dates, but it was to be accepted in 1985 by coroner Hugh Adams because he believed the bingo alibi had been checked by a homicide squad detective.

And Adams was unaware of Tanner's earlier 'trots' alibi: it was part of material implicating Tanner that Kerr's superiors had forced him to remove from the brief before it was submitted to the coroner, a scandalous omission kept secret until Kerr revealed it at a second inquest twelve years later.

Despite the roadblocks put in his way, Kerr discreetly contacted Rosslyn Smith in Queensland, and arranged for her to make a statement to Queensland police about what Jennifer had told her of Denis Tanner's strange behaviour. He got the statement promptly, only to be reprimanded for not requesting it through the chain of command.

Kerr was one man against the system, and he started to keep his beliefs to himself to avoid trouble.

Which is why, when he'd visited the Blakes soon after the funeral, he hadn't told them Jenny was shot twice. Shamefully, they didn't find that out for months, until just before the first inquest.

The Blakes hired a local lawyer to represent them at the inquest. But, by then, the case was too hard to unravel, even for the coroner. At least, despite the skilled efforts of Denis Tanner's barrister, the coroner made an open finding. In the circumstances, it was the best the grieving parents could hope for.

They were left with nothing but memories, and an appalling silence.

334

TEN years later the district was jerked awake by what some called 'another' murder mystery. It began high on a granite-scarred ridge in the windswept hills behind Bonnie Doon. On the afternoon of July 20, 1995, two men with a long rope, a torch and much nerve lowered themselves into an old mineshaft called the Jack of Clubs, known only to a few locals and shooters.

They found more than they bargained for: a skeleton, clothed in faded feminine things. Next day, a homicide crew arrived. By chance, one of the homicide detectives sent to the mine knew the district well.

He was Jennifer Tanner's cousin, and from the ridge he could see the farmhouse where she died – a death he knew nobody in the family accepted as suicide.

In fact, one of the first things he'd done when he'd got into the squad was to pull the thin file with Jennifer's name on it. It hadn't told him anything except how abysmal the 'investigation' was.

Now, fate had dealt him the Jack of Clubs, complete with skeleton.

Two violent deaths in one tiny district. The coincidence gnawed at the detective, and he wondered if whoever had the local knowledge to put the body in the mineshaft might also have had the nerve to kill Jenny Tanner and try to set it up to look like suicide.

Among the bones the police found silicone breast implants that led, with a little luck and a lot of good detective work, to identifying the remains as those of Adele Bailey, a transsexual prostitute who'd vanished from inner-suburban St Kilda in 1978.

By coincidence, Denis Tanner had worked around St Kilda in the late 1970s. By an even greater coincidence, he was the last policeman to write on Adele Bailey's police file before she vanished. And his then fiance – later wife – was the police-woman who was last to sign out Bailey's file.

Two months after the mineshaft find, the old Tanner farmhouse, 'Springfield', burned to the ground late one night, destroying any chance of forensic examination – for stray bullets, or DNA from bloodstains or hair. The house, by then sold to an absentee owner, was empty and locked. There was no electricity or gas in use. The fire started inside, and burned fiercely.

A passing truck driver saw the front gate open and a figure running from the house, yet when fire trucks turned up soon after, the gate was locked and no-one was present.

It began a chain of events that led – after a slow start, and probing of the mystery by this writer – to an exhaustive investigation by a police task force, the quashing of the original inquest, and a new inquiry by Victoria's State Coroner, Graeme Johnstone.

After sitting for 23 days spread over a year, the coroner found that Denis Tanner had shot his sister-in-law to death. The finding finally exposed a police investigation tainted by cronyism and cover-up.

The coroner heard dozens of witnesses. Some should have been called in 1985, and weren't. Some should have been questioned more closely in 1985, and weren't. Some were new to the case.

Those attending the inquest instinctively divided themselves into two uneven camps. Both Jennifer Tanner and her husband come from big families. But on most hearing days her parents, the Blakes, were accompanied by at least two of their three surviving daughters, and several other relatives. They crowded into one side of the court, behind the counsel assisting the coroner, Jeremy Rapke, and task force police.

By contrast, the other side of the court was all but deserted.

336

Although Laurie Tanner is one of five children, though his parents were still alive during the inquest, and though he was secretary of the local show society when his wife was shot, no-one saw fit to accompany him and his brother, Denis. Except, that is, on days that two other Tanner brothers, Bruce and Frank, their mother, June, and Denis's wife, Lynne, were called to give evidence that was singular for its hostility and brevity.

Unlike the Blakes, the extended Tanner family seemed not to feel compelled to know who really pulled the trigger in the old farmhouse on the night of 14 November, 1984. Their attitude was summed up by Denis Tanner's truculent reply when the author reporter questioned him in June 1996. He said the new investigation wasn't 'worth a hat full of busted arseholes.'

Despite this bravado, Tanner again retained Joe Gullaci, then a pugnacious criminal barrister reputed to charge more than $2000 a day, a fee in keeping with a reputation that won him regular work representing police brought before the courts. Gullaci, who also represented both brothers at the first inquest in 1985, has since become a County Court judge.

The thirteen years between inquests evidently did not ease Laurie Tanner's concerns. Whereas he shared Gullaci's services in 1985, this time he retained a prominent barrister who often represents members of the Police Association.

The Tanner brothers sat close together, sharpening the contrast between them. Laurie, about 50 at the time of the inquest, is tall, thin, wrinkled and worried, with curling hair and a drooping moustache under a long, aquiline nose. Long, bony wrists and calloused hands stick too far from his grey, pinstriped suit. He fidgets compulsively.

The only resemblance between the oldest and youngest of the Tanners is the hawk-like nose. Denis is beefy and broad-shouldered, with the hard look and soft hands of the pub bouncer he has been in off-duty hours.

Despite repeated suggestions that he had the motive and the means to kill his sister-in-law, the big detective in the well-tailored navy suit sat calmly, his close-set eyes and stony face elaborately neutral, looking coolest when the evidence seemed most damaging.

It doesn't get much more damaging than the dramatic appearance of Sergeant Helen Golding, a policewoman who is – or was – the best friend of Denis's wife, and godmother to their four children.

Visibly shaken, Golding said she hadn't slept properly, walked her dog or ridden her horse since making a statement to investigators about Tanner's dislike of Jennifer. She said she was 'terrified' after being sent a dagger covered in mock blood, leaflets from funeral directors, a sympathy card with the words 'you're dead' written on it, a .22 bullet in an envelope, a threatening letter, a wreath on her doorstep with the message 'Time runs out', and a marked copy of her police duty roster.

Jeremy Rapke, counsel assisting the coroner, was to submit later there was no direct evidence that Denis Tanner made any or all of the threats. But the inference is that it was probably friends of Tanner's who did. Rapke didn't have to add the obvious: that, if so, they are probably police, too.

Superintendent Peter Fleming, of the anti-corruption unit, assisted the coroner in 1985. His memory is much sharper than that of most other witnesses. He says that the 1985 investigation was 'grossly inadequate', and recalled an angry scene at the homicide squad offices where a Sergeant Albert 'Jimmy' Fry had insisted the death was suicide. 'There were rumours this particular matter was not being handled correctly,' Fleming adds.

Ironically, it was Bill Kerr, first at the death scene, who began a chain of events that led the shooting to be passed off as suicide. Yet Kerr, who describes himself as 'just a dumb country cop', who emerges as the nearest thing to a hero in the whole sorry affair. His reward was to spend hours on the witness stand under withering cross-examination calculated to discredit him. Though he was easily tripped up on detail, one thing survived his ordeal by lawyer: proof of his dogged belief that Jennifer Tanner was murdered.

There were many telling moments in 23 days of hearings. One was when Kerr was asked why he made and kept tape recordings of conversations with several key people, and why he had kept his file when he retired in 1993. He replied: 'Because I probably don't trust them.'

Welch, the former detective sergeant who tried so hard to prove the suicide theory after failing to attend the crime scene, was by now a carpet cleaner.

Asked, after a bruising exchange with Rapke, how he thought the case should have been handled, he hung his head and muttered: 'The scene should have been preserved, and there should have been a full and proper homicide investigation.'

Asked who the homicide squad should have interviewed, he said: 'I believe Denis Tanner should have been interviewed.'

'Anybody else?' asked Rapke softly.

Welch paused uncomfortably. 'No-one else springs to mind,' he said.

Sergeant Denis Tanner subsequently quit the police force and so avoided the risk of being sacked under anti-corruption powers – granted to the Victoria Police Chief Commissioner – dubbed the 'Tanner clause'.

Payback time

The leader of the pack is out there, in the suburbs or some country town. He's in his 40s now, probably with a family of his own. If he has teenage daughters, you can bet he's careful where they go and who with. He knows bad things can happen – he and his mates used to rape girls that age in the 1970s. It was sport to them, like wild dogs killing sheep.

Maybe he thinks about it sometimes when he's mowing the lawn, or washing his car, or when a schoolgirl walks past. Or last thing before he goes to sleep.

No one outside the gang knows exactly how many girls they lured into cars, abducted and violated. There were a lot of gang rapes in the 1970s, and not all were investigated, let alone solved. Often, the victims and their families became part of a conspiracy of silence – gagged by fear, shame and the prospect of blame.

And so the gangs got away with it until something stopped them: they were caught, or close enough to it to be scared off, or they tired of their brutal game. A few of 'the boys' might have taken up other violent crimes and ended in jail, but the rest faded back into suburban anonymity. Family men with secrets.

They might not feel remorse about what they did. But they pay the price of getting away with it – wondering, in quiet moments, whether the past can ever reach out for them.

The answer is that it can. This is the story of how a terrified schoolgirl has become a driven and determined adult, hunting a gang of men who raped her when she was fifteen.

She has traced the man who betrayed her by delivering her and her friend to the gang. This time, she guesses, he will betray the gang. He just doesn't know it yet. Nor that a detective who has worked on the case for ten years has been watching him for weeks.

O N the first Tuesday of November 1976, the rest of the world is waiting for the United States presidential election to start: Jimmy Carter v. Gerald Ford is a cliffhanger. But, in Australia, the Melbourne Cup pushes the White House off page one. Even the worst Cup day weather in memory cannot stop the race that stops a nation. More than 78,000 turn up at Flemington.

It's a day of ominous portents, humid and oppressive, as if the tropical wet season has strayed south. By early afternoon, thunderclouds black out the sun. Anxious drivers turn on headlights even before the first cloudburst hits. Soon, hundreds of cars are stranded in flooded streets. Wind uproots trees and strips roofs. The rain turns Flemington into a paddy field of ruined shoes and shattered hopes, delaying the start of the big race by 25 minutes.

It is the wettest Cup anyone has seen. The deluge is to stick in people's minds for years. The betting ring is swamped with money for a New Zealand 'mudlark' called Van Der Hum, a dour plodder backed to favouritism who duly splashes his way into racing folklore to win the slowest Cup in decades, ears back, rat-tailed and covered in mud.

Hundreds of police are rostered to watch the race crowd. One is Richard Parsons, a constable in uniform, seconded from across the river at Footscray. He is 26 at the time. Another 26 years later, as a veteran detective, he remembers how wet it was and that he found a warm welcome and a few drinks at a party in a double-decker bus after finishing his shift.

There are other attractions on that public holiday. At Festival Hall in West Melbourne, not far across the industrial sprawl between the docks and the muddy Maribyrnong River, thousands of teenagers queue before midday to get into a concert, Cup Day Rock.

The old boxing stadium, dubbed the 'House of Stoush', is a primitive but popular venue. Just nine days earlier some of the biggest Australian acts of the 1970s packed the hall for the annual Rocktober concert promoted by the dominant rock station, 3XY. Now it is full again. The Cup Day concert features Mark Holden, a clean-cut pop idol who tosses carnations into the crowd and draws adoring teenage girls who have seen him on Countdown. Where girls go, boys follow. Not all of them clean cut.

The concert ends about 5pm. Ushers open the back doors into Rosslyn Street to ease the crush around the main doors at the front. The crowd pours into wet streets under a sullen sky.

Among them are two girls, schoolmates who have caught the train in from the eastern suburbs. They are in third form at high school, and have not long started going out by themselves. Donna, curly-haired and vivacious, is dressed in jeans, tee-shirt and a blue lurex cardigan. Angela has more of the hippy look: colourful surfie sandals of the type called 'treads', long skirt and ear rings. The girls are friendly with each other though not each other's closest friends. Waiting in the street are three youths in a station wagon, parked diagonally in the centre of the street. Donna first met two of them at the Rocktober Concert nine days before.

The shorter, better-looking one she knows as Wayne Thompson. He is fair, with hair between blond and brown, cut short in a modified version of the 'sharpie' style. He wears the uniform of the time: collared tee-shirt with a penguin logo and tight Staggers jeans, as if he has stepped off the cover of the Skyhooks album *Living In The Seventies*.

Wayne's mates are both called John. The one Donna has met twice before has pale skin and dark hair with longer 'tails' at the back. The other one she has met once. The three are in the front bench seat of the fawn-coloured station wagon, probably a Holden, the back section of it packed with tools and building equipment. At 18, they are working men with adult tastes in alcohol, cigarettes and sex. Especially sex.

Donna knows the station wagon. It is the one in which the obliging Wayne gave her a lift to Flinders Street railway station after the Rocktober concert two weekends before. The same car that, a few nights later, he drove all the way from the western suburbs to Box Hill to meet her. She skipped a ballroom dancing class to meet him and John that night – and agreed to meet them the following Sunday, October 31. It was a bad move, but an understandable one.

That Wayne would drive across town to see her impressed Donna. He is older, has a car and money, and comes from somewhere else: among her peers, this makes him desirable. She doesn't realise it might also make him dangerous.

But there were clues. During the week a stranger, calling himself 'Tony', telephoned Donna at home asking her to a party. He said Wayne had given him her number. This confused her. She thinks Wayne is her boyfriend. Why would he hand out her number? She refused. On the Sunday, she took the train to the city. Wayne met her at Flinders Street station. With him was his supposed 'brother', John. Who, she later finds out, is called John McNally and not related to Wayne at all. This tendency to fudge names puzzles Donna but does not make her suspicious.

So, that Sunday they had driven west, across the Dudley flats and the Maribyrnong River and beyond, through suburbs she had never seen. To a deserted picnic area, where there was a public toilet block near a creek, some boulders and scrubby trees. There they met friends of Wayne's, including the one who called himself Tony.

It was a trial run, Donna was to realise later. She was naïve. She half expected to have sex with Wayne, as she thought of him as her 'boyfriend'. But when he ignored her refusal and pushed her to 'turn it on' for his mate, Tony, she was upset. Tony forced himself on her and Wayne took photographs, like a trophy. She was angry and humiliated but not scared. She did not yet grasp she was being set up as a target for the gang by being branded a 'slut'...

Which is why, two days later, when Wayne gets out of the station wagon outside Festival Hall, she pauses to listen to him when he apologises for his behaviour. He says he will make it up to her by taking her and her friend to a party.

At first, Donna is cool. She says, 'I know what your parties are like,' referring to the Sunday incident. But Wayne is persuasive and plausible. That's why, as she realises much later, it is his job to 'chat up' vulnerable girls picked out of the crowd at concerts. It is the gang's *modus operandi*.

Donna takes the bait. She and Angela agree to go. As soon as he closes the deal, Wayne smoothly switches things: he says that as his station wagon is already full, the girls can get a lift with his friends. He assures them his mates are trustworthy. On cue, a gleaming red Torana pulls up next to them. It is a two-door manual with black bucket seats, a billiard-ball on the gear stick and a transfer with the word TORANA in big white capitals across the top of the windscreen.

Four young men are in the car. The driver wears a hat. A big man leans forward in the passenger seat and unlatches it so Angela can climb in between the pair in the back. Donna realises she is expected to sit on the big man's knee in the front. She is taken aback at first but having to squeeze in seems so clearly uncomfortable and temporary that it reinforces the impression that the party is nearby.

Wayne assures her he will drive ahead and lead the way. She believes him – and Angela trusts her. It is all organised. In seconds, the situation has changed from the girls going with three people Donna has already met to being in a car full of strangers.

The first thing she realises is that the four men belong to one ethnic group. They are dark-haired and speak with the same accent. She thinks they are Greek but they could be Italian. In itself, that doesn't matter to her. Donna and some of her five siblings were born overseas – to a Canadian father and Northern Irish mother – and the family had been all over the world before immigrating only a few years before, so she knows what it is like to be an outsider.

What makes her uneasy is that these strangers know things about her: which concerts she has been to; that she likes dancing; where she comes from and which school she goes to.

'They were kind of laughing but in a sly way,' is how she puts it later. 'We were being "interviewed" but I didn't know it. They were looking for someone who fitted their criteria: who came from a different area and had no idea who they were or where they were taking us.' The men avoid using each other's names. They call each other 'mate', although she hears the name 'Joe' and one mentions working in a garage.

What the men know about her is harmless enough but the fact they know it unsettles her. Donna glances in the rear vision mirror and catches the eye of one of the men in the back seat. She doesn't like his stare. He is sizing her up.

The longer the trip goes, the stranger it seems. For the second time in three days, she is driven into the western suburbs. When both cars pull up at a service station she is uneasy. The one she calls the 'big guy' gets out and speaks to Wayne secretively. It is as if they are discussing a drug deal.

It is a deal. But not drugs.

THE big guy is boss. He is broad-shouldered, thick set and has a strong accent and a dominant streak. Donna notices the distinctive crease across the bridge of his nose, like the then well-known television personality, Gary Meadows, host of the then popular game show, *The Price Is Right*.

By the time they leave the service station, Donna is spooked but doesn't know what to do. Even if she could get away, Angela is trapped in the back.

They leave the houses behind and pass open country – Williamstown Rifle Range, as it was before being developed – then turn off into a rough dirt track that leads into wasteland between Altona back beach and a row of huge fuel or chemical storage tanks. In the distance she sees the orange tiled roofs of a new housing development, but the wasteland is deserted. Thunder rumbles as the cars stop near a patch of stunted scrub.

Everything is wrong. Donna jumps out and hurries to Wayne's car, checking over her shoulder that Angela is behind her. 'What's going on?' she yells at Wayne.

'What's the problem?' he answers, and one of the other two with him says something odd: 'We're doing a deal'. An admission. She hears a thud, a sudden exhalation of air and a scream. She jerks around to see that the big guy has knocked Angela to the ground and is dragging her along the ground, like a hunter with an animal carcass. Angela's face is contorted with fear. Years later, when Donna sees Munch's painting *The Scream*, it reminds her of the way her friend looked at that moment.

Donna turns back to Wayne and the two Johns and begs them to do something. One mumbles something about going for help. They get back in their station wagon and drive off. She never sees them again. She realises that the whole thing is a set up.

The big man throws Angela into the Torana. Donna runs at him and jumps on his back, clawing at his neck. He grabs her and tosses her into the back seat with Angela, who is sobbing. The other two men are still outside, leaving the driver and the leader in the front. They other two walk off, as if they have rehearsed their movements. The driver speeds off, bouncing over the rough ground, then stops the car.

Donna is terrified but still thinking. 'You don't want to do this –' she says, but the big guy interrupts.

'Why don't you just fucking shut up,' he says quietly, dark eyes staring coldly into hers. Then she sees the glint of the knife in his hand, held low between the bucket seats.

That's when she knows there is no way out. But she can't imagine what is going to happen. She is fifteen and a long way from home.

IT isn't until Donna is twice that age, a successful and sophisticated woman living far from Melbourne, that she finds the words to tell all that happened that day.

She has worked hard and lived fast, a party girl running on adrenalin and deadlines, pushing herself to exhaustion so that she can sleep it off and do it all again, night after night. She left school and Melbourne soon after the rapes, started as a teenage window dresser, moved to nightclubs and then theatre – steadily more frenetic jobs that keep body and mind busy. It is the mask she holds up to the world, a way to keep nightmares at bay. It doesn't always work.

Once, in 1983, drunk in an empty club at 5am, she tells a friend she has been raped, but then she falls silent. He doesn't hear the full story until years later.

After one failed relationship and a few false starts, she stays single for years. Her family knows what happened in Melbourne but talking about it is taboo. Her parents opposed going to the police; they moved interstate soon after the rape and 'left it behind'. Donna was implicitly encouraged to go along with an unspoken conspiracy to keep it buried for the same reasons many rape victims did and still do: shame, fear of blame and fear. Not only fear of reprisals but of being cross-examined in court and judged outside it. In any case, for years she cannot force herself to talk about it.

Until one day in early 1992, when the past finally catches up. It happens with a chance sighting at a mailing house where she is approving theatre subscription brochures. A supervisor asks where she went to school, explaining that one of the men working there thinks he remembers her face from Blackburn High in Melbourne.

It's a harmless query, but Donna is rattled. Being recognised triggers a rush of submerged memories – and fears. From that day, friends notice that her behaviour changes.

One of them is Tom McDonald, an Australian business lawyer then practising mostly in the United States but who often visits the city where Donna lives. He first meets her in 1991, at the club she then managed. They become friends and he helps her with a legal problem. She repays him by cooking him dinner when he's in town.

To McDonald, Donna is 'sparkling company and a damned good cook' but their friendship is platonic. After a meal in early 1992 they are listening to music and having a drink when Donna's breezy charm falls apart. She says she trusts him because he has never made a pass at her. Then she says she has been having 'strange feelings'. Then she breaks down.

The savvy club manager turns into a frightened girl. Crying and disjointed, she pours out a stream of raw recollections. 'It was so traumatic it made her physically ill.'

Afterwards, McDonald feels 'ashamed to be a man for about five minutes'. Then he decides to help. He suggests psychological treatment – and legal remedies. One avenue is crimes compensation. The other is justice – searching for the attackers and seeing them punished.

McDonald helps her launch a crimes compensation case that she is eventually to win. But mere compensation – about six months wages for a dozen rapes and a ruined life – is never going to be enough to put her back together again.

That year, Donna's friends see what one calls 'that sparky, mischievous, bossy girl' unravel. The workaholic can no longer work. Her stylish art deco inner-suburban house is a mess. She stays indoors for days, curled in a ball, crying. On her first visit to a psychologist she hands over a tape recording of an interview with a sexual assault counsellor. It is, the psychologist says later, 'a harrowing account of a harrowing crime.'

Another friend hears the story first hand, with detail that shakes him. 'All the filthy parts she needed to have said,' he says. She reminds the friend of a war veteran he met once, a troubled ex-marine who tells anybody who will listen how his mates were butchered beside him on a far-off battlefield he can't leave behind.

She finally goes to the police on March 17, 1992, while in

Melbourne for a conference. She goes to Nunawading Community Policing Squad and starts talking. It takes ten hours to finish the statement. A kind policewoman takes it all down and shares a piece of boiled fruit cake with her, the only thing either of them eat from midday until 10pm.

She recalls every detail as if it were frozen in time. 'I have these snapshots in my brain,' she explains later. 'It unfolds like a film. A noir film.'

IT'S not just the knife but the look in the eyes of the man who holds it that terrifies her. He drags her out of the car, then gets in the back seat and starts to rape Angela.

Donna is in shock. The driver stays in the car, watching. The other two men walk up. They push and abuse her, working themselves up. They call her 'fucking slut' and 'stupid bitch' and 'hopeless c–' and grab at her breasts. They also call her 'boutana' or 'puttana' – Greek and Italian variations of the word for 'whore'.

She refuses to undress. 'Smart bitch!' snarls one of her attackers, and they shove her face down on the bonnet of the car and pull her jeans and underclothes down, one holding her by the hair. What follows is obscene, violent, and degrading.

She is numb with pain, fear – and concern for Angela, who is a virgin. And who, Donna believes, wouldn't be there except for her. She can hear her whimpering in the car. It rains again. She sees the black clouds and the fuel refinery tanks and watches the drops trickle down the windscreen. She tries to block out what is happening by concentrating on the sky, the refinery tanks, and the drops on the windscreen. Forever after, a wet windscreen jolts her memory to unspeakable acts.

The rapists laugh and taunt Donna as they zip up their flies. She dresses herself and gets in the car with Angela, thinking it is over. It isn't. The Torana goes a few hundred metres and stops. Waiting is another station wagon, a metallic mocha brown Ford with curtains in the back. There are two men in it – a tag team. The big guy drags Angela out and orders both girls into the Ford. He gets in, too, as if he owns them. They drive off. Donna doesn't see the Torana again, except in bad dreams.

She has no idea where they are until the car turns down a sloping entrance to parkland beside the river opposite Flemington racecourse, still crowded after the Cup meeting. It is quiet on the Footscray bank, but a family is nearby trying to have a picnic, despite the weather. The girls are raped again. Donna can see the picnickers through the fogged-up windows. She wills them to realise what is happening and rescue them.

They drive off again. The gang leader puts his arm around Angela in a grotesque parody of affection, as if she is his girlfriend. When the car stops at traffic lights he whispers in Donna's ear: 'I know you'd like to run.' She knows then she will never forget his face.

They drive under a bluestone bridge where water is lying across the road, almost knee deep. They turn into cobbled lanes among warehouses and factories, somewhere in North Melbourne or Kensington, and go up a steep lane and stop in a car park underneath a building. It is dark and deserted but suddenly the space is filled with the rumble of a V8 motor and male voices. More men.

Donna whispers to Angela to cling to the pack leader: 'Just stay with him – he won't let anyone else touch you.' She's not sure this is true, or even if they will survive. She fears their ordeal is heading for some sinister climax: 'I was frightened we were going to be annihilated.' One by one, the newcomers rape Donna. Except the last one, the twelfth man to straddle her that day.

She sees his face. She thinks one of the others called him

'Steve'. He is smaller and fairer than the rest and less sure of himself. She whispers: 'Help me get out of here.'

He quietly helps her get dressed, then calls to the gang leader: 'Mate, it's getting late. Why don't we get rid of them?'

They drive. It is getting dark. Minutes later, the car pulls into a lane beside North Melbourne Railway Station. The girls are shoved out, discarded like pieces of rubbish.

They have avoided death but their life sentences are just beginning.

DONNA'S police statement trickled through the system and across the city from Nunawading to Footscray CIB, a crowded office with stained carpet and strained resources in one of the busiest police stations in Australia.

The file was handed to a detective who was transferred soon after, then to another, who was too busy on recent offences to waste time on something that happened so long before. And so, in mid-1993, the file passed to Detective Sergeant Richard Parsons, who had been a young constable at the 1976 Melbourne Cup meeting.

Parsons had lived and worked in the western suburbs all his life and none knew 'the patch' better. He had seen a lot of bad endings but, unusually in his calling, it had not stopped him being calm and courteous. Only a fool would mistake this for weakness or lack of purpose. No policeman who has worked the Melbourne waterfront is a soft target – but it didn't stop him having a soft heart.

When Parsons read Donna's statement, it touched a nerve. He remembered gang rapes in the district in the 1970s and it bothered him that some went unsolved. Besides, he had a daughter of his own. When he spoke to Donna he struck up a rapport.

Without new leads there wasn't a lot Parsons could do but he did it, anyway. The starting point was the man Donna knew as Wayne Thompson – and his friend John McNally.

Although Wayne had lied that John was his brother, Donna knew his real surname. What she didn't know was that Wayne had also lied about his own surname: it wasn't Thompson. The day after the rapes, Wayne had called her at home and told her his telephone had been disconnected and she would not be hearing from him. She had no idea where he worked, except that he was probably a labourer or tradesman. He had vanished.

Sergeant Parsons soon found McNally, who still lived locally. He had a string of convictions – assaults, thefts and drink driving – and had served time for armed robbery in the 1980s. The detective wasn't surprised when McNally flatly denied anything to do with Donna or the rapes.

On McNally's criminal record, Parsons noticed that one of his known associates was called Wayne, though not Thompson. The surname was a common name starting with S. This Wayne S. was the right age – eighteen in 1976 – and had a record for assault, theft and burglary in the 1970s. He had served time in Turana youth training centre.

When Donna visited Melbourne in January 1996, the detective showed her a series of mugshots of possible suspects, including a poor quality photocopy of Wayne S. She paused over the picture and said the eyes reminded her of the youth she knew as 'Wayne Thompson'. But she wasn't sure.

Meanwhile, Parsons had traced Angela. Whereas Donna had left Melbourne soon after the rapes and had lived interstate ever since, Angela stayed. They had written to each other briefly but it had petered out. They had little in common except their ordeal, which each had tried to bury in her own way.

Angela had married, had children, and moved to an outer suburb. Parsons arranged to meet her discreetly. Angela confirmed Donna's statement but refused to be involved in any possible prosecution. Her husband and children did not know about the rapes and she wanted it to stay that way.

The trail was cold.

IN June, 1996, Donna was going through things she had stuffed into a suitcase when leaving Melbourne twenty years before. She opened a blue satchel full of school English notes. As she put it down, something orange fell out.

It was a ticket to the 1976 Rocktober Concert at Festival Hall. On the back was written WAYNE and a telephone number. She stared at it, then sat down and typed a fax to Parsons. 'You'll never guess what!' it began. 'I'm still shaking with excitement and amazement.' She was sure the old telephone number would lead to Wayne and unravel the rapists' identity. Eventually, it would, but for a long time the orange ticket was a red herring.

In the rush to computer data bases in the 1980s and 1990s, old records and manual systems had not only been superseded, but destroyed. In 1976, a disconnected telephone number might have been used to trace someone who didn't want to be found. But in 1996, the same number seemed useless because it couldn't be cross-checked using modern data systems.

Months after finding the ticket, Donna saw an article about old telephone directories for sale. It gave her an idea. She asked the Victorian State Library to look up Wayne S's surname in the 1976 Melbourne directory – to see if any subscriber of that name matched the number she had. None did.

Donna either had to give up or look for a needle in a haystack. She decided to look. In June 1997, she asked Telstra to let her search an archival copy of the 1976 directory. She spent hours every week at her state's Telstra headquarters, poring over it. She took four months and 655,000 names to find the number. Again, it seemed like a breakthrough.

354

The name listed for the number was T. Fennell, at 175 Millers Road, Altona. Perhaps Fennell was a friend or relative of Wayne's family? It had the allure of the unknown and it seemed to Donna and the detective that T. Fennell was the missing clue.

But when Sergeant Parsons went to 175 Millers Road, his heart sank. It was a block of flats that had been rented out to dozens of tenants over the years. No one knew of a T. Fennell. Parsons and Donna set up stories in local suburban newspapers, appealing for help. None came.

The problem was that the 1976 telephone directory had been out of date. (In fact, as it turned out, respectable tenants called Tony and Doris Fennell had moved out of the Millers Road flat in December 1974 – but Fennell's name and outdated address and number had mistakenly stayed in the 1976 directory. Meanwhile, the number had been allocated to new subscribers: Wayne S's parents. There was no way of knowing this until 2003, when the author traced Tony Fennell to a country district in eastern Victoria.)

For five years, it threw the investigation off course. Without Fennell, it seemed they couldn't prove a connection between the telephone number and Wayne S. As it turned out, when Fennell was found, he couldn't directly make that connection – but he pointed out that Donna had searched the wrong telephone directory. There was still hope.

In January, 2003, on a rare visit to Melbourne, Donna went to see Richard Parsons. Once more they revisited the crime scenes, from Festival Hall to Altona to the Maribyrnong river bank to North Melbourne. This time the detective had unearthed a good quality photograph of Wayne S. taken in the 1970s. Donna said it looked like the Wayne she had known – but she needed to be sure.

Later, she went to the state library and asked for the 1977

telephone directory. She ran her finger down the S– column ... and found the telephone number she had written on her concert ticket 26 years before. Proof that the 'Wayne Thompson' who lured her into a car of pack rapists was really Wayne S.

Proof that the past can reach out.

THE last chapter of Donna's story is not written because it has not happened yet. The ending she hopes for is that the net will tighten around the men who planned and committed the pack rape of two terrified teenage girls all those years ago. And maybe more besides.

She knows they are out there. Time has disguises – thinning hair and thickening waists – but it cannot alter some things. If he's alive, the leader of the pack will still be tall and broad-shouldered and have a Southern European accent and a domineering personality ... and that distinctive crease across the bridge of his nose, like Gary Meadows. Time cannot alter the fact he used to go around with his mates in a spotless red two-door Torana and that he knew someone with a dark brown Ford station wagon with vinyl bench seats and a column shift.

The Torana was the sort of car young men prized. Somewhere, photographs of it will be in an album. Somewhere, people will remember the car and who owned it in 1976.

The rapists are not the only ones with secrets. Richard Parsons is sure Donna and Angela were not the only girls set up and raped who didn't go to the police because they felt compromised by shame, fear, and family pressure to hide it.

Those frightened girls will be women in their early 40s now. Old enough not to be scared any more and to help each other fight back. Each will know something that counts. Some might even know who their attackers are or where they live.

Meanwhile, time is running out for the gang. One day, the patient Sergeant Parsons will knock on the door of a pale brick veneer house on a corner in Hoppers Crossing, on Melbourne's western fringe. It's the house where Wayne S. recently moved in with a new woman. The detective will pick his time – Wayne is an interstate truck driver these days, and isn't always home.

What happens next is up to Wayne. He can help police. Or he can try to protect the members of the gang.

Wayne S. knows what jail is like: he once did time for assault. He was young and reckless then. Now he has family reasons not to go back inside.

Wayne's wife died not long ago and he has a young daughter to worry about. It won't be long before she's at high school and wanting to go out with boys.

After this story was first published in 2003 several potential witnesses came forward, including two rape victims who had been assaulted by the same gang. Donna's friend Angela was moved to co-operate fully and took part in a reconstruction of the crime that corroborated Donna's account. As a result, Sergeant Richard Parsons was able to confirm his suspicions about the identity of the rapists and their collaborators. He found that four of the twelve rapists had become hardened criminals and had died violent deaths. Sergeant Parsons identified and interviewed Wayne S. and his associates and obtained fresh information but at the time of writing none of the surviving men had yet agreed to give evidence against the others. The case is not closed.

Flying backwards

IT'S minutes after midnight, 24,000 feet above Berlin and way below freezing. The Australian tail gunner is hunched in his tiny turret as it swings from starboard to port, port to starboard, searching the black sky for any sign of approaching death.

He recites a mantra to himself, over and over: 'You got yourself up here, now you've got to get yourself back. Concentrate, you bastard.' In his pocket is his lucky charm, a silver cigarette case. Without it, he's certain he'd die.

Despite the intense cold, he's sweating now, adrenalin pumping so hard he stutters when he speaks into the intercom wired into his oxygen mask. Nerves jangle with the ancient instinct for fight or flight, but the gunner and his six crewmates can do neither. As the searchlights blaze and flak explodes below, they must carry out the duty they're quietly certain will kill them – if not on this mission, then the next, or the one after that.

For the tail gunner, flying backwards on his metal stool in the tailplane of the great, shuddering Lancaster bomber, duty means endlessly staring into the blackness behind, eyes strained for enemy fighters. Belts of .303 ammunition loop and coil in hidden tanks, ready to feed his four Browning machine guns. But the last thing the gunner wants to do is use his guns. He's learned fast that his job is not to shoot down the enemy: it's to spy him first. He's the first in the squadron to have a big hole sawn in the perspex bubble so he can see more easily, a flash of Aussie make-do that's quickly imitated.

At exactly 12.15 on this morning he sees a German fighter, a Junkers 88, on the starboard quarter. He stammers a message over the intercom, but by this time the Lancaster is over the target, and evasive action is out of the question. If it were on the way home, bombs gone, the pilot might throw the big aircraft sideways and down, to corkscrew away from the fighter's gunsights. But not now. The bomb load has to be dropped; to do that the Lancaster has to fly suicidally straight and true, a sitting duck.

It's the longest minute in his life, and he is never to forget it. He tells the mid-upper gunner to take aim at the Junkers. 'If he deviates one inch, we'll both shoot,' he says.

But he knows that if they do squeeze the triggers, the tracer bullets will draw fire from the giant flak guns below, and other unseen fighters roaming the sky above.

If they don't fire, they can hope the German pilot hasn't seen them – or hasn't the nerve to risk shooting first.

And so the two aircraft fly on, locked in a strange stand-off Joseph Heller would appreciate. Catch .303.

It was 16 December 1943, the rear gunner's 24th birthday. He's had a lot of birthdays since, but no better gift than surviving that mission – and another twenty afterwards, against awful odds. Most of his mates didn't.

G EOFFREY Williams is now in his 80s. He returned to
Australia after the war and, outwardly, he 'just got on
with it,' like thousands of other war veterans of his generation.
He took back his salesman's job at Myer, married, raised three
children fairly well, and played golf pretty badly.

But hardly a day has gone past in 55 years that he hasn't
thought about the surreal horror of flying over occupied
Europe in the RAF Bomber Command, when 55,500 Allied
airmen were killed, and 18,000 injured or taken prisoner.

In his eight-month tour of duty, each time he flew he feared
he would, in the brusque wartime slang he still uses, 'get the
chop'.

Between missions he and his crewmates had a lot of time to
think about the odds against them getting out alive.

The arithmetic was brutal. His squadron's strength was 30
aircraft. In six months it lost 60, each with seven crewmen. His
was one of only two of the original 30 crews to survive. One
crew shot down had an average age of 21. Some were boys of
eighteen. Crews straight from training were sometimes killed
before they'd even unpacked their clothes.

No wonder the survivors wanted to forget. No wonder they
couldn't.

Williams started recording his memories when he was 79, at
the urging of family and friends. He took a blue exercise book
of the sort primary schoolchildren use, and started writing in
the neat, sloping forehand he learned at Canterbury State
School all those years ago.

Its working title was, naturally enough, *The Geoffrey
Williams Story*. It takes a reader from his boyhood in
Depression-era Melbourne, to his first jobs as a grocery
delivery boy and 'printer's devil' to selling furniture at Myer.

But the story really starts when he decides to go to war in
October, 1941. A friend had joined the Empire Air Training

Scheme, set up to draw airmen from former British colonies, and Williams decided to do the same.

The interviews were held at Preston Motors in the city. 'The first thing they asked', he recalls, 'was to see my intermediate (school) certificate. Of course, I'd left school much too young to get it, but I said in my best voice "Oh, I forgot to bring that with me." They were looking for people with initiative, and as far as I was concerned that proved mine.'

The trainees had to study at night school. Williams was hopeless at maths, so he gave up wanting to be a pilot, navigator or wireless operator, opting for the most dangerous job of all: rear gunner.

After months of mostly useless training, he went to South Australia to gunnery school. Trainees went up in pairs in an old aircraft and fired Vickers machine guns at a 'drogue' towed by another plane. In mid-air, Williams's training partner refused to shoot. His brother had just been killed in the Middle East and he was rattled. Williams stood in for him with the machine gun, but wasn't surprised when the troubled young man was transferred to a desk job in barracks. It was his first lesson in how differently people react to fear.

Williams and his fellow airmen eventually sailed to San Francisco on a fast American troop ship, the SS *Westpoint*, which was chased by enemy submarines across the Pacific. After landing, they were sent across country to Boston to a receiving camp for overseas servicemen on their way to Europe.

They were given leave. They had no money but went straight to the Manger Hotel in Boston, booked in and went to the cocktail bar. A woman in a fur coat approached Williams and asked if he was Australian, then asked his room number. Half an hour later, he was unpacking in the room when she knocked on the door.

'She walked over, kissed me, took off her fur coat and stood there, naked!' He was astonished. Like thousands of other virgin soldiers far from home, it was the first time he'd experienced the aphrodisiac effect of wartime – a mixture of uniforms, danger and dislocation.

'I don't think I was a very satisfactory lover,' he was to write wryly of the encounter. Much later, he was ashamed he had abandoned the woman, leaving her with the hotel bill while he stayed out all night at a party. Back then, he didn't care. He was 21 and on his way to war. He remembers those few weeks in Boston as an endless party. But it was only a taste of the desperate hedonism ahead, on London leave passes snatched between bombing raids.

They sailed from New York on the *Queen Elizabeth*, thousands of men on the luxury liner converted into the biggest troop carrier on earth. The giant ship outran enemy submarines. Had it been sunk, they say, so many trained airmen would have been drowned that it might have cost the Allies the war.

They landed in Scotland, then took a train south. When Williams arrived at Bournemouth in southern England, he wrote later, 'we couldn't help but think that here we were at the front fence in the back yard of the war zone.'

The airmen were billeted in beautiful old guesthouses, but the empty beaches had rolls of barbed wire on top of the sand and thousands of mines underneath it.

They were divided into crews for the final phase of training. To get experience, pilots had to fly two trips with operational crews. Williams's pilot, David Evans, was killed on his second training run. Evans had also come from Canterbury in Melbourne, and the two families knew each other. When his mother received the telegram she assumed that the Williams's son had been killed with her David. The Williams family didn't know Geoffrey was alive until he sent a telegram saying: 'I am all right, David missing.'

In September, 1943, his crew was posted to Waterbeach, near Cambridge, to form RAF squadron 514.

Their replacement pilot was an Englishman called Barney Reid, later to receive a Distinguished Flying Cross. Despite being trained for Stirling bombers, they switched to Lancasters.

There were training flights over Britain. Then, on 11 November, 1943, the first sortie. He was to write: 'Our first operation in our Lancaster Mark II was to La Rochelle on the west coast of France. German ships would harbour there and our job was to drop mines. This was referred to as a gardening trip and we would come in very low and drop these mines from about 15 feet.'

Then came the Battle of Berlin. From November 1943 to March 1944 Bomber Command lost 1047 aircraft, each holding seven men. Most were killed; a lucky few parachuted into enemy territory and, if not butchered by angry German civilians, were taken prisoner. Despite the huge damage inflicted on Berlin, it was, like the German bombing of Britain, an heroic failure – crippling neither production nor morale.

For those who flew, each operation was a nightmare that ended either in death, capture – or a wave of euphoric relief that dissolved into fear as they waited on the order to fly another mission.

Every six weeks the airmen took six days leave. Williams and his friends would go to London, where they booked into the Strand Palace hotel for a binge of drinking and sex to block out what was behind – and ahead.

'I'd be almost incoherent for two days after a mission,' the old man says, studying a photograph of the fresh-faced young stranger that was him in 1943. 'On leave, you'd find women first, then get on the piss. Otherwise, you'd get lumbered – taken up a lane and rolled.'

Bombs and bullets didn't destroy morale, but the shared sense of mortality overturned conventional morality. Threatened by death, everyone lived for the moment. Once, Geoffrey Williams and a friend were picked up by two well-to-do women who'd come to London from the home counties in search of distraction while their husbands were fighting in the Middle East. The four spent five days in the Strand Palace, leaving their bedrooms only to eat and drink. Especially drink.

Another time he sneaked to London overnight for a secret assignation with a distant cousin, only to miss her in the confusion following a German bomb raid. Every haystack in the countryside around the base had an airman with a blanket and a woman, he recalls. He shared one Cambridge girl with a squadron leader, and a London publican's daughter with an Air Vice Marshal. No names, no pack drill, he laughs.

Details of those escapades have faded – 'I can't even recall the girls' names or what they looked like, now' – but not the memory of danger. He still dreams about that.

He describes vividly the claustrophobia of being shut in the gun turret. Rear gunners could hardly move in the bulky flying suit that stopped them freezing to death. They couldn't even wear their parachutes – and had trouble opening the hatch behind them to get out. If the aircraft were hit, they had to scramble out the hatch, find their parachute, put it on and bale out with the rest of the crew.

He knew a rear gunner who, when his aircraft was hit, managed to get out of the turret but, in the confusion, put on another man's parachute. He survived, but the other man was killed. A lifetime later, the old gunner who took the parachute is still haunted by it.

364

That is just one tiny untold story. Geoffrey Williams suspects there are many bigger ones buried in military archives that have never been released.

HE often wonders about fear and its effects, about whether he was naive to take things at face value. Airmen were instructed that if their planes were too crippled to return to England, they should parachute into Sweden, a neutral country. He now wonders if some crews made pacts to set their aircraft on course to crash in the North Sea, then baled out over Sweden. Better, maybe, than facing the aerial abattoir over Berlin.

He wonders, too, how many airmen went 'LMF'– were classified to 'lack moral fibre' for refusing to fly. He thinks they were swiftly spirited away, locked up in secret and later dishonourably discharged, but can't be sure.

Twice Williams flew at short notice with strange crews to fill in for gunners who, he was told, were sick. Now, he wonders if the missing men had reached a point where they couldn't – or wouldn't – go one mission closer to death.

If so, he wonders, were they cowards – or logical? And was he himself brave – or stupid?

The truth, he thinks, is that everyone was frightened, but some were more afraid than others of showing it.

Strangely enough, amid the carnage, the closest he came to dying was when his oxygen pipe froze at high altitude and he fell unconscious. Luckily, his mid-upper gunner, one Dick White, used to keep an eye on the rear turret. When the turret stopped swinging from side to side, White raised the alarm, and the Lancaster's navigator struggled the length of the massive bomb bay with a bottle of oxygen to revive him.

It was White who told him about another incident he's never forgotten. When the war ended, the bombers ferried thousands of prisoners of war back from Europe. To save weight, they carried no parachutes. White saw one Lancaster go into a tailspin and crash, killing all aboard. He thinks it was because someone forgot to tell the passengers not to unbalance the aircraft by crowding into the back.

Only once did Geoffrey Williams pray. That was the night when he accidentally left behind the silver cigarette case that had become his talisman. He realised the cigarette case was missing when he got into the cockpit, and it terrified him.

His prayers were answered. One of the Lancaster's engines wasn't running properly. After several attempts to correct the problem, the engineer declared the aircraft unserviceable. The crew climbed out and returned to barracks.

That night 11 of the squadron's 29 remaining aircraft were shot down. They were among hundreds of casualties in the worst raid ever suffered by Bomber Command. Next morning, there were 77 empty places in the mess. More than a third of the squadron had been killed.

'I still get upset talking about it,' Williams confesses suddenly. He tries to compose himself, and jabs a finger at his manuscript. 'It's all in there,' he says, hands shaking, voice trembling.

But, of course, it isn't all there. What he has written is an outline of one man's war, the bare facts around which layers of the real story can be added. That story, like those of so many ordinary people who survived extraordinary events, is mostly still inside his head. But there are glimpses of it, and it fascinates.

In 1994, he was interviewed by a psychiatrist whose job was to assess if he had enough symptoms of post-traumatic stress to retain his war pension.

He told the young man about how he couldn't forget the mission he flew on his 24th birthday; about how he still

pictured the Junkers 88 in his machine gun sights. The psychiatrist's professional detachment dissolved. Animated, he asked
on which date this had happened. Because, he said, the German
pilot could have been his own father, who'd flown Junkers 88s
in the Battle of Berlin.

The old Luftwaffe veteran, he said, now lived at Apollo Bay.
One day, Geoffrey Williams muses, he'd like to meet him.
Perhaps talking about it will tame the demons.

Meanwhile, he's going to keep writing, adding bits to his
story as they come to him. Then he's going looking for a
publisher, he says. He wants to call his book *Flying
Backwards: Memoirs of rear gunner G.G.Williams.*

Geoffrey Williams's book was published in 2001.

Thylacine hunting

THYLACINUS cynocephalus has had many aliases. The Latin means 'pouched dog with wolf's head'. The thylacine, commonly called the Tasmanian tiger, is or was the largest modern carniverous mammal. It weighed up to 35 kilograms, stood up to 60 centimetres at the shoulder and had from fifteen to twenty dark stripes running across the back from shoulder to tail. The female carried up to four young at a time in her pouch. Thylacines once ranged throughout Australia and New Guinea but lost out to the dingo, a more efficient hunter that came to Australia with early aborigines.

O N an overcast afternoon in the late 1970s, a quiet man called John Anderson set out from his neat brick farmhouse to walk around his property in the coastal grazing country near Longford, between Sale and Seaspray in Gippsland. His red kelpie dog followed him, and he carried a .22 rifle. Anderson, a soil scientist with the Department of Agriculture for most of his career, never lost a chance to rid the farm of rabbits, foxes and

SEX, DEATH AND BETRAYAL

368

weeds. He even paid his two daughters a bounty on each thistle they hoed out at weekends and after school.

This day, while their father checked stock, fences and water, the girls also walked around the farm, which runs more than a kilometre eastwards from the house. They went separate ways, out of each other's sight.

As a young man in the Western District, John Anderson had shot hundreds of rabbits, and he could hit them on the run. At close range, anything bigger was an easy target. So when an animal the size of a large dog appeared in front of him, he could have shot it in the time it took to raise the rifle. He didn't.

A bullet might have solved one of the most tantalising mysteries of the century, but he has never regretted holding his fire.

'I didn't know what it was, so I certainly wasn't going to shoot it,' he says simply. End of argument. And the beginning of a story he's kept to himself for two decades.

Anderson was 74 when he told his story, but remembered every detail of what he saw. He described nearing a belt of tea-tree along his rear boundary fence when his kelpie growled. He looked up – and saw an animal he'd never seen before, nor since.

Like many of his generation, he thinks in chains and acres. A chain is the length of a cricket pitch, about twenty metres. 'It was about a chain away,' he says, 'and looking straight at me. At first I thought it was a wallaby. Then it loped away on all fours.

'It had a peculiar gait, not like a dog. The tail was thickish at the butt. There were markings on the hind quarters. It was coloured in autumn tones: the body was rusty brown and the stripes were dark brown from the loin backwards. It was every bit as big as my kelpie.'

He stared after the animal, then walked home, wondering how to explain his strange sighting to his family. He needn't have worried.

ANNE Anderson, then about sixteen, the younger of the two daughters, had beaten her father home. Her sister Julie was telling their mother she'd been scared by 'something big' creeping on its belly in the bracken. Anne interrupted, stammering out her story.

She'd been chasing rabbits with her favourite dog, a border collie called Devil, near a shallow soak where wild animals came through the fence from the bush to drink.

'The dog ran in to where the dam was,' Anne was to recall twenty years later, sitting in her new house on her husband's farm near Sale. 'This animal ran out of the tea-tree, sort of towards me, then veered.

'It was maybe a bit bigger than the dog. It had heavy shoulders, but was thinner at the back and looked funny in the hind legs. I thought its spine was injured, because it moved strangely – a bit like a Manx cat, which are long-bodied and sort of bound along.'

An expert horsewoman, she was struck by the unusual gait. 'It was as if it was trotting with its front feet and bounding with its back feet. It was a browny tan colour, like a sunburnt red kelpie, but had darker markings around it. The stripes seemed to start mid-loin, and were definite, going back to the tail.

'Devil chased it until it got about fifteen feet from me. Then it spun around to face him. It left its front legs planted on the ground and flipped its hindlegs around. It was a strange movement compared with dogs and foxes. He looked to have short, triangular, thick sort of ears, not really like a dog, and really beady eyes.

'The dog ran towards him. The animal's muzzle stayed straight. That is, the top didn't move, but he dropped his bottom jaw right down ... like a mediaeval drawbridge over a moat.' She mimes this, holding one hand flat, dropping the other down through more than 90 degrees to form a gaping 'mouth'.

'Then,' she continues, leaning forward in her chair, reliving the moment, 'he made this really bizarre sound. It was a weird "yip, yip!" from the bottom of the throat. The hairs went up on the back of my neck. I was terrified. So was my dog. He turned around and bolted. I ran home to tell Mum, but the dog beat me.'

When she told her father what had happened, he pulled down a book of Australian mammals and started leafing through it. As he turned a page she said 'That's it!'

The picture she pointed to was of the thylacine, or Tasmanian tiger, presumed extinct in Tasmania since the late 1930s and, according to the experts, extinct on the mainland for centuries.

It didn't make sense, but father and daughter were certain they'd seen the same animal, and that it was a thylacine. They didn't know then that Anne's account of the animal's unique jaw action and double yipping cry sounded like the most complete witness description of a thylacine since the last one in captivity died in a Hobart zoo in 1936. The yipping she described had been observed only by Tasmanian bushmen who had seen thylacines hunting. Their usual sound was a deep cough.

Anderson warned the girls not to talk about what had happened. He feared 'idiots' would come to try to shoot the animal. Anne stayed quiet for more selfish reasons. She didn't want to be laughed at by her friends. She still doesn't.

Which is why, apart from Anderson reporting the sighting by telephone to a dismissive wildlife officer in Melbourne, they rarely spoke of it outside the family.

A COUPLE of years later, John Anderson's wife Margaret was talking to a neighbour called Alison Alsop. Mrs Anderson looked after Alsops' farm while they spent weekdays at their Toorak townhouse, and the two had become friendly.

Mrs Alsop, sister of Lady (Kathleen) Clarke and a member of one of Victoria's oldest establishment families, was regarded as an honest, intelligent and well-educated woman. She bred racehorses, cattle and dogs and had known animals all her life.

She told Margaret Anderson she'd twice seen animals at the Longford farm she was sure were Tasmanian tigers. The first time, in about 1977, she'd seen one scratching a tree with its paws, the way a cat sharpens its claws. She was to say later it was bigger than her pointer dog, and a ginger colour with dark stripes 'like a zebra'. It had a flat head, a long nose and a long, pointed tail. The second specimen was smaller, about the size of a Queensland heeler, but otherwise identical with the first. She'd seen it two years later, crossing the road near the farm.

'That's funny,' Mrs Anderson told her. 'That sounds like what my husband and daughter saw.'

Before Alison Alsop died, in 1996, she spoke of the sightings to her son Greg Fair, a Collins Street stamp dealer, and brother of the prominent artist, Fraser Fair. She still insisted she'd seen two thylacines.

'She told me that they had a peculiar gait and that their tails were quite different from a dog's,' Fair says. 'My mother was against publicity, because she didn't want hoons coming in trying to shoot it. A lot of the locals accept that it's there. I think there must be a logical explanation. It's feasible, to me, that someone brought some across from Tasmania, a long time ago.'

THE two properties – the Andersons' and what was the Alsops' – back onto country that skirts Lake Reeve, a narrow waterway running parallel with the Ninety Mile Beach to join the Gippsland Lakes near Loch Sport, a holiday-house town squeezed into the narrow spit of scrubland between two lakes.

The soil is lighter than in the dairying districts inland, farms tend to be large and houses scattered. There is ample bush to shelter wildlife, despite holiday and retirement houses being built along the coast since the 1950s.

The climate is mild. Kangaroos, especially, do so well in the bush that borders open paddocks that locals dislike driving to Loch Sport at night because of the risk of hitting them.

Kangaroos and tourists aren't the only hazard. For most of this century, hog deer have bred in the bush along the coast. Although shooters thin them out, the dainty deer wander the empty streets of Loch Sport and Golden Beach at night.

How the hog deer come to be there gives a hint of the 19th century mania for 'acclimatisation' of species in Australasia. Everyone knows rabbits and foxes, cane toads and carp, sparrows and starlings multiplied to plague proportions – degrading vast areas of fragile topsoil, pushing vulnerable native animals, fish and plants to extinction and threatening others.

Not so well-known is that this list of usual suspects is only a few of many species that well-intentioned enthusiasts turned loose in the late nineteenth century and early in the twentieth.

The hog deer, for instance, were reputedly bred at the Chirnside family's Werribee Park, released in the 1870s near Wilsons Promontory, and spread up the coast to East Gippsland. Records are vague.

The acclimatisation and zoological societies that sprang up

in each colony in the mid-1800s mainly imported European animals, birds, fish and plants – but the orgy of meddling with nature was not confined to the recognised societies and foreign species. In his landmark book *They All Ran Wild*, the naturalist Eric Rolls describes how hunters, 'sportsmen', philanthropists, the curious, the concerned, the greedy, the needy and the downright eccentric all joined the haphazard scattering of animal and plant life.

While wealthy landowners imported a Noah's Ark of deer, camels, llamas, ostriches, mongooses, boa constrictors, nightingales and more, poor swagmen carried rabbit kittens across the Nullarbor in billy cans, and housewives cultivated blackberry cuttings. The instinct to experiment ran wild. There was a bizarre attempt to breed African animals in New Zealand, a country with no native mammals but soon to be plagued by deer, pigs, stoats, and weasels – and, interestingly, Tasmanian possums, first sent there in 1840. Wallabies were released on islands off the New Zealand coast and there were attempts to introduce Tasmanian devils and koalas.

Transport and expense didn't deter colonial animal fanciers. Tasmanian-bred deer were sent to NSW and Queensland in the 1860s. The Victorian Acclimatisation Society bought 640 acres of bush near Gembrook and secretly released various game birds there and in other areas away from settlement.

The 'sportsmen' and the acclimatisation societies had good reason to be secretive. Apart from the risk of their stock being poached, their efforts often angered farmers, whose crops and flocks suffered from plagues of imported pests.

Most farmers followed the maxim 'if it moves, shoot it; if it doesn't, chop it down' – and led the way in ruthless extermination of native species, especially predators. On the mainland, this meant dingoes, eagles and native cats, among others. In Tasmania, it also meant the devil and the thylacine.

Thylacines were never common, always elusive. It was two years before the first settlers killed one in Van Diemans Land, in 1805; only four specimens were collected in the first 17 years.

As early as 1863, the naturalist John Gould predicted it faced extinction, but that didn't stop the Tasmanian Government, dominated by graziers, from paying a bounty for its scalp from 1878 to 1909, in which time 4821 were killed.

Soon after, survivors in the wild were hit by a distemper-like virus that also killed the devils. Shamefully, a move to protect the thylacine in 1928 was blocked by landowners, but by then it was too late, anyway.

The devils and native cats survived hunting and disease and came back from the brink of extinction. The accepted wisdom is that the thylacine didn't …

Unless, in the welter of animal trading a generation earlier, well-meaning naturalists had quietly released some in a home away from home. Victoria.

ON the evidence, it would be remarkable if thylacines hadn't been transplanted from Tasmania at the start of the twentieth century. Almost all the other big marsupials were shipped all over Australasia, and beyond, and released.

Remnants of the beautiful Toolache wallabies were taken to an island, where they died. At least four wallaby species went to New Zealand, and red-necked wallabies to England and Germany, where they still live in the wild. Red kangaroos, possums, koalas, wombats, Tasmanian devils, koalas, Queensland tree kangaroos, quolls and pademelons were all released far from home. Some thrived, others didn't.

Eric Rolls, who has studied colonial animal importations and movements for years, argues that 'it is entirely believable' that amateur naturalists could have released thylacines in south-eastern Victoria around the turn of the century. 'Private individuals were breeding all sorts of animals,' he says. 'They definitely had the inclination and the money to import anything they liked.'

He dismisses the absence of known records as proof of anything. Anybody who fancied bringing thylacines across Bass Strait would have faced Victorian farmers outraged at the idea of releasing sheep and poultry-killing 'vermin' that still had a bounty on its head in Tasmania. If thylacines were imported, there were good reasons to keep it quiet. The same reaction conservationists would face from farmers today if they suggested releasing pure-bred dingoes into the Victorian bush.

IN 1900 a record tally of 153 thylacine bounties was paid in Tasmania. Although their numbers crashed during the next 30 years, there were still enough left for traders to trap and sell specimens cheaply in the first years of the new century.

There was a lucrative thylacine trade for Tasmanian trappers, who finally realised the 'pest' was worth more alive than dead. The sketchy records available show that from 1863 to 1930 at least 44 thylacines were shipped to Melbourne Zoo. Of these, some were sent on elsewhere, including the Australian Anatomical Society. No one is sure what happened to the specimens that the society did not dissect.

In 1910 the proprietor of Hobart's zoo, one Mary Roberts, charged London Zoo £25 for one thylacine, meaning that she would have paid trappers considerably less. Before 1909 any more than the one pound bounty was extra profit for trappers.

From 1910 to 1921 Mrs Roberts sent thylacines to three mainland zoos; in the same period about two dozen from various sources went to London, New York, Berlin and Washington. The tragedy was that none of these bred successfully in captivity. That, it seemed, could happen only in the wild – but not in Tasmania, with its snares, guns and poison. A new national park just across Bass Strait would have been ideal.

The question is, did someone make it happen?

MICHAEL Moss thinks they did. The former public servant and amateur naturalist has a simple theory to explain the otherwise inexplicable: that is, why there has been a rising number and range of apparently reliable thylacine sightings in the coastal strip from Wonthaggi to Loch Sport.

He has spent two years researching records and interviewing people who report seeing animals resembling thylacines in the area. He believes there are key differences between claimed sightings in Gippsland and in Tasmania.

In Tasmania the number of sightings has gradually dwindled in the 1990s, as publicity and speculation about the thylacine's fate has faded. But in Gippsland, where there has never been an accepted scientific reason to believe thylacines might exist, reported sightings are rising. This is puzzling, even to sceptics who rank unexpected animal sightings with UFO claims.

The Gippsland reports are overwhelmingly by local people with no previous interest in thylacines. This contrasts with Tasmania, where many if not most people have at least an anecdotal interest, and enthusiasts displaying what one wildlife officer calls 'Lasseter's syndrome' are keen to find the 'hidden treasure' in the wilderness. In Gippsland, in fact, there is a totally different psychology at work. Professor Henry Nix, of the Centre for Resource and Environmental Studies at the Australian National University, says many reputable people who make sightings 'are wary of making idiots of themselves'. He often interviews people who refuse to go public.

Professor Nix and other experts agree that thylacines favoured 'broken country' where trees and foothills meet open land, such as the farming country in north and north-east Tasmania, where records show most thylacines were trapped last century.

This is the sort of habitat favoured by people and grazing animals. The sort of habitat available in South Gippsland.

Michael Moss has traced credible sightings near Wilsons Promontory as far back as 1915, and makes no other claims about sightings claimed for other parts of Australia. In this he differs from 'hard core' enthusiasts belonging to the Rare Fauna Research Society, who suggest thylacines have survived in isolated pockets on the mainland from Queensland to Western Australia since before white settlement.

Moss believes only that sightings – some reported in contemporary newspapers, many not – have spread steadily from Wilsons Promontory into nearby Tarwin Lower, Foster, Leongatha and east to the Gippsland Lakes over 80 years. He thinks the only plausible reason for this – apart from some form of mass psychosis peculiar to South Gippsland – is that at least one pair of thylacines was released at the promontory early this century, and that they bred.

The available evidence is inconclusive, but intriguing. Wilson's Promontory was reserved as a national park in 1898 and gazetted in 1908 – precisely the decade when the thylacine was still available in Tasmania, but obviously in decline.

The search for clues to the puzzle has led Moss to scour the only known records of the park's Committee of Management, a file of annual reports in the State Archives at Laverton.

These hold no proof that the committee ever formally approved release of a known 'pest' like the thylacine. But they do show it made an extraordinary effort to stock the park with native animals from all over Australia, including Tasmania.

And there is a cryptic clue that it would at least have entertained the idea of releasing thylacines: a reference in the 1912 report to consideration of releasing another 'pest', the Tasmanian devil.

Another clue is that the committee corresponded with a well-known Tasmanian animal dealer, James Harrison of Wynyard, who supplied any species if the price was right. Harrison obtained several thylacines for Melbourne Zoo and other buyers around the world, but kept no known records.

It was likely that Harrison and others like him supplied many of the 'outside' native animals of the 23 species known to be released at the promontory between 1900 and 1941. The list, compiled by the National Museum of Victoria, includes Tasmanian brush-tailed possums, King Island wombats, Queensland tree kangaroos, rock wallabies, red kangaroos, bobuck possums, sugar gliders and bandicoots.

The list is vaguely headed *Known Liberations of Native Mammals* – implying, perhaps, there might have been other unknown or unofficial liberations – and does not supply either the number of animals or dates of release for most species.

Moss says he finds it hard to believe that a committee including representatives of Melbourne Zoo and the Field Naturalists Club would import plentiful animals such as wombats, kangaroos and possums from interstate, but ignore the thylacine when it was still available, but regarded as endangered.

He argues that such a release was made all the more likely because the Melbourne Zoo had tried to breed thylacines in 1899, and failed. But the likelihood of angering farmers meant any such release would be a secret kept by a small group. If so, it could have died with them.

The only other explanations for scores of detailed daytime sightings over several decades is that every one is wrong – or the extraordinary possibility there has always been a remnant population of mainland thylacines that not only escaped extinction, but detection, for centuries.

IN the absence of as yet undiscovered – or non-existent – records that support the theory that long-dead amateur naturalists secretly released thylacines to breed at Wilson's Promontory, the only way for an independent observer to test the evidence was to interview people who claim to have seen an unusual animal in the South Gippsland coastal districts.

So, in 1997, I set out with a photographer to interview witnesses scattered from Wonthaggi in the west to Loch Sport in the east, a distance of more than 150 kilometres.

The rules were that they had to have made the sightings in daytime, preferably with other adults to corroborate them. I interviewed only people with no previous interest in the subject of supposed thylacine sightings, as a way to avoid enthusiasts determined to shore up an existing belief.

I carefully followed the same procedure as investigative reporters, detectives and lawyers do when probing a legally-sensitive case: that is, being careful not to 'lead' witnesses by suggesting what they might have seen. No cues were given.

Rather, I asked each to describe exactly in their own words what they saw, as if they were giving court evidence. I was struck by the 'internal consistency' of statements made by people who did not know each other, who had sometimes previously been reluctant to discuss their sightings for fear of ridicule, and who used their own words, similes and reference points to describe what they had seen.

GERALD Lamers is a dairy farmer who knows animals but has no interest in thylacines. That is, he didn't until about 11am on 28 September 1996. He was cleaning a gutter behind his farm in Smiths Road, Leongatha South, when the animal walked onto the roadway about 25 metres away. 'It was bigger than our working dogs, about the size of a labrador but longer and doesn't look like a dog,' he told the author a few months later.

'The stubby ears were the first thing I noticed. Its head was pretty long, and nose pretty straight. It was shiny in the coat. In the front it was brownish, the colour of dead (bracken) fern, with black stripes at the back. Towards the hips it was a bit lighter on top. The stripes ran along onto the tail, but the end of the tail was dark. The tail was thick at the top and straight and long, more like a kangaroo tail. I've never seen a dog with a tail like that. The hind leg is different, too. From the hip to the hock is much longer than the from the hock to the back paw.'

He saw the animal again at night in early 1997. He named two of his neighbours who had also seen it, but who wanted to avoid publicity.

AS a former assistant commissioner in the Victoria Police, the late Fred Silvester was one of Australia's most senior crime investigators. A trained observer aware of now inaccurate some witnesses can be, he was openly sceptical about reported 'Tasmanian tiger' sightings by several other residents of Loch Sport, the sleepy lakeside village where he retired in the 1990s. That is, until 9am on the February day in 1997 when he saw a strange animal standing at the fish pond in his garden in Seagull Drive, which backs onto bush.

Silvester quietly called his wife. They both moved to a veranda about ten metres from the animal, and studied it. 'It was a browny colour, about the size of a medium-sized dog, with a thick tail that came to a point, and dark stripes that went right to the butt of the tail,' Silvester said later.

'We stood for about 30 seconds, then it looked up at me, turned around and loped off. Its action was peculiar. I have never seen a Tasmanian tiger, but I used to shoot a lot, and I've seen a lot of mangy old foxes, and it wasn't that.'

June Silvester described the stripes as 'reddy tan', starting behind the shoulders and running to the butt of the tail, which she estimated was ten centimetres wide at that point, and tapering like a wallaby's.

'It had a long head, a bit like an Alsatian, with ears that were standing up, not floppy.'

L YALL Champion, retired quality control inspector, and his friend Laurie Lavars, an engineer, saw an unusual animal near the local tip late one morning a few days after Christmas, 1996.

'Its head was too big to be a fox, and it was this high at the shoulder,' said Champion, holding his hand 50 centimetres above the floor.

'The ears pointed up but were not long. It's the weirdest thing I've ever seen. It was a dirty greyish-brown colour, with faint strips on the back. The tail was thick but tapered right down. I'd heard the stories but never believed it before. After this happened I wasn't going to say anything, because I didn't want people to ridicule me.'

Lavars said the animal was as big as his german shepherd bitch, but moved more like a cat than a dog. He was puzzled by the faintness of the stripes, but speculated that it had rubbed against fire-blackened trees or rolled in dirt. He said he, too, had previously dismissed other sightings as nonsense but could not explain what they had both seen.

C HRIS Ahern, a mechanic, was fishing from his boat about 75 metres from the south shore of Lake Victoria in 1989 when a movement caught his eye on the beach. 'At first I thought it was a dog,' he said later. 'Then I changed my mind. I looked at it for about 45 seconds, then it strolled along the beach like a cat. It was about 600 (millimetres) high and more than a metre long. It had a bull terrier-type head except that it was finer in the nose and had little ears standing up. The body was dark brown, but had vertical markings on it which were lighter, like a tan, that started behind the front leg and went right through to the tail. The tail was like a kangaroo tail, thick at the base. It had short hair. I didn't tell too many people until later, when I read reports in the paper that other people had seen something.

PETER Connell, RACV mechanic and driver, was driving on a quiet road to the Loch Sport surf beach in late 1996 when he saw an animal 'the size of a greyhound' eating a dead wallaby on the side of the track near a waterhole. 'I jammed on the brakes to get a better look. It was darkish yellow, with stripes halfway down its back to its butt. When it took off it gave me the impression it was going to trip over itself. It gave a couple of hops, then it was gone. I thought before this that it was a load of bullshit. I've been here nine years and seen everything, but it's something I'd definitely never seen before.'

DENIS O'Donnell, optical technician, and Gary Main, a gardener, had two children in the car with them as they returned from Walkerville to Wonthaggi in November, 1993. All four of them saw the animal standing on the right side of the road, in broken bush and farm country near the Ten Mile Road turn-off.

'I could have run him over,' O'Donnell said. 'He was as big as my Weimaraner dog, with a long jaw and cauliflower ears. It looked like a lot of animals stuck together. The tail was like a wallaby's, stuck straight out and thick at the base. The haunches were sort of like a kangaroo's. He crossed the road. It was a sort of a saunter, like a hyena. It went down into a drain and through the fence, then stood on a dam bank. We went back the next day and made a plaster cast of a footprint on the dam bank.'

L OU Caile, builder and social bowls player, was driving from Inverloch to Morwell across the South Gippsland hills one morning in October, 1995, when he and his two passengers saw the animal.

'About 300 yards past the Koonwarra turn-off on the Leongatha Road this thing crossed the road. It had a fairly big head, was as high as a big dog, but thicker and had a long tail. It seemed a greyish colour with dark stripes down the side of it. It loped like a tiger or leopard.

'I said "What the bloody hell's that?" None of us had ever seen anything like it. There's been talk of an animal right back to the 1950s but I reckoned they (people) were nuts. Not now, though.'

L ORNA Moir, a retired farmer, was driving from Outtrim to Korumburra in South Gippsland with her late husband in 1991. 'It was about 9am, between the Outtrim hall and Axeford's Road, when this animal walked across the road. It was greyish with black stripes running on it, starting near the shoulders. It was bigger than my blue heeler dog. The tail was stuck out, the way a cow's is when it's going to have a calf. My husband was the assistant general manager of the SEC before we bought the farm. He had seen it early one morning driving to play golf at Leongatha.'

G ORDON West, retired high school principal, and his wife, Pat West, report seeing the animal twice. 'The first time was coming home to Foster from the Prom (Wilsons Promontory) in 1972, when this animal crossed the road. It was about 5 o'clock on a summer afternoon. It stopped on the edge of the road on the passenger side. It was the size of a small greyhound, striped on the back and had a pointed tail. It had a fox-like head, but was thicker.

'The second time was in February or March of 1991. We'd been playing at Leongatha Golf Club, but didn't stop for lunch, so it was about 1pm. It was a light gingery brown, with dark stripes and pointed tail. There was another sighting on the golf course this year, about six weeks ago, towards dusk.'

GRACE Quattrione, physiotherapist, was driving to Sale from Golden Beach about 8.30 on a summer morning in early 1997 when she saw 'what looked to me like a Tasmanian tiger,' she said.

'It was very different. It had a biggish face. The body was big at the front and narrow at the back. It was fawn with black stripes. It sloped down to the rear quarters. It was chasing a rabbit, I think. It was about as high as an Alsatian dog. It had a beautiful, flowing run, bit like a lioness I saw on television.'

IF the thylacine turns up, it won't be the first time rare animals have made fools of people. Take the case of the Parma wallaby, written off as extinct early this century. In the 1960s, a thriving colony of Parmas was found on Kawau Island, near Auckland, where they had lived happily since being released last century with three other wallaby species – and zebras and gnus. It gets stranger.

Some of the Kiwi Parma wallabies have since been brought 'home' – but even before they got here a colony of Parmas was found near Gosford in 1967. Then more were found elsewhere.

Consider the comeback of New Zealand's flightless parrot, the kakapo. There were only half a dozen (all male) known to exist in the 1980s when, miraculously, a colony of about 50 birds was found on Stewart Island. Some long-forgotten naturalist had sneaked them there long ago, knowing they were being wiped out in their South Island home.

Closer to home, there is the tiger quoll, apparently extinct in most of eastern Australia. None had been seen in northern Victoria for 50 years – until a farmer caught one near Swan Hill in 1991, and rewrote the natural history books.

Meanwhile, at least five large mammal species have been discovered or rediscovered near Australia in the 1990s, making a total of seventeen large mammals found worldwide since 1937. Astonishingly, four of the new-found species were in the war-torn jungles of Cambodia and Vietnam.

In late 1995, researchers looking for the kouprey, a jungle cow believed extinct for 30 years, not only confirmed their existence, but also found a new species of jungle cow.

In 1992 of a new genus of animal, the deer-like Vu Quang ox, or pseudoryx, was found in northern Vietnam. In 1994 a zoologist in the same nature reserve found fresh remains of another new species, the deer-like giant muntjac.

But it was the re-discovery this year of a mysterious wild pig, unseen by zoologists since it was first described in Laos 110 years ago, that proves even large animals can be elusive, even if locals know they're around. A fresh skull confirming the pig's existence was given to a World Conservation Society ecologist by hunters who call it the 'yellow pig'.

But thylacines? Among wildlife experts the jury is still out on whether they survive. But it's clear what the verdict will be unless fresh evidence turns up.

Every year, the spectre of total extinction looms larger for all but the most optimistic. Experts who have spent thousands of hours searching for thylacines have reluctantly concluded the animal is extinct until proven otherwise.

So far, searches have been in Tasmania because that is where the animal was last known to exist. There has never been a methodical search in Gippsland, despite many sightings.

Nick Mooney, a wildlife management officer for the Tasmanian Parks and Wildlife Service, has followed up scores of reported sightings since the early 1980s. Like thylacine expert Dr Eric Guiler, of the University of Tasmania, he has been forced to conclude that if they did survive in Tasmania beyond the 1930s, they've probably since died out through inbreeding or disease. But some of the most sceptical professionals won't dismiss the possibility thylacines have beaten the odds. Mooney and other experts privately admit being tantalised by accurate sightings that, in Mooney's words, 'make the hairs stand up on the back of your neck'.

Former Victorian Conservation Department ecologist Brian Walters feels the same way about some sightings relayed to him when he recorded details of unusual animals seen in Victoria from 1980 to 1993.

Walters, now a wildlife consultant, says people often mistake foxes or dogs with sarcoptic mange for thylacines, because the condition dramatically alters appearance. But he thinks most genuine experts have more open minds than ignorant sceptics who automatically dismiss all sightings as imaginary, mistakes, or hoaxes.

The experts are quick to spot the inevitable 'UFO' syndrome. They know that speculation about any strange phenomena inspires people who report 'seeing' things. Such dubious claims muddy the water, but don't alter the internal consistency and detail of clear sightings by people whose character and testimony are impeccable.

So many sightings were made of thylacines in the area (near Wilson's Promontory) that Fisheries and Wildlife staff tried to trap the animal in the 1960s – the only known official attempt to catch the animal on the mainland. Brian Walters tells a story to show that scientists aren't infallible. In 1983 he and two other wildlife experts spent five weeks on Belabac Island in the Straits of Borneo, looking for the rare mouse deer. They didn't find any.

On the last day, a local man offered to show them one. He took them to a wedding feast. On a plate at the head table was a mouse deer.

Walters rejects assertions that inbreeding would condemn a small number of surviving thylacines to extinction. Isolated groups of rock wallabies in-breed for generations without ill-effect, he says. Many species of Australia's millions of imported pests – rabbits, foxes, Indian mynahs – descend from relatively few animals. Recent research indicates that all Australian dingos could be descended from one female.

The well-known scientist and author Tim Flannery, of the Australian Museum, went to Irian Jaya in 1997 to investigate reports of thylacines there.

He didn't find any. But on his previous trip, in 1994, he did find a 'new' species of tree kangaroo previously unknown to western science.

Professor Michael Archer, of the University of NSW, says he will believe thylacines still exist when a body turns up. But, he adds cryptically, 'Just because you don't see any water babies doesn't mean there are no water babies.'

Dream ride

IT'S a scene straight from every kid-meets-horse tearjerker ever made, by *National Velvet* from *A Bush Christmas*. It goes like this ...

Cup day, 1948. A one-horse town called Birchip drowses in the Mallee heat. It's a day's journey by slow train and a world away from the morning suits and manicured lawns of Flemington. George Neville, battler, is leaning on the bar at the Commercial Hotel. Like most of Australia, he and his mates are listening to the races on 'the wireless'.

George is a racing man, a bow-legged bush jockey who went around once in a Caulfield Cup in the 1920s before coming home to Birchip. He feeds a couple of slow gallopers and thirteen kids, and does the best he can. If Hollywood makes this picture, this is the Mickey Rooney part.

Cut to Flemington. The sun is shining, the champagne flowing, and it looks magnificent, but beneath the lush turf the track is soggy after days of rain. An obscure jumper called

Finentigue has pinched the Cup Hurdle at 100/1. An omen, maybe, that it's a day for outsiders.

The race before the Cup is the Mimosa Stakes, for two-year-old fillies. Regal Gem, the great Bill Williamson aboard, knocks off the favourite, Luck Penny, ridden by another star jockey, Harold Badger. As usual, after listing the placegetters, the caller runs through the Cup field of 30 horses.

The interest is in the topweight, Howe, at 7/4 the hottest favourite since Phar Lap in 1930. Badger is on him, and the combination has pulled a crowd of 101,000.

The odds say Howe has the Cup in the bag, but as the caller ticks off the rest of the field, back in Birchip George Neville automatically listens. All the way through the card to number 25, an 80/1 shot. 'Rimfire, R. Neville, seven stone two,' the caller says.

George almost drops his beer. 'R. Neville' is his son, Ray – a tiny 15-year-old who's had nine race rides since getting his licence just two months earlier.

George bolts for home. On the way he calls in at the school, yelling to several of his offspring in the playground that their brother is riding in the Cup. The boldest of the Neville brood immediately wag school, heading to a cafe where there's a radio.

At home, George blurts the news to his wife. She's stunned. Why would anyone put a raw teenager like her Ray on a Melbourne Cup horse? She grabs her purse.

Flashback to the previous year. Little Ray is working on farms – driving tractors, trapping rabbits, plucking wool from dead sheep – but he dreams of being a jockey, as his dad was and his older brother Max is. He gets his chance when an old local horseman recommends him to a respected Mordialloc trainer, Lou Robertson.

Ray, barely big enough to lug his suitcase, catches the train to the city. His mother doesn't want him to go, but there are too many mouths to feed at home.

The youngster has grown up around horses and competed in shows and unregistered race meetings, and starts riding work as soon as he gets to Robertson's stables. But he doesn't get his race permit until the following season, just two months before the Cup carnival.

By that time Robertson has polished the boy's style. His first race ride is in a field of 40, up the straight six at Flemington. Two hours later, he wins the last race of the day on a stayer called Lincoln.

Cut to Cup eve. Rimfire, a handsome six-year-old chestnut with legs as patchy as his form, is still sore after finishing behind Howe in the Hotham Handicap. A leading lightweight jockey, W.A. Smith, has the Cup ride, but tells Rimfire's trainer, Stan Boydon, he'd rather ride Sun Blast, also an outsider, but one not so likely to break down.

With less than 24 hours to go, Rimfire's connections need another lightweight. Why they pick Neville is unclear. One story is that a stablehand suggests 'the boy from Birchip' because of his win on Lincoln.

Boydon contacts the boy's master and books the ride. But the shrewd Robertson doesn't tell Neville until next morning, so that he sleeps soundly and doesn't have time to get nervous.

Cup morning. Neville is up before dawn and rides work as usual. As he comes off the track before breakfast, Robertson breaks the news. Hurry up and clean your gear, he says. You're on Rimfire in the Cup.

As soon as the trainer is out of earshot, the stable foreman scoffs at Neville, 'If that bastard Rimfire wins, I'll walk from here to Sydney – barefoot.' Later, at Flemington, the public and the bookmakers share the foreman's opinion. No one wants to back Rimfire. The price stays at 80-1.

Little Ray Neville gets to the course in the float that brings Robertson's horses, including a Cup runner, Westralian. In the rooms, the older jockeys laugh when the kid puts on Rimfire's colours. The jacket is so big the sleeves have to be rolled up and pinned; the tail reaches his knees before he tucks it into his breeches.

The kid borrows a lead bag from Smith, the rider who has turned down the Rimfire ride. Smith says kindly, 'He'll be a good ride for you.'

The youngster asks innocently, 'Has he got a chance?' and Smith laughs. 'No, but he'll give you good experience.' He's right.

In the mounting yard, Rimfire looks good – for a crock that has tottered off the track on three legs at his most recent win, months earlier, and pulled up sore after the Hotham Handicap three days before.

His trainer has been putting cold compresses on the horse's front fetlock joints until late the night before, hoping the racing club veterinary surgeon will let the horse run.

The sight of the baby-faced lad perched on Rimfire hardly inspires confidence in a field that includes renowned horses like Comic Court and Carbon Copy, and some of the world's best jockeys: Williamson and Badger, Cook and Hutchinson, Thompson and Moore.

From barrier 23, the boy from the bush eases the handsome crock across well behind the leaders, to be almost mid-field passing the stands the first time. Rimfire gradually improves his position, Neville sitting quietly as a bolter called Royal Scot hares along in front. At the turn, as the leaders tire, Rimfire moves up to seventh place. Photographers stationed there snap the youngster still sitting tight.

Then it happens. Rimfire forgets he is a cripple looking for a place to break down, and sweeps to the front . . . just as the favourite, Howe, falters in his run with an injured ligament.

If it were a film, this is the moment when the audience starts cheering the underdog. In the real world of the racecourse, the punters aren't so generous when longshots beat favourites.

Rimfire hits the front as Howe flounders. But the script calls for a tight finish. The Sydney Cup winner Dark Marne, ridden by the top Sydney jockey Jack Thompson, sets out after Rimfire. Thompson pulls the whip and lifts his horse closer with every stride. They hit the line locked together.

Afterwards, the boy tells reporters: 'I was so excited halfway down the straight at the thought of winning the Melbourne Cup that I hardly realised Dark Marne was so close.'

The taciturn Thompson thinks he's won. So certain is he that he wheels his horse around first and trots back in front, and tells waiting reporters he's got the money.

One of the other senior riders calls to Neville: 'Do you reckon you got there, son?'

'Well, I hope I did,' the boy replies doubtfully. A sea of punters hope he's wrong.

He rides back to scale, as one reporter writes, 'in a hush almost unparalleled in racing.'

FOR the first time in Cup history, the judge calls for a photograph from the new finish camera. It shows that Rimfire has won by a nostril. Angry punters boo the judge. Thompson, who is to ride for another 35 years, swears until the day he dies that the camera was faulty, and that Dark Marne won.

Meanwhile, in Birchip, Neville's parents run to the hotel in time to hear the race. His mother has 'a quid' each way with the SP bookmaker in the bar.

One of the Neville brothers sneaks back to school after the race, and is caught by the teacher, who produces a strap. Luckily, he asks what won the Cup. When the boy says 'Me brother did, sir,' the teacher lets him off – and declares a half holiday for the whole school. It's a big day in Birchip.

Late that afternoon, the boy jockey goes back to Mordialloc in the horse float, clutching '25 quid' Rimfire's owner has given him.

He gets an extra-large serve of steak and eggs to celebrate, and is allowed go to Wirth's Circus to be presented with a trophy whip.

Next day is his sixteenth birthday. He's up at 4am to ride work and muck out stables. The fairy story's over. Fade to black.

Half a century after he piloted Rimfire into Melbourne Cup folklore, it's hard to tell whether the boy from Birchip is tired of recalling his brush with the big time, or just modest. Both, probably.

It's true that the chapter of Ray Neville's life that reads like a film script closed on that golden afternoon in 1948. But, in his own way, he's lived happily ever after.

Which is not to say he went on to a glorious career in the saddle. Neither did he vanish from racing without riding another winner.

The truth is somewhere in between, and not especially romantic. Like many apprentices, Neville got heavy. He won a few more races, but within eighteen months of his Cup win he couldn't make the tiny weights he needed to ride in claiming races.

Too big to be an apprentice jockey, he became a small apprentice carpenter. Not as dashing a trade, but more reliable. At first, he worked in Melbourne, but he soon went home to the bush. And stayed there.

But he didn't stay out of the saddle.

As a schoolboy, Neville loved riding over jumps at local shows. He'd listened to the stories of the old 'jumping men' his father knew. It wasn't long before the only carpenter ever to win a Melbourne Cup decided to dust off his childhood ambitions and try to add the Grand National steeplechase to his record.

It happened like this. He'd been doing riding work at Birchip, and taking the occasional flat ride at country meetings. One day an old jumping trainer, Reuben Fisher, asked him if he wanted to ride in a hurdle race.

Yeah,' Neville replied.

'Ever done it before?'.

'Nah,' said Neville.

'Well, you're the right man for the job,' said the old timer drily. 'Because the horse has never been over jumps either.'

The horse was from Ouyen. The race was on a dirt track at Kaniva. He ran second, and Neville was hooked.

For almost twenty years he built houses Monday to Friday, riding work and schooling jumpers before he started, and on Saturdays he rode in races – against legendary jumps jockeys such as Ted Byrne and Tom McGinley – for 'three quid' a losing ride, more for the occasional winner. It helped feed the kids: he had eight of them.

His biggest win was the Commonwealth Steeplechase. He didn't win a National, the closest he came to winning Warrnambool's famous Grand Annual was fourth, and he ran places in the Hiskens Steeple several times. But he won plenty of other races, including a few for Sir Henry Bolte. 'I never kept records,' he says.

He was stable jockey for a Mallee trainer, Reg Fisher. When Fisher moved from Rainbow to Stawell in 1966, the Nevilles went with him. They've been there ever since.

Neville's second racing career ended in a steeplechase at Ballarat in 1969, when his horse fell and crushed him.

'I woke up next morning in St John's Hospital with one arm in plaster and one leg in plaster and said, "That's it. I've given it away." I came right six months later, but I couldn't go back on my word.'

As soon as he was fit enough, he started riding work again. He kept it up until he turned 60. Old habits are hard to break. He still gets up at dawn to help his eldest son, Geoff, a former rodeo rider, who breaks in young horses for other trainers and prepares a couple of gallopers on his own account. Ray drives to the track with him, does the boxes and offers advice.

The rest of the day he's mostly at home with his wife, June.

A few days before his 64th birthday, Ray is standing in the living room of their cosy old house, on a street running towards Stawell racecourse.

Jumping jockeys are a tough breed. Like a lot of the cross-country fraternity, Neville looks a bit like an old fighter. He's a nugget of a man, with square hands, a strong jaw, a gruff manner and the sort of neatly-parted hair that used to be seen in Brylcreem ads.

A blue singlet shows up beneath a well-filled check shirt. He'd tip the scales at nearly double the feather weight he was in 1948.

He's had his tea, and is looking forward to a couple of beers at his local with the leading Wimmera trainer Terry O'Sullivan and his wife Robyn. These days, O'Sullivan trains city winners, but Neville has known him since he was a skinny kid hanging around the stables wanting to ride work.

There are two big photographs on a mantelpiece at one end of the room.

One is a striking picture of Rimfire with the teenage Neville in the saddle, a set-up shot taken some days after the Cup at the trainer's Flemington stables. The other, in an oval frame, is of Ray and June's wedding in 1955. She was a Mallee bride, born and bred at Beulah, not far from Birchip.

'Isn't everybody sick of this story?' Neville grumbles good naturedly. But he doesn't protest too hard as June proudly produces each piece of Melbourne Cup memorabilia.

Here's a copy of the Cup trophy, the first ever presented to the winning jockey by the GMH car company. The plating is tarnished. 'It's gone a bit black from the gas fire,' she says apologetically.

And there's the gold-mounted whip presented by Wirth's Circus to the winning jockey. It lives on the mantelpiece next to the Rimfire photograph.

Then Mrs Neville produces a miniature set of Rimfire's colours – white, light blue sleeves and red cap – that she ran up herself on the sewing machine. The grandkids love them, she says, eyes shining.

Finally, she produces a recent snapshot of her husband in a jacket and tie, and tells the story that goes with it.

The year before, she says, the Birchip Shire went out of existence because it was amalgamated with others into the Buloke Shire. It decided to mark the occasion by honouring Birchip's most famous sons.

One was the country singer Dusty Rankin, who cut his first record in 1948. The other was Ray Neville.

'Yeah,' he cuts in. 'The old bloke that rang said they usually wait until you die, but this time they decided to do it while we were still alive.'

So he and June put on their Sunday best and drove up to Birchip for the function.

After the speeches Ray was asked to pull back a tiny curtain. Behind it was a metal plaque of a jockey boy on a racehorse.

They've got long memories in the Mallee.

Solomon in a singlet

The morning after we got the news, I went out to your woodheap. There was that big old axe you used in the bush all those years ago, just as you'd left it, stuck in the chopping block like a signature. I split wood until the memories and the tears came flooding in. Then I dropped the axe back in the block, nose down, handle sticking up, as neat as you please. Just like you would, Dad …

REMEMBER how we used to get around in the old Blitz army truck, the one you'd bought when you were sixteen and drove for years before you got a licence? I hadn't started school, but I'd begun my education, sprawled on the petrol tank that doubled as a seat, my head on your lap, lulled by the old side-valve V8 grumbling away behind its thin tin cowling.

I watched the way you used to pat the old girl into gear, those huge work-stained hands easing the gear stick through the unforgiving crash box while you double-clutched and caught the revs just right.

'Listen to her,' you'd say as we laboured up a hill with tons of timber or a bulldozer on the back, 'slurping petrol fast as you could pour it out of a two-gallon bucket.' And you'd laugh and sing *King of the Road*.

You turned 24 the week I was born, so I remember you as a young bloke, a father of three boys by 27. Fair-haired, a touch under six foot and around thirteen stone in the old scale, equal parts bone and muscle, common sense and good humour, wrapped inside a blue singlet with the honest smell of sweat and gum trees. You didn't change much in 30 years. Later, people sometimes took us for brothers born a dozen years apart.

Like the best dogs, horses and people, you were tough, but never mean. We'd marvel at how you picked up hot coals when they fell from the fire, juggle them casually and toss them back. Your heart was a lot softer than your hands. Once, when a visitor produced sandwiches she'd made specially, you saw the one she offered had been fly-blown on the long trip out to see us. Rather than hurt her feelings, you took it, thanked her, and ate it, poker-faced. Chivalry, Mum called it.

Whatever it was about you, we liked it. Little boys in books wanted to be firemen or train drivers, but yours wanted to be sleeper cutters, like you . . .

You'd set up your landing in the shade, preferably to catch a lazy afternoon breeze sneaking up a gully from the lake. You'd fall a tree, measure off nine feet the ancient way, stepping out the log heel to toe, then saw it off and snig it to the landing with the tractor.

You'd belt the bark with the back of the axe to loosen it, then slit it open and lever it off as easily as a slaughterman skins sheep. You'd save sheets of stringy bark and, if it rained, we'd lean them against a tree, shelter under it and drink sweet coffee from your battered old steel Thermos.

You used most tools well, but the axe was your favourite. Your good axe had an oversized head, razor sharp, and a succession of hickory handles worn silky smooth with use. You could do nearly anything with it, and did.

At lunchtime, you'd put the sandwiches on a fresh-sawn sleeper, which smelt so sharp and sweet and clean, and cut them from corner to corner with the axe, as neatly as if you'd used a kitchen knife. You used it to sharpen the stubby carpenter's pencil for marking the ends of the logs. You used it as delicately as a scalpel to notch the ends of the log – right on the pencil mark – ready for the string line.

And, when you finished with the axe, you'd casually drop it, nose first, into the boards and stick it in perfectly, every time, with the handle rising just right. 'As neat as you please' was the way you put it.

You'd shake the battered tin of blue powder to coat the string, stick it in those tiny cuts at each end, pull it taut, pluck it up and twang it. Presto! A straight blue line on the wet, virgin sapwood. You started the swingsaw and backed it rhythmically down the log, the machine straddling it with skinny legs on tiny tyres, the howling circular blade's cruel shark teeth throwing up a plume of sawdust as graceful as a rooster's tail …

And that's when your little boys got a chance to sneak into the bush, dragging the axe. We'd cut a whippy wattle stick, and 'borrow' a length of your good cord as a bowstring. But only if you'd notch the ends of the bow with the axe. You always did, and more besides.

Sometimes, with two sure hits and a quick trim, you'd make a cricket bat from a sleeper offcut. You made us a ripper billy cart, the chassis made of hardwood, the front tapered with the axe, the steering a piece of light rope, like reins.

Your own childhood had been spent fishing, riding, shooting and swimming, and you always had a soft spot for childish pastimes. But you had limits. One day we squabbled too much over the swing you'd made with a tyre and a rope, slung from a big roundleaf box tree. You vaulted the fence, axe in hand, and cut the rope without a word. Solomon in a singlet.

Later, after we'd reflected on our sins, you put the swing up again. That was you, Dad: slow to anger, quick to forgive and forget, always practical. You were never keen on punishment or revenge, and mostly turned the other cheek. About all that made you angry was injustice to another person or cruelty to animals.

You despised callousness or misplaced sentimentality that let animals suffer. If they were sick or injured, and couldn't be helped, you put them out of their misery. With a bullet – or a lightning strike with the axe.

'Quick and clean,' you used to say. You gave an old dog or an old horse a good feed and a pat before they took the walk from which only you returned.

Not that you liked killing anything. Remember your youngest boy conning you to let a sheep go instead of slaughtering it? You decided we could go without fresh meat rather than upset him. One of the few times I saw you angry in public was when you fronted a youth being rough with sheep in the saleyards. He got the message.

Our world was small, and it seemed to us you could do nearly anything in it that was worth doing. You could swim strongly, box a bit, shoot well and drive anything, and you taught us how.

You'd started work at fourteen, got the truck at sixteen, had a bulldozer not long after you got the vote, and a pilot's licence. And, later, a couple of boats that gave us golden memories of summers on Lake Tyers.

You knew a thousand practical things, wisdom won from experience as a farmer and bushman. Like the shine on your axe handle, it came only with time and hard work, but you were always willing to share it. All our lives you've shown people how to do things in that easygoing way, and kept learning yourself. 'You can learn one thing from anybody,' you always said.

You could sharpen any saw. You were a bush carpenter and mechanic, a handy welder and blacksmith. You grew up around horses, and helped drove cattle as a boy. You could stitch harness, use a stockwhip and a branding iron. You once milked 26 Jersey cows every day and raised pigs. You could tan a kangaroo hide, set a wild dog trap, whistle a fox, rob a beehive, butcher a sheep or shear one. You could mend a chair or chair a meeting.

You cleared land, burning windrows and stumps, and sowed down pasture, but never wasted a stick of useful timber. You could quote Paterson and Gordon by the verse and drop a line of Shakespeare, Steele Rudd, Runyon or the Bible to suit most occasions. You could play tunes on a gumleaf, sing a lullaby in the local Aboriginal dialect, or make a bark humpy – a legacy of growing up on Lake Tyers Aboriginal station, where you played in the football teams of the early 1950s.

You played on heart and toughness. You had to. You played hurt every week because of what you nonchalantly called your 'crook foot', a twisted instep caused by childhood polio that left you with a lifetime limp.

But your foot didn't stop you rucking four quarters without a rest in Nowa Nowa's winning grand final team of 1956. Your mates chaired you off the field, and they gave you a trophy for the most determined player.

Mum still laughs about how all the local girls lined up to kiss you after that legendary game.

404

FOR A man who cut down plenty of trees, you loved them. You knew individual trees among thousands, and could find them in the bush years afterwards. You could look at a piece of sawn timber and say if it was grey or roundleaf box, mahogany or messmate, silvertop or stringybark.

Once, you amazed a neighbour by glancing at his new stockyards and telling him exactly where he'd poached the red box timber from, deep in the state forest two kilometres away.

When you went wheat farming on the plains near Bendigo in the 1970s, you missed the tall timber and the whisper of wind in the gum leaves at night.

Perhaps that's one reason you were among the first to re-grow trees on country where a century of ringbarking and burning had made bleak, bare paddocks. You planted, fenced in and watered hundreds of trees in a belt running a mile across the farm. You planted roadsides, and made plantations in places where salt was rising to blight the soil. And still you missed the bush.

Your sleeper quota was gone, but you were younger than most sleeper cutters you'd known, and still strong. You'd been one of the last in East Gippsland to start out with a crosscut saw, a broadaxe and splitting wedges, tools that hadn't changed much since medieval times.

You learnt from axemen who'd worked in the bush since the turn of the century, and you spent your teens splitting logs into billets, then squaring them into sleepers with the broadaxe. And you never forgot how, even after chainsaws and swingsaws took over. Which is why, when Victoria's oldest farm, Emu Bottom at Sunbury, needed authentic mortised posts and split rails to restore it so a television series could be filmed there, you took the contract. The owner, who was to become a friend over the years, was resigned to buying rare old fences to rebuild, but you told him you could split new posts and rails the traditional way. He was delighted. And so began your second life as a bushman. You mortised posts and split rails for Emu Bottom, then hewed bush timber with the broadaxe to restore and extend its historic woolshed. People heard of your work and sought you out. You were invited to field days and demonstrations and started building showpiece fences and entrances all over Victoria.

One of your fences is part of a world-class jumping course at Werribee Park equestrian centre. You and an old mate put on an exhibition with the crosscut saw and broadaxe at the Scienceworks museum in Melbourne. You supplied and helped build more than a kilometre of picture-perfect post and rail on a millionaire's vineyard and stud in the Yarra Valley.

Along the way you befriended a younger generation of timber men in the mountain ash forests above Healesville, loggers who'd grown up with machinery, but liked the way you could use old hand tools to turn timber into something special.

Like your own little boys long ago, they watched you study each log and niggle it with your hook to set it up just right before you struck a blow. They began saving logs for you that would split easily, helped you load up, shared a beer and a yarn with you after work and became your friends.

You were touched when one of 'the young fellas' borrowed your wedges and a little advice to learn how to split rails and shape the ends with an axe. You obliged when a group dedicated to preserving old crafts asked you to give a step-by-step demonstration, which they filmed for posterity. And so, thanks to you, a dying craft has been saved.

But not the craftsman.

It took a while, Dad, but you've finally run up against something you can't fix with the axe. It's cancer, though none of us knew that until it was too late.

As I write this you lie in bed in the next room. I strain to hear you cough and clear your throat, and listen for the murmur of your voice, as you serve out the little time left to us. Those familiar sounds have become precious in a few short weeks.

If courage is grace under pressure, you've got it. As ever, your concerns have been for others, even as that strong body has wasted away, leaving little but strength of character.

I saw you sob for the first time in 40 years when you had to tell your mother you would die before she does. You thanked her for giving you a lovely childhood, and told us later you'd planned a eulogy for her that recalled those happy times. Instead, I'm writing yours, and it's the hardest job I've ever done.

You're sad, too, because you think you've let your grand-children down. You'd decided to retire from farming and cut back the timber work to spend time with them. Only a few weeks before you became ill, you bought a nine-seat station wagon to drive them around. Instead, we used it just a month ago to take you on a last trip to the bush at Lake Tyers.

Well, Dad, you haven't let anybody down, ever. That's one reason so many people have come from all over to see you, as the news has spread on the bush telegraph. Every day, they stream in off the highway and down the gravel road to the old brick house to say goodbye. We knew you knew a lot of people; we didn't realise how many of them loved you, too.

You've always said that material things don't matter – that people do. 'Remember, good friends are like gold,' you told me the other day, your voice as strong as your body is frail.

Now, as the clock creeps towards midnight and the end of another precious day, so many memories still echo around my head, as they have these last bitter-sweet weeks.

You always liked the yarn about the stonemasons who were asked what they were doing. 'Cutting stone,' one says sourly. 'Making a living,' says the next, matter of factly. 'I'm building a cathedral!' exclaims the third. You've always been a cathedral builder. Always believed in what you were doing. Always shown that there can be art and dignity in simple things, in fashioning the functional so it pleases the eye and gladdens the heart.

Once, when you were burning huge windrows of fallen timber, watching a cascade of sparks shoot up to join the stars, you said that's the way you wanted to go. 'I don't want to be buried in the cold, old ground,' you said. 'A man ought to make his own coffin and be put in a windrow.'

Well, Dad, you've left your run a bit late to make your own coffin, but we'll do it for you. One of your friends has offered ironbark and box timber you dressed with a broadaxe for him; another some redgum from an ancient giant you felled, reluctantly, on the Campaspe River flats.

There'll be hand-forged horseshoes for handles, just the way you'd do it, and sprays of gumleaves from trees you planted. Your broadaxe, the one you started with 50 years ago, will be fixed to the lid. We might even get a truck about your own vintage and twitch you down tight with your own chain and twitch 'dog'.

You'll be gone, but you'll never be dead while we're around. You have nine grandchildren, and when we tell them how to do things, it will really be you that's teaching them. When they learn to drive, they'll pat their way through the gears gently, like you did. With 'just a trickle of throttle,' like you always said.

When they cut wood they'll be using one of your axes. We'll show them how you split the tough ones. When they jam the blade, we'll show them how to free it without breaking the handle, the way you showed us.

And when they finish chopping, they'll drop it into the edge of the block, handle up, neat as you please. Just like you.

408

Life is mostly froth and bubble,

Two things stand like stone,

Kindness in another's trouble,

Courage in your own.

– Adam Lindsay Gordon